The Forgotten Debate

The Forgotten Debate

THE KOREAN WAR AND THE ROOTS OF AMERICA'S IDEOLOGICAL DIVISIONS

Dane J. Cash

Published by the University Press of Kansas (Lawrence, Kansas 66045), which was organized by the Kansas Board of Regents and is operated and funded by Emporia State University, Fort Hays State University, Kansas State University, Pittsburg State University, the University of Kansas, and Wichita State University.

Library of Congress Cataloging-in-Publication Data

Names: Cash, Dane J., author
Title: The forgotten debate: the Korean War and the roots of America's ideological divisions / Dane J. Cash.
Description: Lawrence: University Press of Kansas, 2025. | Includes bibliographical references.
Identifiers: LCCN 2025009620 (print) | LCCN 2025009621 (ebook) | ISBN 9780700640126 cloth | ISBN 9780700640133 ebook
Subjects: LCSH: Korean War, 1950–1953—United States | United States—Politics and government—1945–1953 | BISAC: HISTORY / Wars & Conflicts / Korean War | POLITICAL SCIENCE / Political Process / Political Advocacy
Classification: LCC DS919 .C37 2025 (print) | LCC DS919 (ebook)
LC record available at https://lccn.loc.gov/2025009620.
LC ebook record available at https://lccn.loc.gov/2025009621.

British Library Cataloguing-in-Publication Data is available.
EU Authorised Representative Details: Easy Access System Europe
Mustamäe tee 50, 10621 Tallinn, Estonia | gpsr.requests@easproject.com

For my parents, who taught me the value of an education.

Contents

Acknowledgments

Researching, writing, and publishing this book was a lengthy endeavor that would not have been possible without the help of many others along the way. I owe so many thanks to so many people! First, a very special thanks to William Keylor, who first inspired me to pursue the life of an historian and mentored me throughout graduate school. Thanks also to my other role models and dissertation readers at Boston University, including Jon Roberts, Cathal Nolan, Andrew Bacevich, David Mayers, and Bruce Schulman. Of course, I could not have written the first version of the manuscript without the support of Bill Leonard and Javier Marion at Emmanuel College. Further, I was only able to complete the project due to the generous support of my wonderful colleagues at Carroll College: Gillian Glaes, who hired me, and Jeanette Fregulia, who mentored me and helped facilitate the sabbatical during which I finished writing new and revising old material. Many thanks also to David Congdon at UPK, who graciously took on this project and supported it from beginning to end, guiding me through initial submission, peer review, and final revision. Speaking of peer review, I also owe thanks to Steven Casey and the anonymous reviewers who provided invaluable feedback that improved the manuscript considerably. Finally, beyond these academic and professional supports and mentors, I cannot thank my family enough for believing in me and supporting me throughout my life's journey so far. Mom and Dad, I could never thank you enough for your encouragement throughout my education and career and your pride in the fruits they have borne. And lastly, to my wife Wendy and three daughters, Kaelin, Jordie, and Chloe: Being a husband and father brings me the most profound joy every single day. In the immortal words of Bryan Adams's power ballad, "Everything I do, I do it for you."

Note on Transliteration

Despite the widespread use of Pinyin as the preferred transliteration system from Chinese characters to the Roman alphabet, I have decided to use the older Wade-Giles system in this book. I do this for the sake of consistency with the book's source material, which was written in the early 1950s using the now outdated Wade-Giles system. These pages, for example, will regularly refer to Mao Tse-tung (Wade-Giles) instead of Mao Zedong (Pinyin), and Peking (Wade-Giles) rather than Beijing (Pinyin). The same holds for Chiang Kai-shek/Jiang Jieshi, although in this case the former is more commonly used.

Introduction

When the North Korean People's Army poured southward across the thirty-eighth parallel on June 25, 1950, the invasion sent shockwaves around the world. With the Soviet Union boycotting the UN Security Council to protest the fact that China's seat was still in the hands of Chiang Kai-shek's government on Formosa, which had been defeated by Mao Tse-tung's communists in 1949, the remaining members of the Security Council, including the United States and its allies Britain, France, and Nationalist China, were able to bypass the Soviet veto and pass a resolution condemning the North Korean communist aggression and calling for military aid to the besieged Republic of Korea. President Harry Truman had already authorized the use of American air and sea power to help defend South Korea, and within days he also met General Douglas MacArthur's request for the deployment of at least two divisions of ground troops. For the first time in the Cold War, American soldiers would be meeting communist forces on the field of battle.

Initially, things did not go well for the Americans and their South Korean allies. By the beginning of August, they were barely holding on at Pusan, at the southernmost tip of the Korean peninsula. It was not until September 15, 1950, when General Douglas MacArthur directed a risky landing behind enemy lines at Inchon, that the tide of battle turned. By the end of that month, Seoul, the capital of South Korea, along with most of that country, had been retaken. The question then became whether South Korean and American forces should stop at the prewar boundary, having successfully repelled the invasion of South Korea, or press ahead north of the thirty-eighth parallel with the goal of destroying the North Korean regime altogether and unifying Korea under South Korean president Syngman Rhee's pro-Western regime. President Truman, via the Joint Chiefs of Staff, ultimately authorized MacArthur to cross the parallel, barring intervention or threat of intervention by the Soviets or Chinese. The Chinese did, in fact, warn the United States, via the good offices of India, that they would intervene if American forces invaded North Korea, but these warnings were discounted, both in Washington and at MacArthur's general headquarters in Tokyo, as so much empty communist bluster. In early October 1950, American forces began their push north of the thirty-eighth parallel into North Korea. As a result, by mid-October, hundreds of thousands of Chinese began pouring over the Yalu River into North Korea to confront the American army. What began as the North Korean invasion of its southern neighbor had become a war between the United States and communist China. What followed was a hasty American retreat southward, in the winter of 1950–1951, followed by a counterattack that once again pushed the communists out of Seoul and north of the thirty-eighth parallel, by early spring.

Meanwhile, tensions were growing between General MacArthur and the Truman administration. By mid-December 1950, once the scale of the Chinese intervention had become clear, civilian authorities in Washington abandoned their fleeting hopes of reunifying Korea, not wanting to bog the United States down in an open-ended ground war in Asia while leaving Western Europe largely defenseless against a potential Soviet attack. The administration's goal became restoration of the antebellum status quo via a negotiated settlement. General MacArthur, however, was focused primarily on the task at hand—total victory over his immediate enemy on the battlefield. This allowed for no half measures or limited warfare, and he began to regard Truman administration policy as little more than appeasement of communist aggression. MacArthur leveled this charge against Truman several times over the first few months of the war, most notably in letters he penned to the Veterans of Foreign Wars and to Republican House Minority Leader Joe Martin. The final straw for Truman, however, came in March 1951, when MacArthur issued an unauthorized ultimatum to the Chinese, effectively demanding their surrender on pain of an American-led attack on the Chinese mainland. The president relieved the general of his command, making clear once and for all that the United States would henceforth be committed to ending the Korean War by negotiated settlement.

In the spring of 1951, the Korean War entered its final phase: a prolonged military and diplomatic stalemate. On the military front, the war of movement up and down the Korean peninsula had ground to a halt and was replaced by a stalemate along an uneven line near the prewar boundary of the thirty-eighth parallel. Diplomatically, the issue that proved most intractable was whether prisoners of war would be repatriated voluntarily or forcibly. The United States did not want to force thousands of North Koreans and Chinese to return to their communist homelands against their will, especially when they were likely to be tortured or killed for having publicly expressed anticommunist sentiments. The communists, on the other hand, did not wish to suffer the loss of face that would come with so many of their own soldiers choosing to live in South Korea rather than

North Korea and Formosa rather than communist China. Finally, after two long years of diplomatic wrangling and, perhaps more importantly, after the death of Soviet leader Joseph Stalin in March 1953, an agreement was reached whereby those North Korean and Chinese prisoners unwilling to be repatriated would be sent to a neutral third country instead of to South Korea and Formosa, respectively. The editors of and contributors to America's leading political opinion journals thus had plenty to discuss during the three years of war in Korea. As we shall see, the debates that played out in these journals revealed some of the most important ideological currents and fissures of the early Cold War.

Many Americans may prefer not to remember that various strains of Marxism—Stalinism included—were quite popular among the editors of and contributors to American political opinion journals during the 1930s. These writers, however, routinely referred to as the "Old Left" in American intellectual history, found much of their worldview discredited by the Nazi-Soviet Pact of 1939 and, later, the Czech Coup and Berlin Blockade of 1948. By the time of Henry Wallace's failed presidential campaign later that year, the Old Left had all but disappeared from the mainstream of American public discourse. For example, the *New Republic*, that old stalwart journal of the left, had effectively abandoned its leftward leanings by the end of the 1940s. The demise of the Old Left set the stage for the emergence of the next phase in American intellectual history. The publication of *The Vital Center* by Arthur Schlesinger Jr., in 1949, provided the philosophical basis for this new era, commonly known as the liberal consensus.[1] Eschewing extremism on both ends of the political spectrum and based loosely around the containment of communism abroad and the commitment to civil liberties at home, the liberal consensus reigned supreme in American intellectual life until it was shattered in the wake of the Vietnam War.[2] Meanwhile, as Lionel Trilling pointed out at the time, conservatism wallowed in ignominy from the onset of the Great Depression through the Second World War and the immediate postwar period. It was not until the mid- to late 1950s, when conservative voices began to coalesce around the young William F. Buckley Jr., and his *National Review*, that the New Right emerged as a coherent challenge to the prevailing liberalism of the day.

The foregoing is a brief summary of the traditional narrative found in analyses of the intellectual history of the United States in the mid-twentieth century. One could be excused for not noticing it, but the Korean War of

1950–1953 is typically given scant attention in such arguments. What role, if any, does the "forgotten war" play in this story? As we shall see, an analysis of the writings found in the pages of America's political opinion journals during and about the Korean War adds even more complexity to the idea of a Cold War liberal consensus, even among self-professed liberals. Indeed, the divisions between left liberals and hawkish liberals were both significant and consistent, even to the point that hawkish liberals often shared more in common with conservatives than with their fellow liberals. Moreover, conservative journals like *The Freeman* and the *American Mercury* serve as evidence that the conservative movement was much more articulate and coherent in the early 1950s than is typically appreciated. While some historians have already made these arguments, as detailed below, they have done so only briefly or obliquely.

Robert Tomes's *Apocalypse Then: American Intellectuals and the Vietnam War, 1954–1975* stands as one of the more thoughtful works to touch on American intellectual life during the Korean War. Tomes's main focus, of course, is Vietnam rather than Korea, but he does an admirable job of setting the stage for Vietnam by summarizing briefly the intellectual climate of the Cold War prior to American involvement in Vietnam. In so doing, Tomes argues that the "vast majority" of American intellectuals after World War II were more or less of the same mind (i.e., willing constituents of the liberal consensus). Indeed, writes Tomes, they "perceived things in a remarkably coherent way."[3] This does not mean, however, that there were no differences of opinion within the liberal consensus. In terms of global anticommunism, for example, Tomes separates liberals into two categories: "hard" and "soft" cold warriors. According to this analysis, "hard" cold warriors were those who favored opposition to the spread of communism "as fiercely as possible in all parts of the world" (Tomes, somewhat puzzlingly, uses George Kennan as an example), while "soft" cold warriors (e.g., Walter Lippmann) thought such an automatic globalist approach was irrational and impractical, arguing instead that communism should be met on a case-by-case basis. In short, for Tomes, 1950s liberalism "contained inherent tensions, although these may not have been obvious at the time."[4]

In addition to exploring the postwar liberal consensus, Tomes briefly addresses those few intellectuals who can rightly be situated outside mainstream liberalism. During the 1950s, as Tomes puts it, "certain prominent intellectuals were far enough to the political left or right to be placed outside the consensus, but these were a distinct minority." On the right, argues Tomes, was a "loosely assembled group of dissidents to the prevailing liberal consensus," small in number and lacking a unifying, coherent conservative philosophy.[5] This inchoate conservatism went beyond even the "hard" version of Cold War liberalism in that it favored the rollback of communism rather than mere containment. Such conservatives were often former communists (e.g., James Burnham) and would eventually rally around William F. Buckley Jr. and his *National Review*, in 1955–1956 and beyond. These two themes—the coherence of both the liberal consensus and the nascent conservative movement during the Korean War—stand at the center of my inquiry.[6]

Earlier treatments of the path from communism to conservatism that many intellectuals traveled from the 1930s to the 1970s include John Diggins's *Up from Communism: Conservative Odysseys in American Intellectual Development,* first published in 1975 and revised in 1994. Diggins takes a biographical approach to the issues involved, profiling, among others, James Burnham, author of *The Coming Defeat of Communism* (1950) and *Containment or Liberation?* (1952). Burnham, notes Diggins, emerged during the Korean War as America's quintessential conservative cold warrior, and his ideas, in fact, proved rather influential in the State Department, Defense Department, and CIA.[7] After being chastened by the Chinese intervention, though, Truman ultimately decided against trying a second time to turn the Korean War into a war of liberation-rollback, as best symbolized by his firing of General MacArthur. Thus, "to the conservative Right, Korea was the turning point in the cold war at which America failed to turn."[8] By bringing to light such conservative dissatisfaction with American policy in Korea, Diggins laid the groundwork upon which we can build a more extensive understanding of the Korean War's impact on the development of modern conservatism.

Perhaps no other work to date provides a better summary of the debate among American intellectuals during and about the Korean War than William O'Neill's *A Better World: The Great Schism: Stalinism and the American Intellectuals*, published in 1982. O'Neill takes us through some of the salient points of the debate as it developed, particularly during the early part of the war. The only opposition to the initial American intervention in Korea came from the dwindling numbers of communists who had yet to disavow their ideology. But aside from this minority of thinkers, the initial response among intellectuals to American intervention was overwhelmingly positive. Even the editors of the *New Republic*, a previously leftist journal, blamed Stalin for the outbreak of the war and supported Truman's intervention.[9] *The Nation*, however, was slower to turn its back on its leftist past. Although the editors grudgingly supported US intervention in Korea and increasingly distanced themselves from outright support for Stalin, they continued to be critical of containment policy in general.[10] Other liberal journals, most notably the hawkish *New Leader*, did not shy away from support for the war in the least. That publication was so enthusiastic about American intervention in Korea that it continued to call for the forceful reunification of Korea under Republic of Korea (ROK) rule even after Chinese intervention presented the United States with a far more complex and dangerous set of options.[11]

The most recent investigation of how American–East Asian relations impacted domestic political culture is Joyce Mao's *Asia First*, where Mao argues for the centrality of America's China policy to the development of modern conservatism. *Asia First* includes an excellent summary of the significance of the Korean War to the conservative movement, but Mao's chronological scope is large, chronicling the evolution of events in China and the corresponding American conservative reactions from the Second World War through the 1970s. As such, her impressive work has paved the way toward this more detailed investigation of the role played by the Korean War in the evolution of both modern conservatism and postwar liberalism.[12]

The journalistic environment of the early 1950s was, of course, much different from that of the early twenty-first century. There were no twenty-four-hour cable news channels, podcasts, or social media feeds. So whereas we might be able to tap into the ideological divisions in America's political culture by flipping on our televisions, computers, or mobile devices, politically engaged Americans of the early 1950s were limited to more traditional sources of information and opinion, namely, political opinion journals, weekly news magazines, and local daily newspapers. I have chosen to focus on political opinion journals to the exclusion of daily and weekly hard news sources because I am primarily concerned with investigating and analyzing the similarities and differences among the various camps of political and ideological opinion at the elite and national levels. Weekly magazines like *Time*, *Newsweek*, and *Life*, and daily newspapers like the *New York Times* and *Chicago Tribune*, were geared more toward hard journalism than opinion, and more toward a mass audience than toward intellectuals, policymakers, and other molders of public opinion. While Henry Luce and company certainly expressed a distinct political point of view in *Life* editorials, for example, the conservative ideas they espoused were often expressed earlier and geared toward a more sophisticated and engaged audience in a conservative political opinion journal like *The Freeman.* I have also excluded prominent influential syndicated columnists like Walter Lippmann and the Alsop brothers because, while they may have been writing from a generally liberal perspective, they were "free agents," so to speak, whereas journals like *The Nation* and the *New Republic* filled discrete ideological niches of the kind that form the main subject of my inquiry.[13]

Speaking of ideological niches, the analysis in the pages that follow divides the writers in question into three general categories: left liberals, hawkish liberals, and conservatives. Left liberals, under this schema, are those whose foreign policy views often opposed American containment policy as much as they did Stalinist expansionism. They generally felt US Cold War policy was too militaristic and not focused enough on the types of foreign aid that might actually improve the living standards of the masses around the world whose hearts and minds were at stake in the great contest between the superpowers. They favored a global order defined by multilateralism and international cooperation, most obviously to be administered through the United Nations. In terms of Western security against the Soviet Union, they preferred that the American behemoth be constrained by the input of its allies, particularly via the European members of NATO. On domestic issues, left liberals favored an expansion of the New Deal welfare state and were opposed to any and all things related to Joseph McCarthy and his ongoing anticommunist crusade. Generally speaking, left liberals were the editors and contributors to the two flagship journals of the American intellectual left, *The Nation* and the *New Republic.*

Hawkish liberals, by contrast, favored a foreign policy that was much more aggressively anticommunist than those further to their left. They tended to think containment was too passive to defeat the threat posed by global communism. Instead, they often flirted with a vaguely defined offensive strategy in the Cold War, much like self-avowedly conservative writers who were fairly cavalier about the possibilities of provoking a Third World War. Hawkish liberals' commitment to multilateralism was tepid at best, as were their denunciations of McCarthyism. In short, the hawkish liberals of the early 1950s in many ways prefigured the neoconservatives who broke decisively from their liberal backgrounds two decades later. The journal that served as the center of gravity for hawkish liberal ideas was the *New Leader*, with the contributors to *Commonweal* often moving back and forth over the line between left and hawkish liberalism.

Conservatives thought the Truman administration both naive and hopelessly weak on communism. They thought it best to scuttle containment policy altogether, along with America's membership in multilateral organizations like NATO and the UN, so the United States could "go it alone," to not only contain international communism, but destroy it. On domestic matters, conservatives wished to turn back the clock on the New Deal and Fair Deal, while they embraced and supported McCarthy and his mission to eliminate internal leftist subversion. Some of these conservative ideas date back at least to the anti–New Deal and America-First sentiments of the 1930s, but this was now joined by a chest-thumping anticommunism that would allow the various strands of conservatism to coalesce under the leadership of William F. Buckley Jr., in the years immediately following the Korean War. As Buckley's *National Review* was still several years from its inception, however, the two main conservative journals during Korea were *The Freeman* and the *American Mercury*.

This book primarily analyzes six opinion journals from across the political spectrum. Comparing and contrasting the arguments and viewpoints expressed in these journals will illuminate the political and ideological undercurrents of the early Cold War era and will flesh out the arguments of historians like Tomes, Diggins, and O'Neill regarding the fractures in the liberal consensus as well as the origins of the New Right. From left to right, the journals included in this analysis are *The Nation*, the *New Republic*, *Commonweal*, the *New Leader*, the *American Mercury*, and *The Freeman*.

The Nation was the furthest to the left of these six publications. Editor Freda Kirchwey had been a staunch opponent of fascism and a supporter of the Soviet Union in the 1930s. While she certainly viewed the Soviets less favorably after World War II, her leftist leanings continued to inform her view of American foreign relations. She generally opposed containment by military means and tended to see communism, especially in China, as the expression of people's legitimate aspirations for land, bread, and peace. As such, she sometimes viewed American Cold War policy as aligning the United States with those who were on the wrong side of history—quasi-fascists, in her view, like Syngman Rhee and Chiang Kai-shek. Other notable names on staff at *The Nation* include Willard Shelton and Julio Alvarez del Vayo. Shelton was *The Nation*'s Washington editor, while del Vayo covered the UN. Del Vayo, an avowed socialist, had served as foreign minister for Republican Spain before being forced to flee when Franco's forces won the Spanish Civil War. He was sharply critical of what he viewed to be an excessively militaristic and unilateralist American foreign policy. Kirchwey and del Vayo were the recipients of harsh criticism from more hawkish liberals, like those at the *New Leader*, who viewed *The Nation* as the last liberal refuge for the wretched fellow traveler.

Like *The Nation*, the *New Republic* had a recent leftist past. But unlike *The Nation*, the *New Republic* had made a clean break with that past by the time the Korean War broke out. Editor Michael Straight, who had been on the KGB payroll in the 1930s while in England, had turned entirely against his old communist allegiances by the late 1940s. Straight, however, didn't travel all the way along the ex-communist path to conservatism, as others, like Whittaker Chambers, did. Rather, he and his magazine remained squarely in the liberal camp. The *New Republic* under Straight's editorship was decisively anticommunist but never advocated aggressive rollback as conservatives and hawkish liberals did. The editorial line supported the containment of communism by a variety of means, including military means when necessary. Straight's name rarely appeared in the bylines of the *New Republic*, however, as that publication tended to rely on unsigned editorials. The other name of note on staff at the *New Republic* was Harold L. Ickes, prominent New Dealer and secretary of the interior under Franklin Roosevelt. Ickes often employed his considerable wit in attacking General MacArthur in his weekly column. Overall, the *New Republic* shared much in common with its fellow liberal publication, *The Nation*, but ultimately positioned itself closer to the center of the political spectrum than Kirchwey, del Vayo, and company.

Commonweal, a lay Catholic journal edited by Edward Skillin, is harder to pin down ideologically. Its writings represent a curious hybrid of what we might call the Christian Left and the Christian Right. On the one hand, the editors placed a great deal of emphasis on social justice issues like poverty, hunger, and economic inequality, as well as prevention of war. But on the other hand, as Catholics, they took a hard line against the threat posed by atheistic communism. As such, they often hinted that the United States ought to take a more active approach to combating communism than what they considered to be the inherently flawed, passive containment strategy. But they rarely made explicit what such a proactive tack would look like. They never came out and advocated a strategy of military liberation, but they never explicitly ruled it out either. Generally speaking, the *Commonweal* of the early 1950s can be considered a liberal journal of opinion, typically aligning itself with a publication like the *New Republic*, but it did have its more hawkish moments as well, when its line more closely resembled that of the *New Leader*.

The *New Leader*, published by the American Labor Conference on

International Affairs, typified the liberal point of view on most domestic issues but was quite hawkish in its anticommunist foreign policy preferences. The editor, William E. Bohn, wrote mainly on domestic matters, leaving the journal's foreign policy line largely in the hands of David J. Dallin and William Henry Chamberlin. Dallin served as the *New Leader*'s Soviet expert and was a strong advocate of an offensive strategy in waging cold war, as opposed to the defensive posture implied by containment. He was especially enthusiastic about the outbreak of the Korean War, seeing in it the possibility of a liberated China and, with it, the beginning of the end of the Soviet menace. Chamberlin was an ex–communist sympathizer turned enemy of all things collectivist whose writings during Korea were primarily concerned with what he perceived to be American appeasement of communism, particularly Chinese communism. Together, then, Dallin and Chamberlin forged a foreign policy for the *New Leader* that became increasingly critical of American timidity in waging the Korean War. In advocating some manner of offensive war against communist China, the *New Leader*'s line was often virtually indistinguishable from that of conservative journals like *The Freeman* and the *American Mercury*.

The *American Mercury*, founded by H. L. Mencken in the 1920s, came under the editorship of William Bradford Huie in 1950. Huie, a southerner and unabashed conservative, was well ahead of most of his contemporaries in calling for his fellow southerners to leave the Democrats and embrace the Republican Party. In any case, Huie attempted to create a home in the *Mercury* for the nascent conservative movement and hired a young William F. Buckley Jr. as a staff contributor after his 1951 opus, *God and Man at Yale*, made him the darling of the conservative world. Russell Maguire took over the magazine in 1952 and took it in a much more extremist direction than Huie was comfortable with,[14] but through most of the Korean War the monthly journal remained a reliable mouthpiece for the emerging New Right.

The Freeman, edited by Henry Hazlitt, John Chamberlain, and Suzanne LaFollette,[15] espoused a libertarian political and economic philosophy when it came to domestic matters, and a muscular anticommunism abroad, especially in regard to America's China policy. The editors were deeply influenced by Austrian School economists F. A. Hayek and Ludwig von Mises, and counted among their friends Ayn Rand, Max Eastman, James Burnham, and William F. Buckley Jr. In fact, John Chamberlain penned the introduction to Buckley's *God and Man at Yale*. Both the editors and many of the contributors to *The Freeman* later wound up on staff at the *National*

Review. In this way, *The Freeman* was an important stepping stone for the conservative movement and, as such, serves as a window into the state of that movement years before it is typically considered to have arrived at maturity.[16] Because *The Freeman* was published biweekly, it was able to keep up with events a bit more easily than the monthly *Mercury*. As such, *The Freeman* forms the bulk of my analysis of conservative thought during the Korean War as revealed through America's political opinion journals.

An analysis of these six publications reveals that the debate about the issues raised by the Korean War was much more robust than is typically appreciated. Indeed, the significant differences of opinion expressed in the pages of various liberal journals suggest that the notion of a "liberal consensus" during the early Cold War needs qualification. There may have been a general consensus among liberals that Soviet-style communism was bad, but beyond that there was little agreement about anything. We cannot even assume that liberals agreed that communism was bad qua communism, since writers like Freda Kirchwey and Julio Alvarez del Vayo at *The Nation*, as well as some contributors to the *New Republic*, were not quite convinced of Chinese communism's wickedness. And beyond what these six opinion journals can tell us about the coherence of a would-be liberal consensus, they also reveal that the conservative movement was much closer to being unified in the early 1950s than is usually thought.

Chapter 1 will examine the reactions to the issues raised by the outbreak of the war during the first weeks and months of the fighting in 1950. The debates engendered by the beginning of the war were both lively and substantive. Who bore responsibility for the circumstances that allowed the outbreak of war in Korea, Syngman Rhee or the Truman administration? Would the Korean War be a major turning point in the Cold War, indeed, in human history, and what did its outbreak reveal about the shortcomings of US Cold War policy? Finally, had President Truman acted wisely and constitutionally in sending the American military into war in Korea under UN auspices and without congressional approval?

Chapter 2 will detail the debates that were initiated once US/UN forces regained the momentum in the war in the fall of 1950. The first issue discussed will be the desirability and risk of crossing the thirty-eighth parallel in the hopes of reunifying Korea. Of course, this debate was quickly rendered moot by events on the ground, only to be replaced by all manner of hand-wringing regarding the frightening significance of the Chinese intervention in Korea. Once the shock and fear wore off a bit, however, reasoned debate resumed and revealed a gaping chasm between left liberals, on the one hand, and conservatives and hawkish liberals, on the other, regarding who or what was at fault for provoking the Chinese—was it US weakness that invited the Chinese in, or America's unjustified and aggressive march toward the Yalu that painted Peking into a corner until its only option was to lash out in its own defense? There also existed a sharp divide over the extent to which Mao was a stooge of Stalin vs. the extent to which he was a potential Asian Tito. Moreover, that issue informed writers' opinions about whether the United States should recognize communist China, allow its admission to the UN, and encourage its reincorporation of Formosa.

Chapter 3 will examine the "Great Debates" about US foreign policy that arose in the midst of Korea, the first hot war of the Cold War. The first of these debates addressed whether the United States should launch some form of offensive war against communist China. If so, what should such a war look like—should it involve American air and sea power in support of a Chinese Nationalist invasion of the mainland or would American ground troops be required? If war with China was a bad idea, what were the risks and why were they unacceptable? In particular, what would the implications of war with China be for US Cold War policy in Europe? The Europe-first/Asia-first debate, in fact, took center stage in the Great Debate initiated by ex-president Herbert Hoover in late 1950 and early 1951. Hoover proposed withdrawal from mainland Europe, among other things, which horrified Europe-first liberals and titillated Asia-first conservatives. Much of this debate devolved into a somewhat misguided argument about "isolationism," when, in fact, the real issue was unilateralism. Left-of-center liberals favored a foreign policy based on multilateral relationships and institutions, while conservatives and some hawkish liberals argued that the United States should "go it alone" in the fight against communism.

Chapter 4 will address the debates surrounding the MacArthur controversy. Liberals tended to denounce the general for his brash insubordination well prior to his firing, while conservatives defended his common-sense toughness in the face of communist aggression and denied that he had done anything to deserve his dismissal. Just as the events leading up to and immediately following MacArthur's firing reignited the debate about whether the United States should launch an offensive war against communist China, so shall we revisit that debate in the context of conservative support for MacArthur and liberal support for President Truman. Interestingly, as both hawks and liberals, the editorial staff at the *New Leader* was conflicted about the controversy, even to the point of self-contradiction. In the end, that magazine's line amounted to supporting a MacArthur-style American-led war against China while simultaneously opposing a MacArthur-style American-led war against China.

Chapter 5 will provide a brief pause from foreign policy debates to focus on some of the overlapping domestic issues that liberals and conservatives argued about during the Korean War. Specifically, the chapter will explore the debates about the things liberals and conservatives feared the most, respectively, McCarthyism and "creeping socialism." Predictably, left liberals let their disdain for all things McCarthy pour into the pages of their journals, while conservatives enthusiastically defended McCarthyism. For such conservatives, it was the socialism that had been quietly advancing since the dawn of the New Deal that posed the real threat to American liberties at home. Noteworthy about these debates is not only that they anticipate many of the reasons for the partisan divide in our own time, but also that hawkish liberals found themselves caught in the ideological middle ground. They opposed McCarthy's methods, for example, but were almost equally horrified by left liberals' howling about the threat they posed. And regarding the drift toward social welfarism that the United States had undergone since the New Deal, hawkish liberals were dismissive of conservative concerns, citing a sharp distinction between Western social democracy and Soviet totalitarianism.

Finally, chapters 6 and 7 will deal with the debates that took place during the two long years of truce negotiations at Kaesong and Panmunjom. Chapter 6 will address the ideological divides over whether the United States should accept a divided rather than a unified Korea as an outcome of the talks, whether communists were even capable of negotiating in good faith, and what, if anything, the United States should do to break the diplomatic stalemate at Panmunjom. Chapter 7 will focus on the prisoner of war (POW) question, one of the few issues during the entire war about which there was something approaching a consensus, as well as the ultimate significance of the war. Most notably, liberals concluded that Korea was a hard-fought victory waged for a noble cause, while conservatives dismissed such claims, arguing instead that by failing to win a complete victory over the forces of communism in Asia, the United States had ensured that Korea would go down as a historic defeat for a once-great nation.

1. The Outbreak of the War

On June 25, 1950, communist North Korea launched a massive invasion of its southern neighbor, the nominally democratic Republic of Korea. The UN immediately called on its members to provide aid to South Korea, the apparent victim of an entirely unprovoked aggression. President Harry Truman quickly authorized the deployment of American sea and air forces to support South Korea against the North Korean onslaught. Within days, the president had taken the bolder step of ordering several divisions of American ground troops into Korea. While Truman did not have explicit congressional authorization for such a military intervention, he had informed a bipartisan group of senators and congressmen of his decision and had received no objections. In Korea, the early fighting did not go well for the United States and its South Korean allies, whose territorial holdings had been reduced to a tiny corner of the Korean peninsula around Pusan. Only after General MacArthur's daring landing at Inchon in mid-September did the tide of battle turn in the favor of US/UN forces. By the end of September, Seoul, the South Korean capital, had been retaken, and it looked as though North Korea stood on the brink of a decisive defeat.

Back in the United States, these events sent shockwaves through the intellectual community. While the contributors to America's leading opinion journals had been engaged in an ongoing discussion of United States-Soviet relations since the end of the Second World War, that debate now took on an exciting new urgency. Indeed, during the first few weeks of the war, readers of such publications could find commentary on little else but Korea. While the debate during the first several weeks and months of the war was topically wide-ranging, several issues commanded special attention: who bore responsibility for the outbreak of the war; what was the significance of the fighting in Korea for the wider Cold War; and was the American intervention under President Truman wise and constitutional. As we shall see, there were strikingly different answers to these questions from different ideological camps—even from within the so-called liberal consensus.

On the question of who was primarily responsible for the outbreak of hostilities in Korea, voices from across the political spectrum generally agreed that the war began as the result of naked and premeditated North Korean aggression. That said, most writers assumed that Soviet leader

Joseph Stalin must have been the ultimate puppet master behind the attack.[1] The bulk of the disagreement, then, surrounded the extent to which other personalities, including South Korean president Syngman Rhee and various American officials, bore responsibility for the outbreak of war in Korea. Voices on the left, especially those published in *The Nation*, tended to be harshly critical of Rhee, whom they considered a quasi-fascist authoritarian, while conservatives and hawkish liberals were more likely to defend Rhee and place blame on those in the White House and State Department who crafted an allegedly weak-kneed foreign policy during the Roosevelt and Truman administrations—a foreign policy that, they argued, ultimately invited the communist aggression in Korea.

WHOSE FAULT?

William Costello, writing in the *New Republic*, exemplified the liberal critique of Syngman Rhee. Costello wrote that Rhee's "psychopathic nationalism" prevented the United States from adequately arming South Korea, as American policymakers were afraid that large shipments of arms to that country might encourage Rhee to launch his own invasion of the North. Thus, with South Korea left virtually defenseless, the prospect of an easy conquest proved too tempting a morsel for Stalin to resist.[2] In addition to blaming Rhee, albeit only partially, for the outbreak of the war, many liberals used the occasion to let fly their long-held arrows about why Rhee was not worth supporting in the first place. The *New Republic* editorialized that the Rhee regime was "rotten" and had lost the confidence of the Korean people.[3] Harold Ickes, in his weekly column in that magazine, wrote that Rhee ran a "corrupt police state,"[4] while Percy Winner, the foreign editor, did not shy away from discussing Rhee's "barbarous treatment of the Korean people."[5] Despite such commentary, the *New Republic* was actually not the harshest of Rhee's detractors. Prominent thinkers on staff at *The Nation*, including Julio Alvarez del Vayo and Freda Kirchwey, were perhaps Rhee's harshest critics of all.

Del Vayo wasted no time upon the outbreak of hostilities in condemning Rhee, as well as the United States for supporting him:

> Events in Korea have confirmed the position I have always taken on the cold war. The Achilles heel of Western political strategy in that struggle has always been the failure to realize that you cannot fight for democracy in alliance with

> undemocratic forces and regimes. This was the mistake made in China—a mistake which ended in Communist victory. In Korea the attempt to check the Communist drive from the north is weakened and compromised from the start by America's alliance with the government serving reactionary landowners, money lenders, and war-time collaborationists.[6]

Elsewhere, del Vayo compared Rhee's South Korea to Poland and France on the eve of World War II, countries that, according to him, were "politically rotten, infiltrated with fascists," and incapable of rallying their people to fight for a common cause.[7]

Not only did *The Nation* include a weekly column by the obviously anti-Rhee del Vayo but it also consistently published other pieces sharply critical of the Rhee regime, "one of the most repressive police states to ever enjoy our favor."[8] Shortly after the war began, a *Nation* editorial went so far as to suggest that Korean communism offered more to the Korean masses than Rhee's nominally democratic regime. North Korean troops "fight better" than their South Korean counterparts, ran the editorial, "because the Communist program offers them land, hope, and other things not evident in the performance of . . . Syngman Rhee."[9] Then, as US/UN troops regained the advantage after the Inchon landing and the North Koreans seemed on the verge of final defeat, several pieces in *The Nation* argued that a unified Korea headed by Rhee could never bring lasting peace to East Asia.[10] British journalist Alexander Werth, for example, warned of the consequences of a Rhee-dominated Korea by asking, "But now what? Is Syngman Rhee to be reinstated at Seoul and allowed to shed more blood to swell the torrents that flowed after 24,000 tons of bombs were dropped in the name of the UN? Or will a serious attempt be made to take into account the real wishes of the Korean people?"[11]

Finally, Freda Kirchwey described Rhee as a "reactionary" who, with America's blessing, used his "Japanese-trained police" to suppress opposition to his rule. This police force, together with Rhee's youth organization, "a semi-military, wholly fascist body," took the lead in such war crimes in Korea as the "brutal liquidation" of supporters of the northern regime. Thus, the United States effectively gave Syngman Rhee a free hand to repress his people under the guise of democracy, "and in doing so to make the name of America a stench in the nostrils of Asia."[12] For the editors of and contributors to *The Nation* and the *New Republic*, then, Syngman Rhee not only was unworthy of American support over the long term but was portrayed as a threat to the Korean future almost as grave as that posed by the invading communists.

The issues raised by US support for Rhee were some of the earliest during the Korean War about which there was an obvious left-right divide within the intellectual community, namely, between left liberals on the one hand, and conservatives and hawkish liberals on the other. Whereas liberals featured in *The Nation* and the *New Republic*, as noted above, were no fans of President Rhee, the liberals who wrote for the *New Leader* were not so quick to condemn him as a murderous or repressive fascist or reactionary. Rather, while that publication was not blind to Rhee's faults,[13] it generally took a supportive tone. The *New Leader* published pieces by Robert T. Oliver, for instance, who, as a former adviser to and vocal supporter of Rhee, argued that the primary reason Stalin ordered the invasion of South Korea was because that country's flourishing democracy was an obvious threat to his dominion over the Asian continent. "Naturally," wrote Oliver, "the Kremlin found this impressive example of political and economic democracy an intolerable threat to its design for subverting Asia's confused and uneasy millions. Hence, the unprovoked attack from the north on June 25."[14]

Readers of the *New Leader* found another spirited defense of Rhee and his democratic credentials in October 1950, when Indian prime minister Jawaharlal Nehru was working for a ceasefire in Korea, which would have prevented Rhee from extending his authority to any area north of the thirty-eighth parallel. Although Nehru was a favorite punching bag for conservatives and hawkish liberals, Jonathan Stout wrote that the United States must not allow the UN to "appease" Nehru, who was "coldly hostile" toward the Rhee government. Undercutting the Rhee regime to please Nehru, Stout argued, "means handing the Kremlin a large part of what it hoped to achieve in its Korean aggression." And in case this wasn't enough to rally Rhee's supporters, Stout concluded by reminding his readers that Rhee's government was "a child of the UN." Syngman Rhee had been chosen in a democratic election sponsored and overseen by the UN. As such, undermining the Rhee government meant "invalidating the UN's handiwork."[15]

Whereas the *New Leader* supported Rhee because he a) stood against communism, and b) stood against Nehru, the conservative *Freeman* had an additional reason: it supported Rhee because he was opposed by American liberals. In their characteristically sarcastic tone, the editors of *The Freeman* asked why, given that Rhee was constitutionally chosen in an election approved by the UN, "the scurry and the flutter of dubiety about Rhee's claims to the job?" Their answer was a direct attack on what they viewed as the scourge of the twentieth century, the liberal intellectual. "People who never heard of the town of Pusan before last August and September will solemnly swear to you," they editorialized, "that Rhee is nothing but a 'little Chiang Kai-shek.' They will tell you that he is a 'reactionary,' that he is a 'front' for the 'big landlords,' that he is corrupt." As far as *The Freeman* was concerned, this was "the same rigamarole," perpetuated by the liberal dupes of the global communist conspiracy, as that about Chiang Kai-shek prior to the fall of China to Mao's communists. And now the foolish liberals were falling for it again! Could they not see that behind the campaign to discredit Rhee were the same communist masters who had so effectively manipulated American public opinion during the Chinese civil war? In short, for the conservatives at *The Freeman*, "The attempt to grease the slides under Rhee is, of course, part of the never-ceasing Kremlin campaign to subvert the world."[16]

On a separate occasion, the editors of *The Freeman* took advantage of the Rhee issue to take a shot at one of their favorite targets: the Truman administration. "The Syngman Rhee government has been declared by the UN to be the constitutional government of Korea," they wrote. "But Mr. Acheson has suggested that it nevertheless set up an interim government to replace President Rhee, whose term does not expire until 1952." Inspired by Acheson's proposal that the UN replace a constitutionally elected leadership several years before the expiration of its term, they concluded wryly, "Perhaps the UN could be persuaded to do as much for us."[17]

In addition to defending Rhee, the conservative and conservative-leaning writers in the *New Leader*, the *American Mercury*, and *The Freeman* often indicted American liberals in general and the Truman administration in particular, especially Secretary Dean Acheson, for failing to foresee the Korean attack or, worse yet, for unwittingly encouraging the communist invasion of South Korea. The editors of the *New Leader*, most notably David J. Dallin and William Henry Chamberlin, thus distinguished themselves from their fellow liberals at *The Nation* and the *New Republic*, while conservatives at the *American Mercury* and *The Freeman* delighted in attacking the Truman administration for what they perceived to be its de facto pro-communist policies.

Dallin wrote of the "confused writers and political leaders" who, prior to Korea, consistently argued that peace with the communist world was possible. While not pointing a finger at any specific individuals, he argued that the failure to properly arm the Republic of Korea prior to the American military withdrawal from that country was both a symptom of that fallacious naïveté and a necessary condition for the communist invasion. The United States must "never again," he wrote, "repeat the great blunder of Korea—that of withdrawing our occupation troops before a sufficiently strong defense force had been created."[18] Others repeated this same argument in the pages of the *New Leader* in the weeks and months that followed.[19]

But perhaps the greatest liberal critic of the Truman-Acheson foreign policy was Dallin's compatriot at the *New Leader* William Henry Chamberlin. Not only did Chamberlin consistently parrot Dallin's argument about the failure to properly arm South Korea,[20] but he went much further in his criticism of Truman-Acheson policy in the Far East. It was no accident, he wrote, "that the Kremlin's first postwar resort to organized military force occurred in Asia, not Europe." After all, ran his argument, the United States had demonstrated its strength and its resolve to resist communist expansion in Europe. But he wrote that in Asia, on the other hand, "our policy has been weak, fumbling, and contradictory." The Truman administration "withdrew our troops from Korea," he continued, "without giving the government we recognized adequate means to defend itself." What's more, in regard to China, "the attitude of the State Department seemed to be one of waiting expectantly until the Communists overran Formosa." In short, Chamberlin argued that weakness invited the war in Korea, and only strength could prevent such disasters in the future. The onset of the Korean War, he concluded, "affords convincing proof that there is no strength in unpreparedness, no safety in surrender, no security in retreat."[21] If the United States was going to win in Korea as well as in the wider Cold War, implied Chamberlin, it would have to abandon the unfortunate weakness and timidity displayed in East Asia by Truman and Acheson.

While Chamberlin was a contributing editor and weekly columnist on the staff of the liberal *New Leader*, he was also a regular contributor to the conservative journal *The Freeman*. These two publications disagreed on most domestic policy matters, but when it came to foreign policy, they often marched in lockstep. Indeed, writers like the nominally liberal Chamberlin and Dallin, who focused most of their attention on foreign policy, seemed much more at home in the pages of conservative publications than they would have in the leading liberal weeklies *The Nation* and *New Republic*! In one of Chamberlin's pieces for *The Freeman*, he continued the line of argument he expounded almost weekly in the *New Leader*, writing, "Our fundamental blunder in Korea was the almost inexplicable failure to give South Korea an army with sufficient training and equipment to meet

. . . the ever-present threat of invasion from the North." Truman's State and Defense Departments, then, "must share a heavy burden of responsibility for almost inviting the Soviet satellite invasion."[22]

Writing much later in the war, toward the end of 1952, Chamberlin further elaborated his frustrations with Truman and Acheson's pre-Korea policies. Over the origins of the war, he asserted, "there broods an atmosphere of bungling, frustration and futility." Articulating an early form of the domino theory, he argued that once China fell to communism, maintaining a free government in South Korea was the key to preventing a red tide from washing over all of Asia. If Korea had fallen, he wrote, Japan would have been next, followed by other "wavering elements" in Asia. But what was our policy, he asked? It was to inhibit rather than encourage strong South Korean defenses, despite our knowledge that the Soviets had created a powerful army in North Korea. The high point of this failing policy, he added, was Secretary Acheson's "stupid speech" in January 1950, which announced that Korea was outside America's defense perimeter. Thus, he concluded, "the attempt to assure peace through weakness—through 'not provoking' the Communists—was proved bankrupt on June 25, 1950."[23]

While Chamberlin was a prominent voice from within the "liberal consensus" who placed a good deal of responsibility on the Truman administration for the outbreak of war in Korea, there were certainly other, more conservative, voices unleashing even more scathing attacks on Truman, Acheson, and liberals in general. Isaac Don Levine, for example, complained bitterly, in the inaugural issue of *The Freeman*, that former fellow travelers were being too easily forgiven after their conversion to anti-Stalinism in the wake of the Korean War:

> The pastures of opinion in general and the commanding heights in Washington in particular are full of so-called liberals who are now hailed as great patriots because they have joined the beating of drums for action in Korea. These post-Korean patriots are the very ones who helped deliver China into Soviet vassalage, who cried "witch-hunt" when Alger Hiss was put on trial by jury, and who through their consistent appeasement of Muscovite despotism paved the way for the bloody events in Korea. Such is the lot of yesterday's fellow-traveler. Today his path is strewn with roses.[24]

This was an especially jagged pill for Levine to swallow, since he felt that he and his colleague Ralph de Toledano were being scorned in the realm of liberal opinion for demanding a reckoning for those responsible for the loss of China and, by extension, for the outbreak of war in Korea. It was the

Levines and Toledanos, after all, who were, as Levine put it, the "pioneer opponents of Communist totalitarianism."[25] With the advent of this new publication, *The Freeman,* conservatives at last felt they had a platform from which to project their considerable voices. And project they did.

Whereas Levine had vented his frustration with liberals in general, Samuel J. Kornhauser used this new medium to launch a much more specific attack on the Truman administration regarding its responsibility for the Korean War. He called the administration's foreign policy establishment "opinionated amateurs" whose "lack of training and skill" had been exceeded only by their "incurable sense of self-sufficiency, complacency, and capacity to blunder." For Kornhauser, the root of the problem was that America had permitted the "pernicious doctrine" to be established that the executive branch had sole dominion in authoring the nation's foreign policy. As such, Truman, "unschooled in the rudiments of statecraft" and "with only the elegant but feeble courtier Acheson hanging on his sleeve," had a free hand to determine the fate of the nation. His timidity invited the North Korean attack, and now the country was paying a terrible price for his weakness.[26] Clearly, for the contributors to *The Freeman*, responsibility for the outbreak of war in Korea was not Moscow's alone. That burden was also borne by Harry Truman and Dean Acheson.

Perhaps no writer made this argument more explicitly than frequent contributor to *The Freeman* Alice Widener. Writing near the second anniversary of the onset of the war, Widener introduced her topic thusly: "It is now two long years since Americans began to pay in blood for the fatal Roosevelt-Truman-Acheson-Marshall Asiatic policy, which led to the Soviet-inspired aggression against the Republic of Korea in June 1950." The roots of this "Truman-Acheson War of Appeasement," she argued, could be found in the administration's supposed suppression of General Albert Wedemeyer's 1947 report on China and the Far East. In particular, she said, Wedemeyer had recommended that American forces stay in South Korea until that nation had an army sufficient for its own defense. This recommendation was never implemented—an act of negligence which, according to Widener, prepared South Korea for the taking. Then, of more immediate causality, the war launched by the Soviet-inspired North Koreans was "the inevitable result of the Truman-Acheson delineation, in January 1950, of the American defense line in the Pacific."[27] She made much the same argument in a similar piece in the *American Mercury*.[28] In short, for Widener, had Truman and Acheson listened to Wedemeyer and implemented a more forceful anticommunist policy in China and Korea in the years since World

War II, the Korean War likely would have never occurred. As such, the leaders of the Democratic Party had blood on their hands.

Though *The Freeman* was a new journal of opinion, in late 1950, around which angry conservatives could rally, it was not the only such publication. The *American Mercury*, founded by H. L. Mencken in 1924, began taking an avowedly conservative tack under the editorship of William Bradford Huie, who took the reins in December 1950, when the Korean War was only five months old. Pieces in the *Mercury* placed blame for the Korean War on the Truman administration's policy of weakness in Asia in much the same way as pieces in *The Freeman*.[29] But some went even further. Max Eastman, disaffected leftist turned conservative, sarcastically applauded Acheson's "brilliance," once the Chinese intervention in Korea was already an established fact, for his insistence that the United States do nothing further to provoke the Chinese communists. For Eastman, it was precisely this kind of weakness that invited the Korean War in the first place! "The Chinese Communists will be 'provoked' by one thing and one only," wrote Eastman, "another exposed point in our defenses, another chance to win a battle for the totalitarian world-communist crusade." Weakness invited aggression, ran Eastman's argument, while strength deterred it. Yet Truman and Acheson had apparently not learned that lesson. As such, Eastman concluded his attack on the administration with some extreme rhetoric indeed: "Ignorance in the executive, ignorance in the makers of foreign policy, at such a juncture, is more dangerous than treason."[30] For Eastman, not only was Truman and Acheson's bungling timidity responsible for the loss of life in Korea, but their appeasement-minded approach to China was tantamount to disloyalty.[31]

Alice Widener added her own critique of Truman and Acheson's Korea policies to the pages of the *Mercury*. "Either Korea is of strategic importance to us or it isn't," she wrote. "If it is, then Truman and Acheson misled us by withdrawing our troops and opening the way for our enemies to take it. If Korea is not important, then Truman and Acheson misled us by ordering our troops to fight for it."[32] While this may seem a fairly logical argument on its face, one must keep in mind that Korea may not have been of significant strategic importance to the United States at any point, but it came to have tremendous *symbolic* importance to the United States once the communists crossed the thirty-eighth parallel. In other words, if the United States failed to meet the aggression in Korea, then the Soviets would only be encouraged to launch future such aggressions—much as Hitler had been encouraged via the policy of appeasement in the 1930s—not to mention that failing to meet the challenge might send the message to America's European allies that the United States would leave them in the lurch if and when push came to shove with the communists.

While Truman and Acheson were the favorite whipping boys of those on the right, liberals tended to praise the president's courage and resolve in meeting the challenge in Korea. Rather than looking to the recent past, as their conservative counterparts did, the liberals at *The Nation* and *New Republic* focused more on the immediate crisis in the Far East. *The Nation* took up its defense of Truman almost immediately after the war began, editorializing that the president's decisive stand against communist aggression in Korea would leave the administration's critics wondering what would become of their most commonly enunciated arguments: that the administration was soft on communism and would stand aside as the Russians took Asia without a struggle. The editors called such arguments "feeble and contradictory" and mocked the conservative position that the United States had bafflingly "abandoned" Chiang Kai-shek—"that is, we and a few hundred million Chinese." What should Truman and Acheson have done in China, according to *The Nation*'s interpretation of conservative thought on the subject? "Presumably what we should have done was to pour arms into a doomed cause."[33]

Similarly, *The New Republic* editorialized that Korea "has changed everything" about how the country and the world should view President Truman. When news of the invasion first broke, they wrote, everyone in Washington knew what Truman was going to do: "he was going to appease." Yes, conventional wisdom said that "weak, vacillating Truman" would wither under the heat and pressure of open war initiated by Moscow. But when the "diplomatic masterpiece" that was Truman's executive order hit the wires, "Washington took a new look at the President. It found that he had fooled them even more than he did on Election Day, 1948." Finding it strange that the president was so consistently underestimated, the editors noted that his determined leadership wiped out a national mood of "pathetic fatalism" and replaced it with an "almost unprecedented moral unity."[34] Strange, indeed, that the president responsible for the Truman Doctrine, Marshall Plan, and NATO should have been so widely considered "soft" when it came to standing up to communism.

WHAT DID THE WAR MEAN?

We have seen that there was a sharp divide between America's leading liberal and conservative opinion journals on the extent to which Korean president Rhee and American president Truman were responsible for the outbreak of war in Korea in June 1950. Liberals tended to excoriate Rhee whenever they could, while defending Truman and Acheson as strong and wise leaders. For conservatives, it was precisely the opposite: Rhee was the brave champion of democracy, while Truman and Acheson were little more than contemptible scoundrels who invited communist aggression via negligence or appeasement. But what of the larger issue of the war itself: What did the first hot war of the Cold War mean? Would Korea go down as a historic turning point for America and the world? If so, was it because it would be the first step down the path to a new global war of annihilation, or because it would be the first step down the path to the ultimate restoration of peace and justice in the world?

Most of the editors of and contributors to *The Nation* and the *New Republic* doubted that the outbreak of war in Korea meant that the world suddenly stood on the brink of a Third World War. If there was any truly global threat from the localized fighting, they suggested, it was that Stalin might be emboldened to order his satellites to begin or intensify other "little wars" like Korea in hot spots like Yugoslavia, Iran, or Indochina. If this occurred, liberal thinkers feared, the Soviet Union could effectively dictate where and when the United States would have to commit its resources to put out local fires, thus bleeding America white without risking the loss of a single Russian soldier. But generally, left liberals tended not to think the sky was falling.

Other liberals, however, namely, those at the *New Leader* and *Commonweal*, were more likely to think (or, in some cases, even desire) that World War III was in the offing. Writing in the *New Leader*, Daniel James urged the United States to prepare, both materially and psychologically, as though a new world war were imminent. Such a course of action stood to reason, he argued, because Korea had made such a war a very real possibility. "Is there anyone in the democratic camp," he asked, "who can, with certainty, assure us that Korea is *not* the beginning of World War III? There is not." He continued, "Is there anyone on our side who can, with equanimity, guarantee that Soviet planes will not, some fine morning soon, drop atomic bombs on our large cities? There is not."[35] In fact, prior to Soviet development of intercontinental ballistic missiles in 1957, the USSR did not have sufficient bomber range to reach the mainland United States with atomic weapons. But this did not deter James. In a follow-up piece, he elaborated, "The issue is survival—national survival, world survival. Korea was the turning point. Gone is the day when we dared be smug. The only mood we can afford is the one that assumes the worst and prepares for the worst. For if World War III is not in fact already here—and who can prove conclusively that it is not?—then it may be imminent."[36]

Nor was James's thinking unique in the pages of the *New Leader*. Even the editorial staff joined in on the near hysterics of the summer of 1950. Incredulous at how complacent both American leaders and the American people seemed to be in the midst of the world crisis brought on by the Korean invasion, they editorialized, "This country resembles, in our opinion, the classic portrait every schoolboy has of Nero fiddling during the burning of Rome." Had it not occurred to anyone in the White House, they asked incredulously, that Korea may be the precursor to a bigger war? Indeed, they suggested that 1950 "might be recorded by historians as the Year of Catastrophe." What would it take to shock the nation out of its slumber? they asked. "A rain of Moscow-made missiles on Washington itself?" In conclusion, they breathlessly warned, "this is not time for politics-as-usual, business-as-usual, or life-as-usual." At stake was nothing less than national and world survival. "And it takes more than a deftness for platitudes to survive."[37] In a separate instance, the editors brooded poetically, "Few realize that Korea, with its earth almost entirely laid waste and millions of its citizens rendered homeless, is one of the most tragic victims ever preyed upon by the gods of war. Korea could be a preview of things to come, and in that unhappy land, therefore, as John Dunne long ago suggested, the bell tolls for us all."[38]

In the pages of *Commonweal*, as one might expect, the ruminations about a potentially apocalyptic World War III were infused with less secular, more biblical imagery. Erik von Kuehnelt-Leddihn, an Austrian with a decade-long American residence and a future contributor to *National Review*, worried about the fate of his home continent in the wake of the communist invasion of South Korea. Could warfare on that remote Asian peninsula have meant that Europe's halcyon days of postwar peace were numbered? He expressed his pessimistic fears thusly:

> It is later than most of us realize. Holy Year visitors may find Europe a gay continent, full of laughter. Paris or Rome may leave them with a delightful impression. Tyrolean villages, Dutch tulip fields, Swiss mountain hotels, the carefreeness of the Riviera or of Bavarian lake resorts may tend to create an illusion. They may see in Europe a big wonderful garden. A garden it is, but its secret, hidden name is Gethsemane.[39]

Elsewhere, the editors of *Commonweal* described the days immediately following the North Korean invasion as "the very hour the fate of the world hung in the balance."[40] They even wrote that, presumably due to the advent of the atomic age, "the implications, the possible consequences, of the Korean war are, as a matter of fact, more terrifying than those of World War II."[41]

While some liberals casually dismissed the possibility that Korea might be the opening round of World War III and others were convinced that the world stood on the precipice of disaster, some prominent writers almost welcomed the prospect of a global showdown between the United States and the communist bloc. David J. Dallin, who straddled the liberal and conservative worlds, was not merely convinced that Korea marked an epochal moment in history. He was excited about it.

Dallin's initial reaction to the outbreak of war in Korea was to extol the transformative effects that a military clash with communism must have for the United States:

> The whole emotional climate of the U.S. has been transformed. A new, magnificent fighting spirit has emerged. The outside world had begun to treat Americans with scorn, to revile us. The Orient had grown to expect only timidity and confusion from Washington policymakers. Now friend and foe alike are electrified and astonished at our re-dedication to the militant defense of liberty—that secular goddess who must bear a sword as well as a torch if she is to survive.[42]

Indeed, America's "re-dedication to the militant defense of liberty" meant, for Dallin, that "history has begun a new chapter." For the five years since the end of World War II, he wrote, "all manner of confused writers and political leaders" argued that peace with Stalin's Soviet Union was both possible and desirable. But the communist aggression in Korea, he decided, "shattered both of these seductive pipe-dreams."[43] As Dallin's compatriot William Henry Chamberlin put it, "All of these fantasies are gone—and good riddance."[44] From this point forward, in other words, the United States would lead the free world in a decisive crusade to defeat the monstrous evil of Soviet communism once and for all. Korea had changed everything. A new chapter in history had begun.

How would this global crusade begin? According to Dallin, the defeat of the North Koreans was only the first step, to be followed by much larger and more glorious victories for freedom, namely in China. As such, Stalin's error in dispatching his Asiatic minions southward across the thirty-eighth parallel would ultimately prove as fatal an error as when Napoleon and Hitler sent their invading armies into the grinding depths of the Russian winter.

> Intended to obliterate the last patch of non-Communist soil on the East Asian continent, Stalin's Korean adventure will lead, instead, to a contraction of the Soviet empire and the extension of the Western bridgehead in Asia to the very border of Manchuria. Direct contact with China, where an unscrupulous dictatorship is holding down the lid on a seething cauldron of unrest and misery, will have the greatest consequences. A turning point in Chinese history may be at hand, if the campaign in Korea is pressed with sufficient vigor and far-sightedness.[45]

If President Truman seized the historic opportunity given him by Stalin's mistake, then China herself could be pulled back out of the Soviet orbit. From the very beginning of the Korean War, then, this prominent liberal hawk began calling for the conflict to lead to a war of liberation against communist China.

But how did Dallin expect the Korean War to affect the Soviet Union itself? He wrote that, "little war" though it was, it was subjecting the USSR "to great economic, political, and military strain." As the North Koreans required greater and greater support from their superpower sponsors in Moscow, as US/UN troops regained the military momentum, "a large part of Soviet military strength is being shifted to the East," and "the vast supplies needed to keep the military machine running efficiently are rolling constantly over the badly overburdened Siberian railroads." This situation, according to Dallin, would exacerbate the already great strains on Soviet military-industrial infrastructure. After all, "Russia is still a very poor nation whose foreign commitments far exceed its capacity to meet them." For these reasons, Dallin argued that Korea was a necessary step, in the chain of events sure to follow, toward the ultimate defeat of Stalinism: "The Korean invasion is but one link—and by no means the last—in the chain of 'Stalinist Wars,' which will enter history, like the Napoleonic Wars, as the last convulsive spasm of an expiring revolution."[46] Dallin echoed this same theme in a piece for the conservative monthly the *American Mercury*, in which he argued that it was the Soviet Union's hubris, reinforced by the capture of China, that would lead to its ultimate downfall. Once again comparing Stalinist Russia to Napoleonic France and Nazi Germany, Dallin concluded, "It is this new feeling of superiority that has moved the Kremlin to initiate the Korean campaign. But this erroneous notion of superiority may become as fatal as similar notions held by many of the great warriors in world history."[47]

The economic strain placed on the Soviet Union by the need to supply the North Korean army aside, Dallin also saw the inevitable communist defeat in Korea as dealing a heavy blow to Stalin's psychological grip on his satellite empire. As the Soviet-sponsored North Korean army crumbled before the northward advance of US/UN troops in the fall of 1950, Dallin crowed, "The legend of Soviet invincibility is gone; so is the widely held notion that America will supinely acquiesce in every fait accompli Stalin creates." Dallin thus saw Korea as having stiffened the American spine, as well as having planted a seed of doubt in the minds of those millions under Stalin's sway behind the Iron Curtain. If the myth of communist world victory was being shattered in Korea, then the reverberations could not but shake the communist world to its very core: Russia herself. Defeat in Korea would not only lead North Koreans and Eastern Europeans to lose confidence in Moscow, but "the Russian people, too, will be set to thinking." For Dallin, the apparent defeat of communist armies in Korea meant that Stalin's cherished satellite buffer system, so painstakingly pieced together after World War II, was beginning to crumble: "Now American troops are moving toward the Soviet border, American naval patrols are cruising within sight of Soviet villages, and an American army is to be stationed at the gateway to Soviet-controlled Manchuria." These, Dallin mocked, were the "splendid contributions" made to Russian security by Stalin's irresponsibility in the Far East. As a result, doubts about Stalin's wisdom "cannot but preoccupy the minds of the Communist faithful abroad and the average Russian at home." As this doubt spread, so would the satellite peoples' desire for liberation from the communist yoke. Here, then, as the last of the North Korean communist resistance was about to be snuffed out, was how the Korean War would be recorded as one of the great turning points in human history. "North Korea was once a satellite," wrote Dallin, "but now it is free. Obviously, then, there *is* a road to freedom. 'What Korea has done,' the Poles, Rumanians, the Hungarians and the Bulgarians will start telling themselves, 'we, too, can do.'"[48]

Contributors to opinion journals on the left side of the spectrum uncharacteristically agreed that the US/UN stand in Korea was deeply symbolic of the West's determination to stand up to communist aggression in a way that it had failed to do in the face of Nazi aggressions in the 1930s. As such,

Truman's intervention, motivated in large part by the dictates of containment policy, was generally praised. But this doesn't mean that all liberals were altogether pleased with containment policy itself. In fact, left liberals like those at *The Nation* were sharply critical of containment policy for failing to place enough emphasis on food aid and development assistance to the third world, as well as on land reform and political independence for the peoples of Asia.

Freda Kirchwey, editor of *The Nation*, was the most vocal critic of containment policy on the left. She saw containment's primary shortcoming as its inability to deal constructively with what she commonly called the "revolution" sweeping Asia in the years after World War II. This revolution, she explained, was the result of the peoples of Asia waking from a long sleep to demand adequate living standards and political self-determination. By focusing on preventing communist expansion by military means, the United States, she argued, was taking precisely the wrong tack in Asia. America should have instead been focusing its considerable resources on things like food aid and development assistance. Such a course, she argued, would win more Asian hearts and minds in the long run than any amount of military protection from Soviet-style communism. Kirchwey thus viewed the desires of the peoples of Asia and the desires of American policymakers as increasingly incompatible. And the best example of this conflict, she thought, was to be found in Korea, which she called "a case history of the illness of our time."[49]

Kirchwey traced Korea's problems back to the end of World War II, when the Soviet Union and United States proved incapable of uniting Korea under a mutually acceptable form of government. Thereafter, the United States coddled the antidemocratic and reactionary Rhee regime, in effect discouraging the kinds of social and economic reforms that the people of South Korea desperately wanted, because those reforms might have smacked of socialism. "The meaning of it all," she wrote, "boils down to this: In the present stage of American political development we seem incapable of doing what needs to be done in countries ripe for revolution." What's more, whereas American policy fell short of satisfying Korean hunger for, say, drastic land reform, Soviet policy fulfilled that hunger. Then once the United States became militarily involved in Korea, this contrast was made clearer as General MacArthur moved north of the thirty-eighth parallel and allowed Rhee to set "the machinery of revolution" in reverse by restoring farmland to former landlords. The bottom line for Kirchwey was that Korea was a case study of the course of democracy's defeat. In other words, "Korea proves that when the U.S. uses its power to prevent revolution where revolution is inevitable, it sets its feet on a road that leads directly to war."[50]

Implicit in Kirchwey's argument was the suggestion that the communist aggressors in Korea were actually, in some sense, agents of social justice, while the American defenders of South Korea were actually the counter-revolutionary defenders of reaction. As we shall see, conservative critics of Kirchwey's *Nation* went on to raise quite a ruckus over her apparently pro-communist attitude, but Kirchwey seemed more interested in constructively criticizing American containment policy as implemented in Korea. She in fact urged the United States to transform its foreign policy in order to more effectively counteract the appeal of communism among the Asian peasantry, writing that the only way to meet the Russian challenge was "a drastic overhauling of our foreign policy in the direction of more courageous, aggressive democracy." In other words, she urged America "to put our own strength behind the forces of change. We must become, and quickly, the new sponsor of revolution, helping the peoples of the world to win all that communism promises or provides—plus liberty."[51] Indeed, even if American military intervention in Korea should succeed, wrote Kirchwey, it would accomplish little unless "fortified with a political program that revives the faith of Asia in our liberating purpose."[52]

Lest we conclude that Kirchwey stood alone on this point, it is worth noting that the editors of *Commonweal* also criticized the United States, though in a less strident tone than Kirchwey, for ignoring human needs in its twilight struggle against Soviet communism. Containment policy, editorialized *Commonweal*, fell short of its purposes because it lacked the drive necessary "to relieve the poverty of the Far Eastern peoples, something that has been so skillfully exploited by the Communists. The hunger of the Asiatics is for food and land and it does little good for us to sit back and watch the Communists satisfy that hunger."[53]

Such liberal critiques of containment policy's shortcomings were not necessarily just criticism for criticism's sake. Kirchwey and other writers for *The Nation*, as well as some of the more hawkish liberals at the *New Leader*, provided an alternative vision for how US policy could be transformed to meet the actual human needs of the peoples of Asia, even as it continued to meet the military necessities of containing communism's various armies. "If this country hopes to play the role of liberator in Asia," editorialized *The Nation*, "it will have to tie its intervention in Korea to a far more drastic and revolutionary policy than it has pursued in the past." This new "revolutionary" policy, if it was to succeed, needed "to offer now the concrete pledge of national freedom and basic economic reform" to all of the struggling countries of Asia, which were at once potential friends and potential enemies, including Indochina, Malaya, Korea, Formosa, and the Philippines.[54] *The Nation*'s foreign editor, Julio Alvarez del Vayo, put the matter thusly: "'Realists' tend to think only in terms of bombs, guns, and bases, but it is the crucial issue of giving bread and land and social justice to the peoples of the earth which will in the end decide the cold war."[55] If such promises of national freedom and economic reform sounded a bit vague, the editors of *The Nation* later offered more specific proposals, namely, that the United States assist the relevant countries in building roads, health-care infrastructure, and a more just and efficient system of agricultural production.[56]

Hitching a ride on the back of an Asian revolution for social and economic justice may seem like a perfectly fitting suggestion for left liberals to have made, but the more hawkish liberals at the *New Leader* did not disagree. They viewed Korea as "a highly unorthodox war" in that it was one "which will not be decided by force alone, but a war in which men's minds and spirits will assume pre-eminence." Previewing the debate over Vietnam that would come more than a decade later, they concluded the issue as follows: "For the nub of the whole issue in Asia is this: The Asians want, more than anything else, freedom from oppression in all its forms, native and foreign; and it therefore follows that the U.S. must frame a policy in line with—and not opposed to—the aspirations of the Asian people."[57]

Daniel James was even more explicit. America's function in Asia, he wrote, "is to become an ardent sponsor . . . of the Asian revolution." While strongly supporting US military action in Korea, he added that "our fight against communism can have meaning only if it is joined with a crusade to fight poverty, ignorance and disease." His specific recommendations included 1) urging European imperial powers to withdraw from and grant independence to hitherto colonized Asian nations, 2) ending America's cozy relationship with Asian reactionaries (he presumably had in mind Chiang Kai-shek, Syngman Rhee, and Bao Dai), and 3) giving vast economic and technical aid with no strings attached. Only in this way, he argued—such as via a marriage of military containment and proactive and altruistic aid—could America's strategy in Asia, up until then "foredoomed to defeat," stand a fighting chance.[58]

Still, even if the United States did change course to focus more on the human needs and national independence of Asian countries, liberals cautioned the fight for hearts and minds would not be easy. *The Nation* pointed out that "the Asian peoples, by and large, are less hostile to communism than they are to imperialism—and to them imperialism means Western intervention and control."[59] And while the *New Republic* editorialized, "Sooner or later we must recognize the fact that wars are not won merely by guns but by ideas," its editors also noted, albeit paternalistically, that among the "uncomfortable realities" in the Korean situation was "the difficulty a capitalist democracy faces in trying to proselytize a primitive people."[60] In any event, it is clear that most contributors to the leading liberal journals were quite critical of Korea-style containment methods to the extent that those methods were not adequately coupled with other, nonmilitary, means.

WAS THE WAR JUSTIFIED?

Whereas liberal voices generally supported America's involvement in Korea, many to the right of center took issue with President Truman's decision to send American boys to fight on Asian soil. It is worth noting that most of this criticism came only after the Chinese intervened, threatening to turn the tide of battle against the United States for good. Nonetheless, these debates remained squarely focused on some of the central questions surrounding the outbreak of the war, namely, the wisdom (and constitutionality) of Truman's intervention in Korea. In any event, conservative disapproval of the American entanglement in Korea not only recalled an earlier era of isolationism but also anticipated its unexpected resurgence in the early twenty-first century.

Writing in December 1950, *Freeman* coeditor Henry Hazlitt called the Korean intervention a "disaster," and one that demonstrated the "incompetence and unfitness" of the Truman administration. Indeed, Truman and Acheson's responsibility for this disaster was "as clear and direct as it could possibly be." In sending troops to Korea, Hazlitt contended, Truman ignored the judgment of military experts that Korea was strategically indefensible by US ground forces. But Truman disregarded the military wisdom of these unnamed authorities and acted "on the impulse of the moment." Now, several months later, the results of such a foolish decision were apparent, especially in light of the restrictions placed upon American freedom of action by the UN. "We have maneuvered ourselves into a preposterous situation," Hazlitt complained, "in which American boys do 90% of the fighting and dying, while our token-fighting or non-fighting 'allies' in the UN tell us what we can or can't do."[61] Hazlitt was here registering his disapproval of those American allies at the UN who objected to a MacArthur-led expansion of the war into China. In any event, so onerous were the mistakes and miscalculations of the Truman administration, thought Hazlitt, that he went so far as to call for the removal or resignation not only of President Truman but of his entire cabinet! Hazlitt's proposed mechanism to accomplish such a clean sweep? A constitutional amendment giving the people the power to change leaders "at any time"—the almost certain and constant political chaos this would engender apparently notwithstanding.

Nor was Hazlitt alone in his call for Truman to resign. *The Freeman*'s other editors joined in the chorus, writing that the president, via his Korea policy, was "leading the country down the road to calamity." They were quick to pronounce the Korean War, a full two and a half years before it ended, "the worst military defeat in our history." Chiding Truman for calling Korea a "symbol," they retorted, "It surely is. To the rest of us it is [a] symbol of a major and wholly avoidable defeat, a symbol of the folly of acting on the basis of wish-fulfillment rhetoric rather than of hard realities." What's more, they continued, Truman's stubbornness and incompetence would prevent him from changing course in any case. Where this editorial differed from Hazlitt's recommendations was in the proposed mechanism to remove Truman from office. A constitutional amendment was not needed, they asserted, because the Constitution already allowed for impeachment on the grounds of "inability to discharge the powers and duties" of the presidency. "Inability," they said, surely included gross incompetence, as to be determined by the Congress. However half-baked this theory of impeachment, they nonetheless looked forward to the removal of Truman and his cabinet, "whom many suspect, rightly or wrongly, of having permitted a continued useless involvement in Korea . . . in preference to permitting an earlier withdrawal and thereby admitting their original mistake in ordering our troops into the Korean trap in the first place."[62]

The *American Mercury*, *The Freeman*'s conservative monthly cousin, published similar views. Walter Trohan wrote in 1951 that the Korean intervention "is now conceded to have been one of the most foolish and disastrous decisions ever made by an American government." He made no mention of who, exactly, was making this concession. Instead, he maintained that, after 50,000 casualties, "we are now struggling to get out of Korea so that we can exploit the advantageous position which we were in before Truman, Marshall, and Acheson committed our ground troops."[63] How would sitting back and watching North Korean tanks steamroll an outgunned South Korea have placed the United States in an "advantageous position"? *The Mercury*'s editors argued that if Truman had relied on air and sea power instead of ground troops, all would have been much better for the United States in Korea. The United States, in this scenario, should have set up a World War II–style Korean government-in-exile in Japan and unleashed a furious air bombardment of North Korea while simultaneously imposing a crippling blockade on that country. South Korea, then, would not have been devastated, and American troops would not have had to suffer through the cold Korean winter. But, as it was in reality, they reminded their readers, the administration acted rashly and without input from Congress in ordering ground troops into Korea, and, as such, "all of the blood and devastation in Korea are, as a matter of fact, on the heads of Truman, Marshall, and Acheson."[64]

It is clear that many conservatives, writing in both *The Freeman* and the *American Mercury*, felt that American intervention in Korea was doomed to failure from the beginning. And the wisdom of taking a nation to war under a given set of circumstances is indeed a deadly serious topic. But conservatives laid a second charge, perhaps just as serious, at Truman's feet: that he had acted not only foolishly in ordering American troops to defend South Korea but also unconstitutionally. After all, unlike McKinley, Wilson, and Roosevelt before him, Truman neither asked for nor received a congressional declaration of war.

The first to launch an arrow at the president's claims of authority as commander-in-chief was Samuel J. Kornhauser, in the second issue of *The Freeman*. Kornhauser began:

> We are at war in Korea. Our young men are being killed and maimed there. Our army, our navy, our air force are engaged. Huge quantities of munitions and materials are sent to the scene of action. Hurried preparations are in progress to levy heavy additional taxes on our citizens, and to impose drastic restraints on their normal liberties. We are at war. Yet our Congress, the one agency vested with constitutional authority to declare war, did not do so. We are at war by Presidential edict.[65]

Kornhauser, unlike many of his fellow conservatives, did not take issue with the need for the United States to intervene in Korea. Rather, his focus was on Harry Truman's usurpation of congressional authority in doing so. "Now where, I ask," he continued, "is there any constitutional provision which by word or implication empowers the President to be the 'author and director' of our foreign policy?" For Kornhauser, questions of foreign policy needed to be aired in the crucible of congressional debate. That was, after all, why the Constitution gave Congress the sole power to declare war. To assume that foreign policy decisions did not fall under the ordinary process of self-government, he proceeded, would be to abandon democracy. Here, Kornhauser argued that an increasingly imperial presidency, at least in the realm of foreign policy, was a threat to the very existence of the Republic. "Unless we eliminate or drastically curtail the prevailing extra-constitutional functions of the Presidency," he wrote, then the United States, "the last competent force in the defense of human liberty," was "desperately imperiled" and democracy doomed.[66]

The Freeman later editorialized on these same points, slamming Truman for "the usurpation of power in the foreign field"[67] and dismissing as a fiction the president's claims that he had the right to deploy troops as part of a UN police action.[68] Such an abuse of presidential authority, the editors charged, amounted to "a menace of the utmost gravity to our security"[69] and could be remedied most effectively if the president were to step down immediately. "True," they admitted, "there is still no historic precedent for the resignation of an American chief executive who has lost the confidence of the country. But someone should call Mr. Truman's attention to the fact that the Constitution explicitly permits him to resign."[70]

The low likelihood that Truman would resign over Korea aside, the upshot of all of this is that Truman's conservative critics viewed his unconstitutional "usurpation" of Congress's war-making powers as the first step down a slippery slope, the end of which was the death of the Republic itself. This warning note, first sounded by Samuel Kornhauser, was a heady charge indeed, but one *The Freeman*'s editors returned to repeatedly. Harry Truman, they seemed to suggest, was a Caesar in the making, and Korea was his Rubicon. "A habit of contempt for the uses of Constitutional procedure," the editors insisted, "is the beginning of the end of government by law. What follows is government by men."[71] Garet Garrett further dramatized these dark possibilities by asking his readers to imagine a future historian, say, a thousand years in the future, "who may be trying then to trace the departing footprints of the vanished American Republic." State Department documents pertaining to the Korean War, he suggested, would be a precious find. The unconstitutional Korean precedent, Garrett concluded, would cast a long shadow over American history. "The simple question is," he wrote, "whose hand shall control the instrument of war? It is late to ask. It may be too late, for when the hand of the Republic begins to relax, another hand is already putting itself forth."[72]

The Freeman's conservative cousin, the *American Mercury*, was a bit more prosaic in its assessment, opting for straightforward language instead of grand comparisons between modern America and ancient Rome. "For the first time in the history of our nation," explained the *Mercury*'s editors, "the Constitutional authority of the Congress to declare war has clearly been bypassed."[73] In any event, it is clear that conservative thinkers thought Truman's Korean intervention to be, at best, unconstitutional and, at worst, a threat to the very existence of American republicanism.

But how did liberals deal with the question of the war's constitutionality? Writing in the liberal weekly *New Leader*, Cornell professor of government Clinton Rossiter agreed with conservatives that the answer to the question at hand—what was the constitutional scope of the president's authority to use force—"may well be decisive for the democratic future." But that is about where the agreement ended. Far from taking the Manichean approach of *The Freeman*, Rossiter called the issue "one of the most perplexing questions in constitutional law," and admitted that "a final and precise solution to the constitutional problem is impossible to achieve." Despite this disclaimer, Rossiter ultimately concluded that the president's power as commander-in-chief must be "unqualified." As for Republican senator Robert A. Taft's charge that President Truman had acted unconstitutionally in sending troops to Korea without congressional approval, Rossiter opined that Taft's argument was more political than constitutional. If Truman and Taft had been members of the same party, he implied, then Taft would never even have raised the issue. Besides, he added, "the Constitution has always been the last refuge of the out-argued politician."[74]

The Nation also took aim at "Mr. Republican," Senator Taft. He was, after all, the leading voice in the Senate on the issue of Truman's supposed usurpation of congressional authority. Like Rossiter, Kirchwey and company condemned Taft's attack as disingenuous, since the Republican leadership in Congress was apparently not seriously considering a move to impeach the president—the only punishment seemingly fitting for such an outrageous abuse of presidential authority. "To bring a grave indictment of this sort in a period of national emergency," they editorialized, "is extremely drastic in any case; to do so without intending to take appropriate action is the depth of recklessness and should stamp Taft as a man without scruple."[75]

The following week, in an editorial titled "Who Makes War?," *The Nation* once more dismissed as pure political grandstanding Taft's argument that Truman had unconstitutionally usurped authority. To make their case, they first noted that Senator Taft "wholly approved" the president's decision to dispatch sea and air forces to Korea in the immediate wake of the North Korean invasion. They then pointed out that when Truman took the more significant step of ordering in ground troops, he made sure to disclose his decision to a bipartisan group of senators and congressmen, and "none dissented; nor was [a] single voice raised on the floor of either house against the move, which, incidentally, was made at the request of Louis Johnson, then Secretary of Defense, and General Douglas MacArthur." They made sure to mention MacArthur in this regard because, by January 1951, battle lines over MacArthur's vision for the war were already drawn, with conservatives tending to place the good general high on a pedestal of virtual infallibility. Thus, if Taft objected to Truman's unconstitutional usurpation of authority, ran the argument, then he must surely also acknowledge MacArthur's complicity in that usurpation. In any event, the editors argued that there was naught but hearty approval of Truman's Korean policy from the Republicans until the Chinese flooded across the Yalu, eventually turning the tide of battle against US forces. In short, "the President's 'offense' became 'heinous' at exactly the moment when the military reversal set in."[76]

Whatever Taft's motivations in condemning the president, be they crudely political or genuinely principled, the editors of *The Nation* did move on to tackle the issue on a more substantive level, writing, "Anyone who has ever opened an American history book knows that the record is replete with such 'police actions.'" They argued that US history held "literally more than a hundred" examples, from Jefferson dispatching the navy to deal with the Barbary pirates, to Polk ordering troops to the Texas-Mexico border, to McKinley sending troops to China to put down the Boxer Rebellion, to Wilson's interventions in Mexico and Russia, to the countless police actions in Latin America under the umbrella of the Roosevelt Corollary. "In almost all these cases," they wrote, "ground forces were used without prior Congressional sanction." Moreover, they argued, such executive actions on the part of these commanders-in-chief were perfectly consistent with the original intent of the Constitution. An early draft of the Constitution, they noted, assigned Congress the power to "make" war, but "after some debate the verb was deliberately changed to 'declare' so that the President might have the power to use force, in Madison's words, 'to repel sudden attacks.'" And lest there had been any confusion on the matter, they added that, given the newfound responsibilities of the United States in containing global communism, "resistance to an invasion of Korea may well come under the head of 'repelling sudden attack.'"[77] In short, many American liberals defended the constitutionality of the Korean intervention almost as forcefully as conservatives attacked it.

CONCLUSION

In the pages of America's leading political opinion journals, different ideological camps had very different answers to the issues raised by the outbreak of war in Korea in the summer of 1950. Left liberals placed a great deal of blame for the outbreak of war on South Korean president Syngman Rhee, while conservatives and hawkish liberals used the occasion to lambaste Truman and Acheson. Some liberals feared Korea was an ominous sign of an impending war of global destruction, while others actually welcomed the prospect of a showdown with Stalinist Russia. Many liberals disapproved of the Korean intervention to the extent that it reflected a policy that was excessively militaristic and insufficiently humanistic, while conservatives disapproved of American intervention in Korea for reasons both political and constitutional. In sum, the debate that dominated the pages of American opinion journals in the first weeks and months of the Korean War was both heated and robust, and it exposed substantive fissures within the "liberal consensus." At the same time, conservative voices utilized their newfound platforms in *The Freeman* and the *American Mercury* to articulate a much more coherent agenda than we might have expected to find some five years prior to the founding of William F. Buckley Jr.'s *National Review*. As we shall see, as the war grew more complicated upon the intervention of communist China in the fall of 1950, these trends would only be exacerbated.

2. Chinese Intervention

Having regained the momentum in the war, US/UN forces first liberated Seoul during the final week of September 1950, then forged ahead, north of the thirty-eighth parallel, during the first week of October. The move, desired by General MacArthur, was supported by President Truman and the Joint Chiefs of Staff in Washington, despite Chinese warnings that Peking would intervene in Korea should American forces invade the North. But even before US/UN forces recaptured Seoul, in September 1950, some writers had already broached the subject of crossing the thirty-eighth parallel to unify Korea by force, to rid that country of communism once and for all. As the possibility of unification by force became a much more realistic one, after MacArthur's successful landing at Inchon, the issue briefly became a central focus in the pages of America's leading opinion journals. The left liberals at *The Nation* argued that the fighting should stop once Americans reached the prewar boundary, while their counterparts at the *New Republic* were a bit more willing to contemplate the potential benefits of pressing on into North Korea. Meanwhile, more hawkish liberals at the *New Leader* and *Commonweal* voiced their full-throated support for transforming Korea from a war of containment into a war of liberation.[1] As that debate quickly became moot due to the fait accompli, new, more dire discussions filled these journals following China's intervention in Korea. This, agreed most contributors, might be the start of a third and final world war. While most agreed that the United States bore the greatest responsibility for such a catastrophe, conservatives and hawkish liberals tended to blame American timidity for emboldening Moscow, while left liberals blamed the reckless militarism of American foreign policy. Finally, once war panic had subsided a bit, writers disagreed about the possibility and desirability of good faith negotiations with communist China. Was Mao merely Stalin's stooge or a potential Asian Tito? What concessions, if any, would it be wise for the United States to offer China, especially regarding the Chinese seat at the UN and the future status of Formosa? Or would the very act of negotiating be tantamount to appeasement?

CROSSING THE THIRTY-EIGHTH PARALLEL

During the earliest days of the war, *The Nation*'s Washington editor, Willard Shelton, was already arguing that the American war aim should be to preserve South Korea, not to forcibly unite all of Korea under one democratic banner.[2] To push for the latter, he implied, was to take the unacceptable risk of provoking a Soviet-American war. "All that is needed to forestall any immediate danger of general war," he wrote, was that the United States "stop—as promised—at the line approved by the UN."[3] Shelton continued to argue for this limited policy through the end of the summer of 1950.[4]

Once it became clear, in September 1950, that UN forces had already crossed the thirty-eighth parallel, *The Nation* voiced its grave disapproval. The primary reason for the editors' objection was the likelihood that a US/UN invasion of North Korea would provoke Chinese intervention in the war. They noted China's "solemn warning" that it would not tolerate enemy forces north of the thirty-eighth parallel and thus concluded that the theretofore limited struggle in Korea was about to turn into a vastly larger conflict. If this were to happen, then the justified American resistance to the North Korean aggression "might quickly and perhaps half accidentally be transformed into a general war against the Asian revolution." In other words, what the editors of *The Nation* most feared was an American-led crusade (in partnership with an Asian reactionary like Chiang Kai-shek) against the forces of social change and economic justice throughout Asia. The editors of *The Nation* may here have been flirting dangerously with becoming apologists for Mao Tse-tung's regime in Peking, but their more immediate concern was to prevent the United States from getting bogged down in an open-ended ground war in Asia, especially against zealous Asian revolutionaries who, in one form or another, represented the legitimate aspirations of the peoples of Asia for land, bread, and self-determination. Thus, "the decision to cross the border," they concluded, "carried with it the threat of staggering consequences."[5]

Freda Kirchwey added yet another reason why she disapproved of UN forces crossing the thirty-eighth parallel: that the invasion would further ingrain suspicion of America in the minds of the people of North Korea, "ordinary folk who have felt the weight of American bombs and seen their factories and roads and bridges blown to dust." MacArthur's move into North Korea, she wrote, could only serve to convince the North Koreans that the Americans planned to install "the distasteful Rhee regime as the government of all Korea." Faced with the prospect of such a government being imposed on them, the people and army of North Korea, according to Kirchwey, would commit themselves to a desperate fight-to-the-end to prevent such an eventuality. Thus, "nothing could be less conducive to a quick ending of the struggle than the counter-invasion by the South."[6]

For Kirchwey and her fellow editors at *The Nation*, then, crossing the thirty-eighth parallel brought with it the danger of a significantly expanded war (most likely with China) as well as the danger of losing hearts and minds throughout Asia. As MacArthur's troops pressed ever farther northward toward the Manchurian border in October 1950, Kirchwey became progressively more pessimistic. She noted almost resignedly that her fears were all coming to fruition, as Rhee began sending governors and police to take charge of the newly liberated areas of North Korea, not to mention his right-wing youth organizations, which were there to "teach democracy." Moreover, nothing would seem so likely to provoke Chinese intervention as to permit Rhee's forces to occupy the border area near the Yalu River. Though at this point there was nothing anyone could do to reverse the damage already done, Kirchwey still felt that ultimate disaster (i.e., Chinese intervention) could be averted. "The most prudent as well as the most humane course," she counseled, "would be to call a halt some distance south of the border."[7] Thus, by mid-October 1950, Kirchwey had resigned herself to the reality of an expanded sphere of influence for President Rhee but was still hopeful that war with China could be avoided. Little did she know that even as she expressed this hope, Chinese troops were already crossing the Yalu in large numbers, about to present the United States, in MacArthur's words, with "an entirely new war."

While the left liberals at *The Nation* consistently opposed crossing the thirty-eighth parallel to unify Korea by force, their counterparts at the *New Republic* were not so insistent. Although the *New Republic* did at one point warn, with some concern, that Korea "could still be the spark for a general war" between the United States and Russia if and when UN forces launched an offensive north of the thirty-eighth parallel,[8] this did not represent that magazine's general line. Rather, when the editors weren't matter-of-factly and without objection taking for granted that US/UN forces would ultimately occupy the whole of the Korean peninsula, they were dismissing the border between North and South Korea as "artificial,"[9] and therefore unworthy of the sanctity normally accorded to the boundaries of a sovereign nation. Writing in the pages of the *New Republic*, journalist Peter Kihss answered the question of status quo ante or forced reunification thusly: "It would seem sounder to decide now to press for a unified Korea and to drive on to a situation where the UN might occupy the entire country."[10] Finally, a *New Republic* editorial suggested that the primary US/UN war aim ought to be a united and democratic Korea (though not necessarily one governed by Syngman Rhee), despite the very real danger such a policy would carry of provoking either Russian or Chinese intervention.[11]

Clearly, the two most prominent liberal journals were far from unified in their assessment of the risks and rewards of unifying Korea by force, with *The Nation* opposed and the *New Republic* in support, however tepidly. *Tepid* is not the word one would use, however, to describe the liberals at *Commonweal* and the *New Leader* on this point. They were unabashed in their support for crossing the thirty-eighth parallel.

During the first few weeks of the war, Waldemar Gurian, frequent contributor to *Commonweal*, was already writing that a mere victory for containment (i.e., pushing the North Koreans back above the thirty-eighth parallel) would not be satisfactory. The status quo ante, he wrote, was simply unacceptable. In his own words, "Avoiding appeasement is not enough. Positive steps and policies are necessary."[12] A *Commonweal* editorial was more detailed in its policy preferences. The editors rejected the idea, floated by *The Nation*, of a UN trusteeship for Korea, instead calling for the Republic of Korea to be "a sovereign, undivided nation."[13] Here they were also going beyond what the *New Republic* had advocated. They were calling not only for a unified Korea but for one administered by the Rhee government. Later, they were even more insistent that Korea be unified by force. An American failure to reunite the country after the fighting stopped, they suggested, would amount to a devastating defeat in the Cold War, as little else would so delight communists around the world. Therefore, it was precisely the possibility of a still-divided Korea that needed to be prevented at almost any cost. And to prevent it, they concluded, US/UN troops may be forced to move north of the thirty-eighth parallel.[14] Even the possibility of Soviet and/or Chinese intervention left them undaunted: "If we can keep the offensive moving at this pace," they wrote, "we would stand a good chance of doing away with Russia and China's opportunity to intervene. Eliminating the temptation, this is called."[15] For the editors of *Commonweal*, then, so long as Soviet and/or Chinese intervention was merely a potentiality, the invasion of North Korea should proceed unhindered.

The editors of the *New Leader* were more strident, if also more poetic—especially David J. Dallin. Almost immediately upon the outbreak of the war, Dallin called for Korea to be a war not merely of containment but of liberation. "One thing is clear," he proclaimed, "there can be no return to the status quo ante. That geopolitical monstrosity, a partitioned Korea, must be relegated to the attic of history." For the people of Korea, he exulted, "the hour of liberation and unification has struck."[16] Dallin may have been the first of his contemporaries to call openly for the forced reunification of Korea, but his was not the only voice to do so. Robert T. Oliver wrote in the following issue that the United States must not only halt the communist attack but move all the way to the Chinese-Korean border. A dangerous precedent would be established if the United States was content to win a victory for containment and stop at the thirty-eighth parallel, Oliver suggested, as Stalin would conclude that he had nothing to lose by any other military adventure he chose to launch.[17] In other words, unless the communists were faced with actual *loss* of territory, as opposed to mere failure to acquire new territory, they would have little incentive to abandon their expansionist ways.

Dallin's fellow editors at the *New Leader* also agreed very early in the war that the thirty-eighth parallel ought not stand as an inviolable border, writing that the UN must prosecute the war in Korea "to the very fullest degree, relaxing only when the invader is driven off that unhappy peninsula."[18] Later, once US forces actually approached the border, the editors asked, "Shall Korea be permitted to become another Germany—divided, and a source of division—or will we prove capable of making our military victory stick by quickly unifying Korea under a democratic regime?" Their preference, of course, was the latter, and they derisively called those who disagreed with them the "apostles of confusion and retreat." In case there was any doubt about where they stood (unlikely though this may have been given the title of the editorial, "Unite Korea!"), they concluded by writing that MacArthur should immediately occupy all Korean territory north of the thirty-eighth parallel.[19]

In the first week of October 1950, as American forces stood poised to enter North Korea, the editors of the *New Leader* couched their argument in the context of what they perceived to be the West's most glaring diplomatic failures of recent memory: Munich and Yalta. "Just as democracy was tested at Munich, but was found miserably wanting, so now it is being tested in Korea," they wrote. Their fervent hope was that the American government had learned the hard lesson from Munich and Yalta that timidity only emboldened aggressive totalitarianism. The only way to ensure a meaningful and lasting victory in Korea, then, was to boldly press northward to eliminate any and all communist presence on the Korean peninsula. Even if the communists came away with a partial victory in Korea, they wrote, "they will be wholly victorious—for a compromised peace in Korea will reveal to the world, with somber finality, that the democracies are unwilling and unable to lead mankind to peace with freedom." Thus, there could be no honorable alternative to unifying all of Korea under democratic government. They concluded by painting the issue of whether or not to cross the thirty-eighth parallel in grand, almost Churchillian terms:

> The future of the West is at stake, both in Asia and Europe. To Asians we have the opportunity to prove that our policy can bring peace and security, as well as freedom; to Europeans we shall be able to say that resistance pays. But if a Munich, or a Yalta, is brought about in Korea, then we will have sacrificed all Asia and all Europe to the Soviet Moloch, for after that no one will believe that the United States and its allies want or know how to lay the specter of Red fascism.[20]

This debate over whether to cross the thirty-eighth parallel, brief though it was, reflected two very different approaches to the Cold War, even from within the so-called liberal consensus. The left liberals at *The Nation* counseled restraint, arguing that to invade North Korea was to risk too casually provoking a wider war with China or the Soviet Union. The hawkish liberals at the *New Leader*, *Commonweal*, and to a lesser extent the *New Republic*, urged an aggressive boldness, based on the premise that restraint (or weakness, according to their way of thinking) would only encourage the communists to continue their aggressive ways. While both sides of the debate thought that disaster would befall the West if their specific recommendations weren't followed, it was *The Nation*'s concerns that were borne out by succeeding events. By the end of October 1950, it was clear that China had decided to intervene in force in Korea, confronting the United States with an entirely new set of challenges.

WORLD WAR III

In mid-October, as US/UN troops pushed ever closer to the Korean-Chinese border, Chinese troops began pouring across the Yalu River into Korea to engage the Americans. Apparently taken by surprise by the Chinese, MacArthur's overextended troops had to beat a hasty retreat southward, returning Seoul into communist hands. Such was the magnitude of the military reversal that by mid-December American officials had given up any hope of reuniting Korea under democratic auspices. Washington's new war aim became the restoration of the status quo antebellum—a divided Korea. Thus, when General Matthew Ridgway led a successful American counter-offensive against the Chinese between January and March 1951, recapturing Seoul in the process, most in official Washington expected a negotiated end to the war would soon follow.

In short, upon the Chinese intervention, the editors of and contributors to America's leading opinion journals, like MacArthur, were faced with "an entirely new war." Whereas the debate about whether or not to cross the thirty-eighth parallel in the first place was quickly rendered moot by the fait accompli, these writers had the opportunity to spill plenty of ink regarding the significance of this "new war" in Korea. Initially, at least, something unusual happened once it became apparent that China had decided to intervene substantially in Korea: opinion journals from across the ideological spectrum found themselves in agreement. Specifically, they agreed that the situation was extremely grave and might even lead to a Third World War. Almost all major opinion journals included some exceptions to this rule, but overall there was a fairly clear consensus that the circumstances facing the United States and the world were far more serious than they had been at the start of the war.

Writing in *The Nation*, Julio Alvarez del Vayo said that, now that China had intervened, "a long and terrible war seemed in prospect," and called the situation "extremely grave."[21] Freda Kirchwey wrote of the "end-of-the-world mood" that had enveloped Washington, and for good reason. The option America seemed most likely to exercise, in her view, was "to fight a limitless war against China, committing all available resources for an indefinite period, with a good chance that Russia would intervene in support of its ally either in the East or in Europe."[22] Willard Shelton added to the furor, writing that Washington had been "gripped by as bad a case of war jitters as just before Pearl Harbor," and noted that government officials "have bluntly discussed the imminent threat of World War III." Shelton feared, at best, "the full-scale commitment of China's battle-tested armies," which "could drag us into an endless war of attrition" on the Asian continent, and at worst, the Soviets taking advantage of the moment to strike in Europe, possibly leading to nuclear war.[23] Poet and playwright Archibald MacLeish even added his considerable voice to the pessimistic discussion:

> It may already be too late to discuss means of avoiding the unspeakable catastrophe of atomic war. The Chinese and Russian regimes are beating the drums of

> hate in every village across the north of Asia. Chinese soldiers have crossed the Yalu River in force. The army of the UN will not evacuate the peninsula. . . . Nothing but a Chinese withdrawal, either by choice or under pressure, can now prevent a conflict which would be no longer Korean but continental, and not continental only but world-wide.[24]

Thus, as Christmas 1950 drew near, the editors of *The Nation* were in no mood to celebrate. Instead, they marked the season in tones approaching despair:

> Only those of very tender years will be able to enjoy this Christmas fully: for the rest of us, listening to the bells with one ear cocked to catch the distant rumble of the guns, it will be hard to sing hymns of peace and good-will without consciousness of their ironic overtones. Nor can we wish our friends a happy New Year with any confidence when we must recognize the possibility that it may see the world plunged into a war which would wipe out civilization, if not mankind.[25]

The editors of the *New Republic* were similarly frightened about the possibility that Chinese intervention might mean World War III, especially in light of the West's "appalling lack of information" about Chinese intentions.[26] "The situation is really quite terrifying," they wrote. "Chinese reinforcements are crossing from Manchuria into Korea, and what happens after the buildup we don't know. It might be World War III."[27] Several weeks later they still could find no clear answers: "Has the Soviet thrown us so far off balance, while Western Europe still is weak, that World War III is now approaching in accordance with the Soviet timetable? Is the danger of World War III now so great that we should get out of Korea and put all our efforts in strengthening Europe?"[28] They finally seemed to inch closer to a concrete, if slightly dark, prognostication by Christmas 1950, when they editorialized that the *New Republic*, "deliberately and reluctantly, sets down its opinion that the global odds have shifted and that chances of war are now somewhat greater than those of peace."[29]

The editors of *Commonweal* seemed also to think that the sky might well be falling. Though it may appear hyperbolic in retrospect, they wrote in the wake of the Chinese intervention in Korea that the United States "has never before been confronted with so great a threat to its existence."[30] After all, it was clear, as they put it, that "a showdown is coming between the U.S. and China," and that what would begin as a limited war "is terribly likely to become less and less limited."[31] What they feared perhaps more than anything else was that America would prove excessively cavalier or even reckless in its response to the Chinese attack, relying wholly on force to do a job that only delicate diplomacy (or divine intervention) could finally solve. Indeed, as MacArthur's troops became increasingly locked in a death struggle with the Chinese, they wrote, "We become emotionally and intellectually hardened and committed to nothing much but force in Asia, an attitude which can only lead to war with China and eventually with Russia."[32] And such a war would mean, of course, the near certainty that many "irresponsibles" in the halls of government,[33] the "small boys among us who already kick the wall," would give in to their "swaggering emotionalism" and begin to call for the use of atomic weapons.[34] So could the unleashing of atomic war be avoided? They weren't so sure but, nonetheless, clung to the hope that it could. "Whether the world can achieve peace again without some belligerent's using the dread bomb looks, the way things are going, improbable. But . . . [t]he bomb, we have told the world, is a last resort. And while there is life there is hope."[35] In the end, the editors could do little but turn the fate of the world over to their God. "It is a time," they wrote, "for resolution and for prayer."[36] They gave no explicit indication that they might have been rash, if not altogether wrong, in their earlier calls to forcibly unify the peninsula, come what may.

The hawkish liberals at the *New Leader* were less afraid of nuclear war than they were of communist expansion, but even so, they tended to agree with their counterparts at *The Nation*, the *New Republic*, and *Commonweal* that Chinese intervention in Korea likely meant the dangers of a significantly expanded war. "Mao's entry into the Korean war," they wrote, "virtually guarantees that it will henceforth become a major war—if not actually a world war—whose ramifications will extend far beyond Korea itself."[37] Columnist David J. Dallin thought it an open question whether the Soviet Union would launch the Third World War rather than suffer an ultimate defeat in Korea, but he advised that we should be prepared for that eventuality: "It is by no means too soon—if anything, it is late in the day—for this country to train its sights upon the issues which may assume a tragic immediacy in the not-too-distant future."[38] Elsewhere, lead editor William E. Bohn wrote that the Chinese intervention, "obviously arranged by Moscow, brings us close to the horrors of the worst war of all time,"[39] while various editorials compared the global crisis created by the Chinese attack to that at the outset of World War II, and Stalin, in this way, to Hitler.[40]

It is quite clear, then, that liberals of various stripes shared the same fear in the immediate aftermath of the Chinese intervention in Korea, namely, fear of an imminent and likely atomic Third World War. But what of conservative writers? How did they view these developments in East Asia? As it turns out, conservatives too feared for the future of the world. But in expressing this fear, they never missed an opportunity to blame liberals for the whole mess. Prominent conservative intellectual Ralph de Toledano excoriated the liberals of the Roosevelt and Truman administrations for allowing, nay, encouraging, the evil that was the postwar Soviet accumulation of power, which, according to his interpretation of events, was approaching a destructive crescendo in Korea. As a result, the world now stood on the precipice of disaster. Framing the crisis in rather theological terms, fittingly enough for the Christmas season, Toledano wrote:

> In the past, when too much evil filled the world, God rained destruction and terror on humanity. With the passage of time, God developed a taste for irony. He put the punishment in man's own hands by letting him create the atom bomb. God let us manipulate destruction and terror and struck us with fear, not of His wrath but of ourselves. . . . in the wilderness of our time, in the Year of Our Lord 1950, the only sound was the distant, rising note of requiem.[41]

While Toledano's expression of lament sounded not unlike the hand-wringing of liberal writers, other conservatives went much further in their state of alarm. Also writing in *The Freeman*, Lawrence R. Brown asserted that the communist attack(s) in Korea were but a prologue to the Soviet Union's ultimate goal of attacking the United States. Although "respectable" opinion typically refused to consider a direct Soviet attack on the United States a realistic possibility, he argued that Stalin had both the ideological motive and the technological means to launch such a war of annihilation. He acknowledged that his argument presupposed that the Soviet Empire would be satisfied with nothing less than world conquest, but this he considered self-evident. Why did Stalin desire or even require the possession of more territory in East Asia, namely, in Korea? Because the Soviets needed an unbroken chain of territories to transport oil from Indonesia to Siberia, which would then serve as a base from which to launch attacks on North America, presumably via Alaska. Fantastic though this scenario may seem to us today, he urged that its plausibility required the United States to "recognize the state of war that now exists between ourselves and that department of the Soviet Government which calls itself Communist China." After all, better to risk general war now than to have the conditions of war dictated by Stalin later. Could Stalin be dissuaded by means short of war? According to Brown, it was too late for that. Not to disappoint his fellow conservatives, he laid the usual blame for America's vulnerability at the feet of Roosevelt and Truman: "We have, I fear, already assisted the Soviet Empire to become so mighty that I doubt its willingness to forego [*sic*] its great objective."[42]

Liberals and conservatives alike, then, both feared that the conflict in Korea, upon Chinese intervention, was about to spiral out of control and turn into a global Armageddon. But they disagreed entirely about who deserved blame for the coming catastrophe. Some liberals feared that it would be irresponsible American conservatives who would, via their emotional saber-rattling, push the world into atomic annihilation, while conservatives argued that it was soft-headed liberal policy that allowed the Soviet Union to rise to the position it now occupied: that of controlling much of Asia while bearing down on the West with the full weight of its own atomic arsenal.

Beyond what China's intervention might have meant for general war and peace, what did the editors of and contributors to America's leading opinion journals think it revealed about US foreign policy more specifically? Virtually all of the opinion journals examined here concluded that China's intervention revealed the bankruptcy of US policy, though in very different ways and for very different reasons. Continuing the debate that had begun about the origins of the war in the first place, hawkish liberals, most notably William Henry Chamberlin, and conservatives alike argued that the Chinese intervention proved once and for all that the Truman administration's weakness had not only failed to check communist aggression in the past but continued to embolden the master planners in Moscow and Peking. Left liberals, on the other hand, particularly those at *The Nation*, thought the Chinese intervention proved that US policymakers got drunk on military success and thus allowed themselves to be swept up in the illusory prospect of a quick, easy, and consequence-free military conquest of all Korea, even up to the Chinese border.

William Henry Chamberlin was his usual polemical self in assessing the West's response to the Chinese intervention. "Since Red China's inauguration of large-scale war" against the United States, he wrote, "the free civilized world has put on an exhibition so disgraceful that one hopes it will soon be ended and never repeated. If the meek spirit in which Mao Tse-tung's truculent aggression was accepted is indicative of the free nations' morale, then Stalin has won world domination without the need to fight a Third World War." Chamberlin was especially critical of the US/UN response (or lack thereof) to the Chinese delegation's rhetoric at a special session of the

UN—rhetoric that he called "more offensive and abusive than the Japanese declaration of war, delivered immediately after the attack on Pearl Harbor." What was worse, for Chamberlin, was that China was invited to this UN session in the first place. After Pearl Harbor, he noted, "No one suggested that Japanese special envoy Kurusu be permitted to follow up the attack by rising before an international forum in New York and delivering an abusive harangue against the United States."[43] Chamberlin in fact thought the similarities between the Japanese attack on Pearl Harbor and the Chinese attack on UN forces in Korea were much stronger than they actually were. He called the parallels "complete," despite the obvious difference that the former was an attack on US soil, the latter on Korean. What's more, he claimed both attacks came "without any warning," whereas, as noted above, China gave Washington plenty of advance notice that it would intervene in Korea if and when US forces crossed the thirty-eighth parallel.

In any event, Chamberlin continued with the tenuous analogy, if mainly to point out how the US reaction to Pearl Harbor was appropriately strong, while that to Korea was hopelessly weak. "How different has been the reaction to Mao Tse-tung's Pearl Harbor!" he exclaimed. Not only had that "inveterate appeaser," UN Secretary General Trygve Lie, disgraced the UN by inviting Chinese representatives to Lake Success but the British, far from breaking off relations with Peking, attended a dinner with the Chinese delegation! And when the Chinese met with India's "appeasement-minded government," many observers hailed it as a great diplomatic achievement. Meanwhile, he pointed out, UN forces in Korea "are compelled to fight against overwhelming numbers with one hand tied behind their back. There is no bombing of Chinese bases in Manchuria. Chiang Kai-shek is not being permitted to raid the Chinese coast and organize anti-Communist guerrillas." In short, for Chamberlin, "We are getting the worst of two worlds: war and appeasement." His conclusion was equal parts dark and frank: American and UN prestige, not to mention European morale, simply could not survive the "super-Munich" that was Korea.[44] Apparently, Chamberlin considered any kind of accommodation of the de facto Chinese government, whether its admission to the UN or its incorporation of Formosa into China proper, as nothing less than a "surrender" to Chinese military aggression—an aggression that he viewed to be as bad as or worse than the Japanese attack on Pearl Harbor.

This was neither the only occasion when nor the only angle from which Chamberlin argued that the Chinese intervention exposed the timidity of the United States and its allies. In February 1951, several months into the "new war" in Korea, he lambasted the West for having been overcome by "a wave of pessimism and defeatism" regarding its position vis-à-vis China. The standard argument, according to Chamberlin, of those who wanted to surrender was that standing up to China with force would provoke a larger war. In other words, Chamberlin was criticizing the spirit of what he considered US weakness, as evidenced not only by the Truman administration's refusal to bomb China and/or support a Chiang Kai-shek invasion of the mainland but by UN consideration of withdrawing from Korea altogether. "The assumption that peace can be safeguarded by continual one-sided retreats and surrenders," he warned, "is one that contains the seeds of ultimate demoralization, leading to the loss of our freedom or to war under desperately unfavorable circumstances." Suppose, after all, the United States left Korea, and Red China were admitted to the UN and allowed to take over Formosa. What then? "Can anyone in his right mind suppose that the Chinese Communists' avowed hatred and contempt for the United States would be transformed into love and esteem?" No, he answered. Rather, China would simply gobble up what remained of noncommunist mainland Asia, placing almost irresistible pressure on Japan in the process. Continued appeasement, in short, would lead either to a war against an immeasurably strengthened communist foe, or to a "Soviet satellite-world."[45]

Here Chamberlin was almost certainly attacking a straw man, as the Truman administration never seriously considered such measures as leaving Korea in the lurch or admitting China to the UN and handing over Formosa under military threat—the statements of some American allies at the UN notwithstanding. But Chamberlin nonetheless repeated many of these same themes, from the comparisons with Pearl Harbor to assertions of US weakness for not bombing China and unleashing Chiang, in the conservative publication *The Freeman*. Once more, his conclusion was that a strategy of appeasement, or, alternately, "a surrender to blackmail," was taking the United States down a slippery slope that could only end with the establishment of a communist-dominated world.[46]

While Chamberlin may have been the leading voice on this point, he was certainly not alone in his thinking. What made him unusual was that he was writing primarily for a nominally liberal publication, the *New Leader*. Most of those who felt similarly were of an avowedly conservative persuasion. Writing in *The Freeman*, for example, Forrest Davis, Washington correspondent for the conservative *Saturday Evening Post*, argued that the Chinese intervention in Korea was only the most recently harvested bitter fruit from twenty years of a weak-kneed diplomacy that was tentative if not "downright appeasing." A particularly egregious manifestation of this, he maintained, was the sight of the Chinese delegation visiting the UN: "the sight of our Chinese enemies basking in American luxury, slandering the United States while [our] sons fought their minions in a glacial Korea." In all, the fight against the Chinese in Korea was the culmination of years of postwar diplomacy that had failed to grasp the "full malignancy" of Soviet intentions. Why had it thus failed? Because of communist sympathizers in the American and British governments that had aided Mao's victory in China and were now unwilling to stand against his regime, however precarious his hold on power.[47] William Bradford Huie, editor of the *American Mercury*, made a similar argument about American postwar weakness of spirit empowering the communists in both Moscow and Peking, culminating in the emboldened Chinese Reds striking directly at American power in Korea.[48]

Whereas hawkish liberals like Chamberlin and conservative contributors to *The Freeman* and the *American Mercury* thought the Chinese intervention had exposed US policy as hopelessly timid, the left liberals at *The Nation* complained that it revealed US policy to be blindly militaristic. Indeed, Freda Kirchwey, editor of that liberal journal, blamed American adventurism for the Chinese intervention in the first place, noting that, in the immediate aftermath of the apparently successful UN drive north of the thirty-eighth parallel, "only a few voices, *The Nation*'s among them, continued to warn of a probable Chinese reaction as the UN troops approached the Manchurian frontier." But neither American nor UN authorities reined in General MacArthur, and "now the expected has happened. Chinese troops, in numbers still unknown, have joined the North Koreans in a powerful counterattack . . . and savage warfare has replaced the easy sweep toward the Manchurian border."[49] Thus, where Chamberlin and company saw excessive timidity leading to China's sweep across the Yalu, Kirchwey saw only reckless arrogance.

Nation staff contributor Andrew Roth agreed with Kirchwey. After the unexpected military difficulty US forces had in dealing with the North Koreans, he was dumbfounded that the West "accepted so blithely the risk of fighting the Chinese." Specifically, he thought it "incredible" for the United States to risk Chinese involvement simply on General MacArthur's "dogmatic estimate" that the Chinese were bluffing in their warnings, via India, that they would intervene if American troops entered North Korean territory. To help his American readers empathize with the Chinese point of view, he asked them to imagine Red Chinese forces marching northward through Mexico toward the Rio Grande! As such, he wrote, the Chinese were entirely justified in feeling directly threatened by American actions. And their unease could hardly be dismissed while the UN forces were under the command of a general "whose violent antagonism to them has never been disguised."[50]

Though the bulk of Kirchwey and Roth's criticism fell on General MacArthur, Kirchwey especially did not absolve the civilian leadership in Washington. On the contrary, she laid much of the blame at the feet of the Truman administration for trying to sound "more belligerent than the opposition [Republicans] in an effort to disprove charges of pussyfooting and appeasement." In other words, domestic politics had gotten the better of the administration, and their resultant saber-rattling only increased the already considerable animosity between the United States and China.[51]

Freda Kirchwey and others at *The Nation*, then, drew almost the exact opposite conclusion from the Chinese intervention in Korea from that of William Henry Chamberlin and other conservative-leaning writers. Writers on both sides of the divide agreed that Chinese intervention in Korea exposed the fatal flaws of US foreign policy. The issue was what those flaws were. For Kirchwey and her fellow left liberals, China's intervention revealed US policy to be wanting in that it was too reckless, perhaps even aggressive. But for Chamberlin and his fellow hawks, it exposed the United States and the rest of the Western world as weak and frightened appeasers.

A GENERAL SETTLEMENT WITH CHINA

In addition to the disagreement over whether the Chinese intervention revealed US policy to be too hard or too soft, there was also a split among the self-acknowledged liberal publications regarding the extent to which Mao was a potential "Asian Tito." The *New Leader* thought the notion demonstrably absurd, while *The Nation* was not yet ready to write off the Chinese leader as nothing more than an unquestioning stooge of Moscow. Since Mao's victory in the Chinese civil war, left liberals had been holding out hope that the Chinese communist leader would prove to be independent of Moscow, or maybe even pose a challenge to Soviet leadership of the communist world, while hawkish liberals and conservatives tended to assume that all communists, Marshal Tito of Yugoslavia notwithstanding, were cut from the same Stalinist cloth. Chinese intervention in the Korean War seemed to support the latter position, as the *New Leader* loudly proclaimed, while *The Nation* still clung to their faith that Mao was, at least potentially, at the head of a different and less threatening kind of communism, an Asian/agrarian communism.

The obvious lesson of Chinese intervention in Korea, editorialized the *New Leader*, "is that Mao Tse-tung has defied all prognosticators of a Titoist turn in China, and has conclusively sealed his pact with Stalin to join forces in Communism's bloody and ruthless march of world conquest." This fact, as they saw it, "should be clear to the most myopic observer."[52] Several weeks later, however, they apparently still saw the need to correct such myopia, complaining that American liberals continued to deceive themselves with wishful thinking, believing that Mao was somehow different from Stalin, and Chinese communism different from Soviet communism. How long would liberals hold on to this illusion, they asked, adding with emphasis, "*When shall we learn that Communists are Communists, whether Chinese, Russian, British or Czech*?"[53] The good editors seem to have thought the better of including "Yugoslav" on their list.

In any event, it is clear that they felt confident about their assumption that Mao, in sending his "volunteers" south of the Yalu, was simply doing Stalin's bidding, and naught more. Soviet Russia's, they claimed, "is the hand that guides Mao;"[54] the intervention was "obviously arranged by Moscow;"[55] and "Chinese Communism is and always has been committed" to the Soviet drive for world conquest.[56] The conservatives at *The Freeman* did not disagree. The Chinese offensive in Korea, wrote Forrest Davis, "finally swept away the Acheson-Lattimore thesis that Mao Tse-tung is a potential Tito" or the Chinese communists mere "agrarian reformers."[57] Here is one more example, then, of hawkish liberals and conservatives making common cause, especially against the left liberals at *The Nation* who, on the question of Mao's potential Titoism, took a position decidedly out of line with the conventional wisdom.

Even in the darkest days of the UN cause in Korea—during January 1951, when the Chinese had overwhelmed MacArthur's forces—*The Nation* continued to take the long view of Sino-Soviet relations. The editors acknowledged that the "popular American theory" was that Mao moved into Korea on Moscow's orders, but they nonetheless raised the plausibility that Mao might have acted "independently and against the Kremlin's wishes in order to assert China's dominance in that embattled land." Indeed, they cited reports that the Soviet Union and China were jockeying for position and influence in Korea, even as they publicly marched in lockstep. While they acknowledged that these reports were not conclusive evidence, they argued that they "certainly support the theory that in the long run the historical rivalries between China and Russia will dissolve the ideological cement that has bound Peking to Moscow."[58] As *The Nation* had been correct about the danger of provoking Chinese intervention by crossing the thirty-eighth parallel, so too were its editors correct about the seeds of discord sown into the Sino-Soviet relationship from its very inception. It may have taken until after Korea for those seeds to blossom into the full fruit of animosity between the two communist giants, but it was once again the left liberal analysis that ultimately proved correct.

After the initial shock of Chinese intervention wore off, left liberals, hawkish liberals, and conservatives began to come to very different conclusions as to what Chinese involvement meant for the United States and the world. These differences were all the more marked when it came to the various groups' prescriptions for action vis-à-vis the Chinese. Should the United States be willing to enter into negotiations and possibly even make painful diplomatic concessions to avoid a wider war, including seating Mao's regime at the UN and recognizing the communists' right to rule Formosa? Or were any such concessions tantamount to the appeasement of an aggressor—an "Asian Munich"? Of the leading liberal journals, most agreed that some form of negotiation with communist China was both desirable and necessary to bring the war in Korea to an end without the fighting spiraling out of control and possibly leading to a Third World War. In fact, the staffs at *The Nation* and the *New Republic* had long favored seating communist China at the UN and allowing that regime to rule Formosa.[59] The fact that US soldiers were now fighting communist Chinese in Korea only reinforced their conviction that negotiation and compromise was the only way out of the Korean bear trap.

Immediately upon learning that China had decided to intervene in Korea, *Nation* editor Freda Kirchwey viewed the situation as grave, but also as an opportunity for a broader peace. "It seems to us," she wrote, that the moment had come "for reassessing the whole situation." She argued that the "volunteer" aspect of the Chinese intervention was a sign that Peking did not desire a big war. If China had wanted to involve the United States in an all-out war for Asia, Mao would have had no compunction about making China's involvement official. Thus, "the apparent desire on all sides to avoid general war affords a little leeway for efforts to find a road of escape." Specifically, Kirchwey proposed that the United States give China public assurance that Syngman Rhee's domain would not be expanded, regardless of how much North Korean territory the UN might occupy, and that the power resources along the Yalu would continue to be available to China. "Such promises," she concluded, "would not be 'appeasement'; they would be no more than a clear statement of what must in any case be the premise of a just settlement."[60] For Kirchwey, then, from the very beginning of the "new war" in Korea, diplomacy was the best and only way to avoid a catastrophic war while also achieving a just resolution of the conflict for all parties involved.

The Nation's foreign editor, Julio Alvarez del Vayo, went so far as to suggest what the ultimate outcome of any negotiations with China regarding Korea should be: the seating of communist China at the UN. Regardless of how jagged a diplomatic pill this might be for the United States to swallow, he called it "an inescapable prerequisite to any peaceful settlement in Korea." In fact, he wrote, admission to the UN was the single most important issue on China's agenda.[61] Elsewhere, del Vayo intimated that the entire Korean crisis could have been prevented had the UN (read: US) been sensible enough to seat the communist Chinese earlier. Communist China's exclusion from the UN was the original cause, he wrote, "of present difficulties in Asia."[62] Thus, "no solution is possible unless [the UN] accepts the inescapable necessity of recognizing the Peking government as the real government of China." Moreover, this principle included, for del Vayo, a recognition of Peking's sovereignty over not just mainland China, but also Formosa.[63] Finally, in January 1951, by which time the Chinese unmistakably held the military momentum in Korea, del Vayo continued to express a similar sentiment. The UN, as he saw it, had to choose between the Scylla of a negotiated settlement favorable to the Chinese or the Charybdis of a complete withdrawal from Korea. And negotiation, in his view, demanded that the UN "accept the political conditions attached by Peking to a military truce," namely, admission to the UN. This may be "a bitter pill to swallow," he concluded, but such a concession remained "the wiser course," as compared to an outright withdrawal.[64]

It is noteworthy that del Vayo, one of the most prominent voices in one of the most prominent liberal opinion journals, was willing to allow, indeed, welcome, what many of his centrist or center-right contemporaries would have considered China "shooting its way" into the UN. The rest of the editorial staff at *The Nation* also continued to favor American diplomatic recognition of Mao's government, which they had been encouraging ever since the Chinese communists came to power, even if it meant losing a bit of face in the process.

> Since we refused to recognize Mao's government at a time when we had no real quarrel with it, a reversal of this position is obviously difficult after our forces have been attacked by Mao's army. . . . Yet how can we hope to negotiate with a strong government holding powerful cards if we refuse to concede its right to exist? And what alternative to negotiation do we have save a war, declared or undeclared, against Communist China?[65]

The US government, of course, had no intention of recognizing the Peking government or granting it Formosa so long as there were open hostilities in Korea. Nor did this please *The Nation*'s editors. As the war seesawed back and forth in the early months of 1951, they complained that the United States stubbornly refused to negotiate an end to the war, regardless of its military position. The prospect of an end to the war, they resignedly acknowledged, "is more somber than ever." Certainly there was no possibility of a peaceful solution so long as the United States refused to negotiate out of considerations of prestige, they continued.[66] And that was not all. When the United States announced that it would not accept any would-be UN decision about the future of Formosa that collided with its own interests, Kirchwey harshly proclaimed that the United States was demonstrating "a contempt for UN authority equaled only by that of the Russians themselves."[67] The editors of *The Nation*, then, were tremendously frustrated by the Truman administration's apparent distaste for common sense diplomacy in the face of war, even to the point of comparing American behavior on the international stage to that of the very bane of America's existence, the Soviet Union.

The *New Republic*, like *The Nation*, was willing to accept a general settlement with China as a reasonable means to end the war in Korea and the threat it posed to world peace. "If the price of compromise in Korea proves to be negotiation for a general settlement," it editorialized, "then we should pay that price." To the editors of the *New Republic*, such negotiations did not amount to "appeasement" in any way. Rather, "negotiation which seeks to prevent aggression and to restore vital principles is necessary and honorable." More specifically, they argued, no vital American principle would be sacrificed either in extending recognition to China or in allowing China's communist government to be seated at the UN.[68] Elsewhere, they were even more explicit in their calls for a settlement based on transfer of the

Chinese seat at the UN from Chiang to Mao: "We should cede to China's claim of membership in the UN which is a universal organization and not an alliance of like-minded nations," "we should withdraw recognition from Chiang Kai-shek as the ruler of China which he obviously is not,"[69] and "the logical and proper conclusion . . . is that the Communists should represent China in the UN."[70] The editors of the *New Republic*, then, agreed with *The Nation*'s del Vayo that the United States should be willing to not only recognize the Peking government but also admit it to the UN as part of a larger settlement to end the Korean fighting.

Whereas left liberal publications *The Nation* and the *New Republic* embraced the need for a negotiated settlement with China, hawkish liberals at the *New Leader* and conservatives at *The Freeman* and the *American Mercury* were much less inclined toward a give-and-take with Peking. Instead, the writings found in these journals regularly denounced the path of negotiation and diplomacy as the path of appeasement, weakness, and surrender. Here is one more example, then, where conservatives and centrist liberals found common ground against their left liberal contemporaries at *The Nation* and the *New Republic*.

As usual, William Henry Chamberlin was the most strident of the *New Leader*'s contributing editors. Not only did he oppose negotiations with China but he scathingly denounced the UN for even trying diplomacy. "It is time for America . . . to awaken from the opium sleep of appeasement, from the harmful dream that anything decent, honorable or stable can be achieved by trying to negotiate with an armed aggressor on the rampage." To those Americans, say, like those on staff at *The Nation* and *New Republic*, whose main interest was to avoid "all-out war with Red China," Chamberlin retorted that China, by intervening in Korea, had already "declared and waged all-out war on the United States and the UN."[71] The time for negotiation, for Chamberlin, had long since passed.

On the specific issue of Formosa, Chamberlin, like his left liberal counterparts, saw the ultimate fate of Korea as bound up with that island. But whereas Julio Alvarez del Vayo, for example, thought the only way to save Korea was to bargain Formosa away to the Chinese communists, Chamberlin thought that maintaining Formosa as an American ally was absolutely critical to the future of a democratic Korea—indeed, to the future of all Asia. "It is to be hoped that the fruits of struggle and sacrifice in Korea will not be lost by flabby irresolution on the issue of Formosa," he wrote. "It is of paramount importance . . . that this vital island should not pass under Communist control."[72] Why was Formosa so important? Chamberlin thought it to be, in General MacArthur's words, "an unsinkable aircraft carrier" necessary to safeguard US interests and allies in Japan, in the Philippines, and throughout Asia. He failed to see how anyone could contemplate turning over Formosa, with all its economic and strategic value, "to a regime that loses no opportunity to proclaim itself our implacable enemy." For Chamberlin, such a concession to communist China would amount to nothing less than a "one-sided retreat," a "unilateral surrender."[73]

Chamberlin also railed against proposals to seat communist China at the UN, since it was "a government that has openly sabotaged the UN police action in Korea." He found the idea absurd. After all, he argued, "that would be like rewarding a gangster with a seat on the magistrates' bench."[74] He further mocked the "quaint thesis," advocated by del Vayo, that seating China at the UN was the cure for all that ailed the Far East. "What a pity," he sneered, "that someone did not suggest, after Pearl Harbor, that all the subsequent unpleasantness could be avoided by pleading with Hitler and the Japanese militarists to rejoin the League of Nations!"[75] Once more, Chamberlin had conjured up one of his favorite, if flawed, analogies: The communist Chinese intervention in Korea was akin to the Japanese attack on Pearl Harbor. As such, any attempt to negotiate with Peking or its partner in Moscow was the equivalent of appeasing Japan or Nazi Germany after December 7, 1941.

Chamberlin and *The New Leader* were hardly alone in espousing the point of view that the United States must neither seat the communist Chinese at the UN nor hand over Formosa to Mao. In fact, they were joined by voices on the right, namely the editors of and contributors to the expressly conservative publications *The Freeman* and the *American Mercury*. The editors of *The Freeman* explained the importance of holding Formosa in terms of its deterrent effect on Mao. "As long as Formosa is denied to the Chinese Communists," they wrote, Mao's "Red divisions must stick to the East China coast to provide insurance against invasion."[76] Thus, ran their argument, as long as Formosa remained in Chiang's hands, Mao could not afford to strike southward against vulnerable areas such as Indochina, Burma, and Malaya. Therefore, according to the editors, not giving Formosa over to Peking was of paramount importance for the future security of noncommunist Asia. In short, abandoning Formosa "would be tantamount to abandoning the whole eastern half of the oceanic world."[77]

This sentiment was echoed elsewhere in the pages of *The Freeman* when writer George Langdon argued that "throwing Formosa to the Communist wolves" would "cut through the Japan-Okinawa-Philippines perimeter that represents America's line of defense in the Pacific."[78]

Edward Hunter, contributing editor to the conservative monthly the *American Mercury*, was convinced that the Red Tide would sweep over all of Asia if Formosa were abandoned—or if the United States even recognized the communist Chinese government and allowed it into the UN. Indeed, he titled his piece, "The Suicide of Recognizing Red China"! To the peoples of Asia, he wrote, "Far from being a mere diplomatic debate, the recognition issue is a naked contest for power." What he meant here is that throughout Asia, UN recognition of China would determine whether or not people accepted the inevitability of a communist takeover of Asia. As he explained it, communism in Asia was an all-or-nothing proposition. It would either conquer the whole of Asia or be destroyed. Recognition by the UN, he argued, would acknowledge the inevitability of the former rather than the latter course. In other words, "This would be that the Western world, the proud and powerful Western Powers, had capitulated and agreed that Communism was the permanent form government in Asia would take." And because this admission would effectively determine the future of all of Asia, recognition would be a tacit green light from the United States for Asians to psychologically accept their communist fate.[79]

There was quite a sharp divide, then, between left liberals, on the one hand, and conservatives and hawkish liberals, on the other, when it came to the general question of negotiations with China and the specific issues of Formosa and representation in the UN. The liberals at *The Nation* and the *New Republic* thought negotiations were the only sensible way to end the fighting in Korea and to bring lasting peace to East Asia. Specifically, these left liberals were prepared to allow communist China to take over the Chinese seat at the UN and even to see Formosa incorporated into the People's Republic. Hawkish liberals and conservatives, on the other hand, had concluded that negotiating with a communist aggressor was an exercise in futility, and that handing over Formosa or allowing Peking's entry into the UN would doom Asia to a dark future of communist tyranny. From this conclusion, it was but a short step, for these thinkers, to the argument that the United States must, in order to prevent the loss of all of Asia, expand the war in Korea to China herself, the threat of starting a Third World War notwithstanding.

CONCLUSION

The issues raised by the potential for and reality of Chinese intervention in Korea reveal important fissures in the "liberal consensus," as evidenced by this examination of the leading political opinion journals of the early 1950s. In fact, hawkish liberal positions often aligned more closely with those of conservatives than they did with those of their fellow liberals. Even prior to Chinese intervention, for example, the left liberals at *The Nation* were a voice crying in the wilderness, warning that crossing the thirty-eighth parallel risked provoking the Chinese and turning the limited war in Korea into a vastly expanded (and vastly more dangerous) conflict. More hawkish liberals at the *New Leader* and *Commonweal* dismissed such warnings rather cavalierly and supported MacArthur's move north of the thirty-eighth parallel. Then, once the Chinese, as per the warnings of Freda Kirchwey and *The Nation*, actually did intervene, editors and journals from across the ideological spectrum entered into a consensus of fear of an impending Third World War. Here, what set liberals and conservatives apart was the issue of who deserved the blame for the precarious position in which the world found itself. Liberals blamed what they perceived to be the gun-slinging recklessness of US foreign policy, while conservatives and hawkish liberals like William Henry Chamberlin blamed twenty years of Roosevelt-Truman "appeasement" of the Kremlin. Similarly, conservatives and liberal hawks made common cause in arguing that "a communist was a communist" and that Mao was therefore nothing more than a stooge of Stalin, while left liberals held out hope that Mao and the Chinese communists might eventually chafe under the influence of the Soviet Union and go their own quasi-Titoist way. Finally, when it came to how to bring about a satisfactory end to the fighting between the United States and China, left liberals favored a negotiated settlement marked by meaningful concessions to the Chinese, while hawkish liberals rejected the very idea of negotiating as just one more example of appeasing communist aggression. Of course, looming over this debate about whether to negotiate with Peking was the mostly unspoken and much graver issue of whether the United States should go so far as to launch an *offensive war* against China. As we shall see, this issue was hotly debated as early as late 1950 and early 1951, ultimately culminating, in the spring of 1951, in a rogue general, Douglas MacArthur, who had forced it to the forefront of Americans' attention, being relieved of his command.

3. Great Debates

Once China had entered the fray in Korea, the United States was faced with, in General MacArthur's words, "an entirely new war." Some writers took the phrase more literally than others and began advocating that the United States retaliate against China not only on the battlefield in Korea, but in China itself. Whether to revert to fighting a war of containment in Korea or to respond to the Chinese intervention in Korea by launching an *offensive war* against Mao's regime became perhaps the central question in American political opinion journals in late 1950 and early 1951. As with most of the major issues raised by the Korean War, different ideological camps had very different perspectives regarding China policy. The conservatives at *The Freeman* and the *American Mercury* forcefully advocated that the United States launch some form of an offensive war against Peking, while the liberals at *The Nation*, the *New Republic,* and *Commonweal* believed such a course of action was nothing less than unthinkably mad. Perhaps most interestingly, the hawkish liberals at the *New Leader* found themselves caught in a web of contradictions on this issue, first supporting an expansion of the war into China, then making an about-face and hedging considerably once the MacArthur controversy reignited the fires of the war-with-China debate in the spring of 1951.

This debate about China dovetailed with a larger "Great Debate" about the fundamentals of US foreign policy, kicked off by former president Herbert Hoover, who argued that the United States should withdraw forces and aid from mainland Europe and Asia, pulling back to a series of global island defenses, including Britain and Japan. This suggestion was derided as "isolationism" by left liberals, who instead advocated for a multilateral internationalist approach to global affairs, while conservatives tended to agree that Hoover's speech pointed toward a more common-sense nationalism marked by a unilateralist approach to foreign policy.

TO RESTART THE CHINESE CIVIL WAR

The evolution of conservative thought on China, as revealed in *The Freeman* and the *American Mercury*, began with a rather simple premise: that

China's fate was far more significant in the long run than Korea's. The fate of Korea, with its population of 30 million souls, editorialized *The Freeman*, could not possibly be as important to the free world as that of 500 million Chinese. The editors railed, moreover, against the idea sold to America by its "Russia-first diplomats and press" that China was forever lost and could never be regained.[1] Rather, their faith was that China not only could, but *must* be re-won for the free world, so that its long border with the Soviet Union could perhaps replace Germany as the central front in the Cold War. The obvious question, then, was how exactly this ambitious project, namely, the retaking of China for the free world, was to be accomplished. The conservative answer was a perfect blend of traditional isolationism and newly discovered muscular anticommunism: re-conquer China without using any American ground troops. In other words, the answer was to reignite the Chinese civil war, this time with the support of American air and sea power.

As early as November 1950, the pages of *The Freeman* began to be filled with the explicit argument that the United States should restart the Chinese civil war. Rodney Gilbert, editorial writer for the *New York Herald Tribune*, wrote that Formosa could be made a "base for counter-revolution" if the United States provided Chiang Kai-shek with the necessary moral support to retake the mainland. Gilbert was short on specifics but concluded that this could be accomplished without the use of a single American combat trooper.[2] A more prominent and controversial figure was leader of the China Lobby and, later, founding member of the John Birch Society Alfred Kohlberg.[3] Kohlberg recalled a personal conversation with Chiang in which the generalissimo had pointed out that, in China, nearly 500 million people could swing from one side of the Cold War to the other. "How important this difference would be to us," he wrote, "is now fully apparent from the havoc that just eight million North Koreans . . . have created." The allegiance of China's population was, to Kohlberg, the decisive factor in the Cold War in Asia. Were China to remain communist, "the best we could hope for would be a stalemate."[4] Kohlberg may actually have been correct on this point, but his argument left open the question of whether "victory" over communism in Asia was even desirable from the American perspective, given that devoting the resources necessary to defeat Asian communism would have almost certainly left Europe unacceptably vulnerable to Moscow.

In any event, the editors of *The Freeman* agreed with Gilbert and Kohlberg. They argued that conditions in late 1950 were in fact ideal for a Nationalist invasion of the mainland, but that it was the Truman administration that stood in the way. Under Truman's orders, they complained, the US Navy "continues to 'neutralize' Formosa—thus ensuring Mao Tse-tung against any Nationalist attack, and thus permitting him to throw the bulk of his forces against the US Army." Truman, according to this line of thinking, was directly responsible for the "macabre paradox" that US military action, via the disposition of the Seventh Fleet in the Formosa Strait, was actually partially to blame for the heavy losses US ground troops were suffering at the hands of the Chinese in Korea. As an amusing footnote to this argument, the editors made use of President Truman's infamous and coincident tirade against the music critic who slammed his daughter Margaret's singing abilities. Whereas other writers were embarrassed by the president's behavior, *The Freeman*'s editors sardonically praised his pugnacity. "If we could only contrive," they smugly wrote, "to have Mao Tse-tung reflect upon the bel canto of a certain soprano!"[5]

Other contributors to *The Freeman* saw a rekindling of the Chinese civil war as even more of a cure-all. Malcolm Wheeler-Nicholson, perhaps better known for inventing the modern comic book, of all things, was also a military veteran and analyst. He, like Kohlberg, stressed the anticommunist manpower that was supposedly left unexploited in China, namely, half a million Nationalist troops on Formosa and 1.5 million guerrillas on the mainland. "They want to fight," he wrote. "They are able to fight *today*." More specifically, he argued that south China was particularly ripe for a "free Chinese" attack, since that region had seen communist forces transferred to fight the United States in Korea. Such action, he explained, "would immediately convert our present, useless Korean fighting into strategical common sense." What is more, like the editors, he harshly criticized Truman's policy regarding the Seventh Fleet: Truman's "amateur strategy" was effectively to use the American Navy "as aid in inflicting unnecessary casualties upon, and ensuring the defeat of, our own Army!" But Wheeler-Nicholson thought an American-aided renewal of the Chinese civil war would have salutary effects not only in China, but globally, since Stalin dare not move against Europe until the 2,000-mile-long Soviet-Chinese border was secured. "By backing the free Chinese on Formosa," he wrote, "we could make them the spearhead to stir all China to revolt, thus keeping Stalin so busy at home that he would not have time or energy to make more mischief abroad. This would relieve pressure on Europe."[6] So all America had to do, in Wheeler-Nicholson's view, was back the free Chinese against the communists, and everything all around the world would be wonderful for the forces of freedom. This was perhaps more comic book fantasy than strategic reality but was nonetheless the nearly universal view expressed in the pages of this leading conservative opinion journal.

The editors of *The Freeman* elaborated on the themes raised by Wheeler-Nicholson, namely that continued fighting in Korea made sense only if the United States had a larger plan to overthrow the communists in China:

> Our commitment in Korea would have made sense on one condition: that the Administration had up its sleeve a whole vital program for the re-winning of Asia for the forces of democracy. As part of a campaign to unseat Mao Tse-tung in China, the decision to hold on in Korea would be intelligible. But if we merely intend to sit in Korea and feed more and more Americans as a continuing blood sacrifice into the maw of the Chinese dragon, then what is to be said for our brains?

Further,

> Why, then, do we hobble ourselves in our Korean venture? Why do we use the 7th Fleet in Formosan waters to guarantee Mao Tse-tung against being harassed on his middle and southern flanks while our armies take it on the chin as Mao hits us in the North? And how is it that both Mao and Stalin can continue to be assured that Chiang Kai-shek's armies will not be used against them along the China coast while GIs are dying around Seoul?

And finally, President Truman "the other day took a crack at those Americans who 'would withdraw from Korea and from Europe.' He spoke of 'quitters.' But who is the 'quitter' in Korea if it is not an Administration that refuses to go after the enemy that has struck us in Korea—to wit, Red China?"[7] So as *The Nation*'s editors were intensely frustrated with Truman for not making peace, so were *The Freeman*'s editors frustrated with Truman for not making war.

Yes, the United States should take an active role in relaunching the Chinese civil war. That much was clear to readers of conservative opinion. But how, specifically, should the United States go about implementing such a policy? No one explicitly suggested the large-scale use of American ground troops to invade a country as vast and populous as China, but that did not mean conservatives opposed the use of American power, primarily through sea and air, against the Chinese mainland. Nevertheless, the application of any American power at all would, of course, leave open the possibility for a greater commitment of resources in the future, including the use of ground troops. Not even the editors of *The Freeman* could altogether sweep this under the rug.

The editors of *The Freeman* seemed to have a bit of trouble walking the fine line between advocating direct US involvement in a renewed Chinese civil war and insisting that such action would not necessitate the large-scale use of US ground forces. They first attacked "the cliché that we must get out of Asia for fear of becoming 'bogged down' in China," pointing out that there was much room between the poles of total abstention and total commitment. It mustn't be all or nothing, in other words. The United States could fight a *limited* war in China—precisely the kind of war conservatives so objected to in Korea! So if US ground troops would not constitute the primary fighting force against Mao, who would? The answer was Chiang's forces on Formosa and/or the supposed million-plus anticommunist guerrillas on the mainland. While this army was waging war against Mao on the ground, the United States would be "using what we have—our naval supremacy, our power of blockade, our economic ability to create a superior air force." Such a recipe might have sounded quite appealing to staunch anticommunists in the United States: we use our navy to weaken China via blockade and our air forces to bomb railways and support our free Chinese allies on the ground without having to worry about the bloody mess of all those dead and wounded GIs. Yet, to the editors' credit, they were honest enough to admit the possibility that American troops might inevitably have to be deployed to China. While they prefaced their remarks by saying that no large American expeditionary force would have to fight in China, they concluded by acknowledging that some ground troops would likely be needed to offer "auxiliary aid" on the Chinese mainland.[8]

"Such a program," the editors concluded, "would be wholly within our means. It would be a program of limited warfare in Asia for limited ends. It would be 'warfare without bogs.'"[9] Again, while this rosy scenario may have been tempting to Americans with a soft spot for the old China, it contained serious flaws. The use of American sea and air power in support of anticommunist forces may have started as limited warfare wholly within our means, but what of the very real possibility, if not likelihood, that things went badly for Chiang? What then? Would the United States simply "abandon" him once again? Or would the initial commitment to regime change in Peking place American prestige on the line to the extent that ground forces would have to be sent in sufficient numbers to complete the job numbers obviously well beyond those initially needed to provide "auxiliary aid" to the

Kuomintang? Moreover, what of the more frightening possibility of Soviet retaliation for an American attack on China? Might the Soviets themselves intervene in this would-be war in China? Would they take such US actions to be a declaration of World War III, prompting them to attack across the Elbe? These were considerations not broached by the editors. In the end, then, they were advocating a course of action that, via any number of realistic possibilities, might involve the United States in an endless morass of war on the Asian mainland or even around the world—an ironic upshot of a piece titled, "Keeping Out of Bogs."[10]

Whereas conservative opinion journals advocated war against China, however nominally limited, as a panacea for the ills of US Cold War policy, the liberals at *The Nation*, the *New Republic*, and *Commonweal* recoiled at the mere suggestion, thinking war with China a fool's errand at best, the spark that would ignite a global catastrophe at worst, and an action that, in any event, would split the United States from even its closest allies.

Even before Chinese intervention in Korea, *The Nation*'s Willard Shelton warned against the perils of too aggressive a policy toward China. "Most Americans," he wrote, "should be able to comprehend that a war with China is the last thing we should invite, and that to prop up Chiang indefinitely or to 'seize' Formosa as an American base would alienate Asian public opinion disastrously."[11] By way of contrast, Asian public opinion, or "hearts and minds," as a later generation would come to think of it, was something the conservative editors of *The Freeman* simply did not consider. As for Chiang's regime on Formosa, Julio Alvarez del Vayo agreed with Shelton that it was not worth supporting. As he commonly did, del Vayo expressed his own opinion by explaining the views of "observers" abroad and at the UN. Here, it was the generic "European" who served as the vehicle for his own views and who opposed renewed civil war in China at least in part on anti-imperialist grounds: "To imagine that this immense country [China], freed of the overlordship of the West, full of confidence in its new-found strength, hardened by 30 years of continuous warfare, with the vigor and élan of a revolutionary regime recently come to power, could ever be reconquered for the colonial interests with the aid of Chiang Kai-shek and his Formosan army seems to the European the height of madness."[12]

And del Vayo was not the only contributor to *The Nation* to point out that Europeans were not necessarily on board with a potential American war against China. Well-known journalist Howard K. Smith pointed out that if, in fact, the United States led the West toward war with China, minds in Europe "would be clouded with doubts, and the effort would be half-hearted." Such an uneasy commitment, thought Smith, was "hardly a proper mood" with which to begin what he assumed would become "the greatest struggle for freedom of all time": the long-expected global war between the West and communism.[13] Finally, Freda Kirchwey added that neither America's European allies nor its potential Asian allies would support a war to help Chiang retake control of the mainland. "No single development," she wrote, "could so profoundly alienate the independent Asian countries or so reinforce Europe's dread of headlong American decisions unilaterally announced or carried through."[14] Thus, the editors of and contributors to *The Nation* were quite clear: China was lost and it was not coming back, and any foolhardy attempt to win it back for the Nationalists was sheer folly, not least because it would leave the United States without the support of its allies, both actual and potential, in Europe and Asia.

Like *The Nation*, the *New Republic* strongly opposed expanding the war into China, though at times for slightly different reasons than its liberal sister publication. The editors of the *New Republic*, for example, initially thought the Soviet Union was trying to bait the United States into an East Asian trap by tempting it into an unwinnable war against China. The United States had the choice between two defeats, the editors wrote in December 1950, as US/UN forces were reeling from the Chinese onslaught, "the Little Defeat which means cutting losses in Korea, or the Big Defeat which means falling into the Moscow trap and making all-out war with China." The editors feared that Americans would fall hook, line, and sinker into this would-be communist trap: "Every temptation of Jingoism is to slap one's chest, denounce 'appeasement' and charge madly ahead. It is what Moscow wants."[15] Elsewhere, they agreed with their liberal brethren at *The Nation* that to "charge madly ahead" would lose hearts and minds in China and, indeed, would help consolidate communist power in that country. Blockading the Chinese coast, bombing mainland targets, and helping Chiang's forces invade, they wrote, "would surely turn the Chinese people against us and aid the Chinese communists in unifying the country behind their leadership."[16] After all, few things are likely to create more nationalistic solidarity among a people than bombing and invading their country. British historian and Sinologist Victor Purcell only reinforced the view that military action against China would backfire. It would "gravely endanger" the solidarity of the Western alliance and "swallow up all the reserves of men and munitions in an insatiable morass," he explained. Thus, "the Chinese menace (if there is one) must be met by the peoples of Asia and not by the West on their behalf." Chinese dominance in Southeast Asia, he concluded, could not be met "by any military action whatever."[17]

Even the editors of *Commonweal*, who at times took a fairly aggressive anticommunist line, refused to support a military adventure in China. Supporting a Nationalist invasion of the mainland, they warned, "would almost certainly bring on a full-scale and futile war between the U.S. and Communist China, a disaster that would merely compound Asia's misery and sign away the continent to Stalin at one stroke."[18] Thus, most of the liberal opinion journals were of one mind on the prospect of war with China: they were staunchly opposed. Such writers thought war with China would cost the United States allies in Europe, lose it hearts and minds in Asia, involve it in an unwinnable war of attrition on the Asian mainland, and possibly be the start of a Third World War. But there was one liberal publication that threw most of its weight behind the notion that American military might should be used to destroy the Chinese communists. Not surprisingly, that publication was the *New Leader*.

The editorial staff at the *New Leader*, particularly the fiery William Henry Chamberlin, talked tough about China in the fall and winter of 1950–1951. When it came to arguments about whether to expand the war to China, they did not sound unlike their conservative counterparts at *The Freeman* and the *American Mercury*. Although they would hedge significantly once MacArthur was relieved of duty in the spring of 1951, they were initially about as hawkish on China as any anti-Truman conservative.

Immediately upon Chinese intervention, the editors began to harshly criticize the Truman administration for its "spirit of appeasement." One of the most frequent arguments against military action vs. China made by Truman's State Department was that the United States could not hope to defeat a country with such immense reserves of manpower, nearly 500 million strong. But the editors casually dismissed these concerns: "as if even one percent of them could be equipped for modern war, and as if all of them would be furious at being liberated from their famine-provoking dictators." So whereas the left liberals at *The Nation* and the *New Republic* insisted that making war on China would surely turn the Chinese population against the United States, the hawkish liberals at the *New Leader* argued that the Americans and their free Chinese allies would be welcomed by the Chinese as liberators. Moreover, fears of getting bogged down in a land war in Asia were apparently overblown, since China's lack of a modern industrial base would prevent Mao from capitalizing on China's manpower advantage. While they were not yet explicitly calling for war, they concluded this editorial with some fairly suggestive language. "No concessions to dictators," they warned, "can be tolerated. If the U.S. is at all interested in fighting Stalin's power, it can ill afford appeasement of his Chinese satraps."[19]

From denouncing "appeasement," it was a short step to calling for the very same thing conservatives were calling for: US support for anticommunist Chinese forces in a renewed Chinese civil war. William Henry Chamberlin thought that there were only two options in China—war or appeasement. He acknowledged that most Americans would agree with Secretary of State Dean Acheson that war with China would be a "colossal tragedy," but he held that such a tragedy was the only real alternative to "the slippery slope of futile appeasement." As such, some form of offensive war against China was the lesser of two evils for Chamberlin, as it was "decidedly preferable to the pussy-footing" of the Truman administration. It was time, he wrote bluntly, "to put an end to the pitiful make-believe that the bullets fired by Chinese Reds against American and other UN troops are not real bullets, and to demand a showdown." To bring about this showdown, he suggested that the Chinese be given a peace-or-war ultimatum, demanding that they withdraw from Korea entirely by a certain date. If they refused, then the United States should begin bombing Chinese bases in Manchuria and supplying Chiang's forces for raids on the mainland.[20] Elsewhere, Chamberlin called for a naval and air blockade of the Chinese coast, to be combined with "heavily supported coastal raids by Chiang Kai-shek's Nationalists, developing into full-scale invasion if possible."[21] It is no wonder that Chamberlin, in addition to his role as contributing editor at the liberal *New Leader*, was a frequent contributor to the conservative biweekly *The Freeman*.

The *New Leader* also published pieces by individuals not on the editorial staff who made similar arguments. Jonathan Stout wrote that the United States should support the anticommunist forces in China because "full-scale civil war in China could well become a serious drain on Soviet war industry" and prevent the Russians from launching an immediate attack on Western Europe.[22] Christopher Emmet wrote that Formosa, which represented "China's last chance to be liberated," should form the home base of a reactivated Chinese resistance. After all, "until China is liberated, its Red cancer will remain a threat to all Asia." What's more, support for Chiang and his forces would divert Soviet and Chinese communist resources to the East, thus not seriously affecting the defense of Europe.[23] This was essentially the same "warfare without bogs" argument made by the editors of *The Freeman*. Finally, William Caldwell viewed a renewed civil war in China through the same panacean lenses as the conservatives previously discussed. With the United States delivering small arms and radio gear to the nearly two million mainland guerrillas, bombing communist railways and supply centers, and providing the air and sea forces necessary to assist Chiang in invading the mainland, the United States could defeat Mao "without involving a single American foot soldier."[24]

Here is yet another example, then, of where hawkish liberals and conservatives took the same position on a critical foreign policy issue, against that of left liberals. As we shall see, however, whereas conservatives would remain consistent in their demands for an expanded war in China, the hawkish liberals at the *New Leader* would wind up scrambling to qualify and make sense of their position in the aftermath of MacArthur's dismissal. But before that fateful firing could take place, a series of related issues were brought to the forefront of American public life by former president Herbert Hoover. Thus began the "Great Debate" on foreign policy, which was mainly focused on whether the United States should act in the world multilaterally, with and through international institutions like NATO and the UN, or resort to what liberals tended to describe as conservative "isolationism"—more accurately, unilateralism—leaving most of Europe to fend for itself while "going it alone" if and when threatened.

THE GREAT DEBATE

In December 1950, things looked bleak for US/UN forces in Korea as they fell back southward, reeling from the unexpected Chinese onslaught. Many Americans became discouraged by the steady stream of bad news from Korea and began to wonder if the new US role in the world, global anticommunist policeman as per the Truman Doctrine, was worth the cost. Perhaps it would be better for the United States to withdraw from most of its overseas commitments, particularly in Europe, as it had after the First World War. Into this atmosphere of questioning and confusion stepped former president Herbert Hoover, who launched the "Great Debate" on foreign policy by delivering a high-profile speech on December 20, 1950. The premises of Hoover's speech were rather simple. The United States should no longer provide any defense for Western Europe unless the countries of Western Europe began providing more for their own self-defense.[25] Meanwhile, the United States should withdraw from any mainland commitments on the great Eurasian land mass and move to a global defense line of island chains, including Britain, in Europe, and Japan, Formosa, and the Philippines in Asia. The United States would thus cease to be overextended, as Hoover thought it had become under Truman, particularly since the beginning of the Korean War, and could rest secure in its own hemispheric Gibraltar, a fortress America.

Political opinion journals in America immediately voiced their praise or condemnation of Hoover's proposals, with liberals almost universally denouncing his "isolationism" and conservatives lauding his common-sense nationalism. Hoover's proposals were, in fact, among the few foreign policy issues of the day around which a "liberal consensus" was actually realized. Both left liberals and hawkish liberals denounced Hoover's ideas, while conservative publications embraced them. The debate spread to Congress, where "Mr. Republican" Robert A. Taft became the chief spokesman for the Hoover point of view, even arguing that expanding the Korean War into China by supporting Chiang was perfectly consistent with such principles. Taft and company thus became derided by liberals as "Asialationists," willing to risk World War III in Asia while leaving Europe wholly defenseless. Indeed, Hoover's de-emphasis of continental Europe drove much of the debate. Liberals, who were typically proponents of a Europe-first foreign policy, opposed Hoover for proposing the "abandonment" of Europe, while conservatives, more likely to be of an Asia-first disposition, embraced Hoover's vision for America's reduced role in Europe even as they continued to advocate war with China.

The left liberals at *The Nation* reacted to Hoover's speech by proclaiming boldly that world communism had effectively captured Herbert Hoover "and a good section of the Republican Party of the United States." The editors were, of course, not accusing Hoover of being a communist sympathizer himself, but simply stating that his ideas would play right into Moscow's hands. "No doubt the former President and those who have praised his speech," the editorial continued, "still think of themselves as the arch-foes of the Cominform, but the line they are laying down for their country should set the bells ringing in the Kremlin as nothing has since the triumph of Stalingrad." In particular, the editors of *The Nation* objected to Hoover's call to effectively cut off any further aid to America's European allies, save Great Britain. For if the United States really did withdraw to Britain, then there would be nothing to stop the Soviets from incorporating the industrial power of Germany, Belgium, and France into their empire, which, combined with the vast manpower of Russia and China, was a frightening prospect indeed for any Westerner who feared communist expansionism.[26]

The editors then focused their attack on what motivated Hoover's remarks, calling his speech "a rallying cry for all the discredited forces of isolationism, to all men who since Pearl Harbor have covertly nursed their infantile illusions of a hemispheric 'Gibraltar' without having the courage to give them voice. Its appeal is to the provincial little souls who have always looked with a jaundiced eye on the UN and all its works."[27] The editors of *The Nation*, then, were dismayed to see that isolationism, as opposed to their brand of Europe-first internationalism, still had life, and were alarmed by the geopolitical implications of Hoover's ideas. Elsewhere they condemned the Hoover thesis thusly: "that the best hope of humanity was for the mighty United States to pull into its shell and avert its gaze while the rest of the world fell into the Soviet orbit."[28]

The liberals at the *New Republic* often agreed with their brethren at *The Nation*, and their reaction to Hoover was no exception. In proposing that the United States provide no more aid to Europe unless Europe undertook all its own defenses, they wrote, Hoover intended to "abandon Europe." In effect, they continued, Hoover's position "is that we and Russia should undertake a *de facto* division of the world in which Western Europe is ceded to Stalin." And such a bilateral division of the world would not bring peace, they feared. Rather, "just as our strategic abandonment of Korea led to the Korean War, so our strategic abandonment of Europe will lead at once to a world war."[29] Here they did not specify exactly why this would be the case, but they presumably meant that an undefended Europe would be too tempting for Stalin to resist, and that the United States would have no choice but to intervene if and when the Red Army marched into West Germany. Further, like *The Nation*, the *New Republic* thought Hoover's ideas were nothing more than the same old isolationism, stubbornly refusing to adapt to the new geopolitical realities of the postwar era. "As the big debate continues," they wrote, "isolationism again rears its stupid head, wearing a tight Hoover collar."[30]

Harold Ickes, for good measure, added his own personal denunciation of Hoover's suggestions in the pages of the *New Republic*. Hoover's idea of defeating Russia, thought Ickes, was "to run away from Russia," and his idea of fighting for democracy was "to abandon the democracies." Hoover, according to Ickes, would have the United States "cower, pusillanimous and inglorious, as the 'Gibraltar' of the Western Hemisphere." Thus, if the ex-president had his way and the United States left Europe to its fate, then Hoover would outdo the infamous appeaser Neville Chamberlain, "who was only willing to serve up to Hitler on a highly decorated platter such tidbits as Czechoslovakia."[31]

The editors of the hawkish liberal weekly *New Leader* typically expressed a foreign policy viewpoint more closely related to that of conservative publications than that of their fellow liberals at *The Nation* and the *New Republic*. But in their reaction to Hoover's address, the editors of the *New Leader* proved that—every once in a while, at least—there really was something of a consensus among liberals.[32] In this case, that consensus was strongly opposed to the idea of a renewed isolationism, especially regarding America's interests in Europe. The *New Leader* editorialized that "conservative isolationists" like Hoover were "substantially at one with the Communists in wanting to surrender Europe and Asia to Stalinism." This was precisely the same charge against Hoover's policy as that made by *The Nation*. What's more, while this applied more to Hoover's followers, such as Senator Taft, than to the ex-president himself, the editors noted the "seemingly paradoxical policy toward Asia: there, isolationism counseled armed intervention against Chinese Communism." In any event, the hawkish liberals at the *New Leader* shared the alarm of left liberals at the unexpected renaissance of isolationism in the wake of Hoover's speech. In 1951, they wrote, "the margin between self-preservation and catastrophe is so thin that a major resurgence of isolationism—united in practice with Stalinism—could destroy not only Europe but along with it the fool's dream of an American 'Gibraltar.'"[33] Elsewhere, one Republican contributor to the *New Leader* wrote off Hoover's speech as "the disillusioned mumbling of a very elder statesman."[34]

Whereas the internationalists at the liberal opinion journals rejected Hoover's calls for withdrawal from the mainland of Eurasia, conservatives at *The Freeman* and the *American Mercury* were much friendlier to the former president's proposals. After all, according to *The Freeman*, if voters had listened to him in 1932, then the economy would have recovered without being encumbered by the New Deal, which "served only to institutionalize the depression." Regardless of *The Freeman*'s almost laughable argument that the free market would have quickly corrected itself without massive government intervention in the early 1930s, it is obvious that the magazine's editors still had a soft spot for old Herbert Hoover. Now, in 1950, he had come up with some more "excellent advice," namely, that the United States make its military aid to Europe conditional upon Europe's willingness to defend itself. While liberals called this position "abandonment," the editors of *The Freeman* called it "plain common sense." For no sane man, they argued, would give a gun to an ally who had shown no inclination to fight on his own behalf. Rather, "to arm a thoroughly reluctant friend is tantamount to handing a gun to one's enemy—for the friend will not object strenuously when the enemy comes to pick up the weapon for his own uses."[35] Apparently the irony of their advocating for continued aid to Chiang Kai-shek was lost on the editors.

Later, as the "Great Debate" began to flower more fully, *The Freeman* continued to support Hoover's ideas. Whereas liberals viewed the resurgent specter of isolationism with horror, the conservatives at *The Freeman* thought Hoover had "raised the whole foreign policy argument to a higher level." Moreover, they were disgusted with liberals' dismissals of Hoover's speech "by smearing it with such all-embracing labels as 'isolationism'" or "abandonment of Europe." Such knee-jerk liberals, they wrote, "ignored the unpleasant military facts that Mr. Hoover had set forth, and talked as if the Russian hordes could be stopped in Europe by a few American token troops."[36] In this same editorial, however, the editors betrayed the conservative "paradox" noted by the *New Leader* that, while arguing that Europe didn't deserve American aid, they nonetheless demanded increased American involvement in battling communism in China by aiding Chiang and the mainland guerrillas while bombing Manchuria.

In fairness to the editors, in the face of this apparent contradiction, they later wrote with greater consistency that "American strength cannot tip the balance across two wide oceans unless *both* Europeans and Asiatics can first be galvanized into action on their own behalf" (emphasis mine).[37] And in the end, the editors were at least sensible enough to acknowledge that "we cannot do anything to give Stalin the impression that it is safer for him to march into Europe tomorrow than it was yesterday." Thus, rather than resulting in an undefended Europe, *The Freeman* hoped Hoover's speech would "shock Europe into a recognition that it must immediately begin to prepare for its own defense," such that NATO could become a true "bargaining table, and not merely another demoralizing American giveaway table."[38] So the editors of *The Freeman* did not necessarily favor isolationism per se, but they did seek to more fully "Europeanize" Western defenses against the Soviet threat, even as they sought to increase American involvement on the Asian mainland. In one editorial, for example, they complained that President Truman was seemingly and disingenuously using the need to send American troops to Europe as an excuse not to aid Chiang in a war of reconquest in China:

> The Administration has begun a whispering campaign in Congress that, much as it would like to do so, it unfortunately cannot give serious support to the Chinese Nationalists because everything must be sent to Europe. We dislike to suppose that the sole reason for the Administration's sudden and unnecessarily public passion to arm Europe was to gain this dishonest excuse for neglecting the vital war in Asia. But what other intelligible motive is there?[39]

Over at the *American Mercury*, *The Freeman*'s monthly cousin, the editorial staff had little patience for the "neo-isolationism" that had begun to take root among conservatives in the wake of Hoover's speech. They had instead moved decisively toward the kind of muscular unilateralism that has characterized conservative foreign policy in the early twenty-first century. Where they agreed with Hoover, however, was in his claim that stationing American ground troops on European soil to deter a Soviet march westward was ridiculous. "Western Europe," they wrote, "is only an enlarged Korea. It, too, is a peninsula of the Asiatic heartland." As such, they argued, "no intelligent military man believes that an invasion of Western Europe can be prevented by ground armies." Instead, they thought, deterrence ought to take the form of "unchallengeable air atomic-power":

> If, after we implement this plan, Russia marches across Western Europe, we will have Russia at the same disadvantage that we could have had the Communists in Korea if we had not sent in our ground troops. We will be able to assault all the sources of Russian power, yet Russia will lack the means to retaliate in kind or degree. *We will have forced Russia into an air-atomic war where we hold the advantage, instead of allowing Russia to force us into a ground war where she holds the advantage.*[40]

While some of the language here is rather frightening, especially considering that the peoples of Western Europe would likely have borne the brunt of any Soviet retaliation for American atomic strikes against Russia, the editors of the *Mercury* were here previewing the Eisenhower-Dulles "New Look" that would be implemented after the election of 1952 and which, all things considered, proved to be a successful policy. So whereas *The Freeman* indeed flirted with a neo-isolationism—at least isolationism vis-à-vis continental Europe—during the so-called Great Debate, the conservatives at the *American Mercury* took a more nuanced position, supporting Hoover in his call not to send American ground troops to Europe, but going beyond the ex-president by laying out an early version of what would come to be known as "massive retaliation."

The "Great Debate" that was launched by Herbert Hoover, especially as it bled into the MacArthur controversy, was ultimately more about nationalistic *unilateralism* than *isolationism*. That said, the issue still cut to the core fundamentals of American foreign policy. Should the United States act multilaterally in the world, taking its allies' often dissenting views into consideration and modifying its behavior accordingly, or should it disregard its weaker allies and act unilaterally according to its own interests? This is often what writers of the early 1950s were actually talking about when they wrote of "isolationism." In other words, genuine isolationists were increasingly difficult to come by. But the debate about the extent to which the United States should lead an international community in the spirit of adherence to international law, as opposed to acting as a law unto itself as the mightiest nation on earth, had yet to be settled. And in answering this question, liberals tended to argue for a multilateral approach to international affairs, while conservatives were more willing to see the United States "go it alone" in the battle against communism.

Perhaps the most articulate mouthpiece for liberal internationalism was the *New Republic*. On the occasion of Truman's 1951 State of the Union address, the editors of that magazine decided to deliver a State of the Union of their own, in which they defined the interests of the United States as necessarily intertwined with the interests of America's allies around the world. "The State of the Union in 1951," they wrote, "means the state of all free peoples. They share a common faith in human rights. They hold a common trust in the UN. They fight on a common front in Korea. They face a common peril in Soviet imperialism. They cannot withstand it alone." Without the unity of the noncommunist world, they continued, the Soviet Empire would spread, unstoppable, across both Asia and Europe. "But when the free nations stand together," they implored, "aggression cannot win." After all, the free nations "comprise two-thirds of the world's peoples. They turn out four-fifths of the world's production. They control three-quarters of the resources needed for war. As long as the free nations are united, no aggressor is likely to risk war. Unity is our rock of salvation on which we can build world peace." Still, they cautioned, "the unity of free nations is not yet firmly established." Indeed, there were forces even within the United States working to divide free country from free country. One such force of disunity, they claimed, was American isolationism, the proponents of which wanted the United States to disregard the wishes of its European allies, both by withdrawing from that continent and by forging ahead to pursue its own belligerent course against China. How the United States dealt with and respected (or disrespected) its allies, concluded the editors, would be "the test in 1951," for there was much greater strength in unity than solitude. So, when Americans defined strength, they asked, "Do we mean limited strength of the U.S., or do we mean the strength of all free peoples?"[41]

Elsewhere, on the one-year anniversary of the outbreak of the war, the editors of the *New Republic* addressed a frequently heard conservative argument: that America was left by its allies in the UN to do most of the heavy lifting in Korea, therefore the United States should forget the UN and its allies and "go it alone." Their counterargument was an appeal to the better angels of America's nature. For a "mature people," they wrote, "leadership is a cause not for resentment of others but for pride in ourselves." Thus, "that we have borne a heavy responsibility should fill us not with contempt for the cause we led but with new pride in the record of the UN and new confidence in its future."[42] Such an argument was unlikely to sway unilateralist conservatives, however, as they would argue that a "mature people" should have learned from the world's experience with Hitler that appeasement leads to catastrophe.

In any event, the *New Republic* did not stand alone in its defense of internationalism. The editors at *Commonweal,* for example, took a similar line when they lamented the "new surge in isolationism" in the midst of the Korean War. The United States was not, they were sure, engaged with Soviet Russia "in a rivalry for dominion over nations." Rather, the United States was attempting to defend the free peoples of the world from communist subjugation. As such, they concluded, "We cannot do this alone." Indeed, with the advent of the Cold War and the future likelihood that the United States would become increasingly vulnerable to a Soviet nuclear attack, "we must admit that whatever logic there was for isolationism has long since vanished."[43]

Center-left liberals, then, were firmly committed to multilateralism in American foreign policy and firmly opposed to unilateralism, or "isolationism," as they were more likely to call it. But what of more hawkish liberals like William Henry Chamberlin? Chamberlin was no Hoover-style neo-isolationist, but he was decidedly less enthusiastic about the liberal internationalist project than his left-of-center counterparts. Indeed, Chamberlin attempted to weave himself a nuanced position, urging the United States to be simultaneously multilateralist and unilateralist in its foreign policy. Chamberlin complained that the population of UN member states numbered in the hundreds of millions, yet the non-American member states "could supply only a pitifully small token handful of ground troops" to the military effort in Korea. "The lesson for us," he wrote, "is that America must rely primarily on its own armed strength for its own security." But then he followed this up by claiming that Korea also demonstrated the need for a well-equipped standing UN military force.[44] Thus, without explaining precisely how to square this circle, Chamberlin called for the United States to "go it alone" while simultaneously calling for the creation of a UN rapid reaction force to meet future aggressions on the Korean model.

Later, as he explicitly jumped into the "Great Debate," he decried what he considered to be extremists on both sides of the issue: dogmatic isolationists and dogmatic interventionists. Both extremes, he wrote, contained "dangerous fallacies." The isolationist, he explained, "is living in an escapist dream-world when he imagines America withdrawing from Europe, withdrawing from Asia and then leading a normal, peaceful life." It is unclear whether Chamberlin was cognizant here of how much he sounded like one of his favorite targets, Franklin Roosevelt, in the late 1930s. In any case, Chamberlin viewed the United States as the only power capable of checking Stalinist expansionism in the postwar world. He thus rejected the Hoover thesis and argued that America had the responsibility to step up to the plate in defense of the free world. At the same time, however, he also held that there was a "contrary fallacy in extreme interventionism," namely, the assumption that America could and should act as a global policeman. If such a role were taken on, then he feared America's strength would be "frittered away on relatively unimportant enterprises," leaving it insufficiently strong for the possible "last decisive struggle." So Chamberlin favored neither isolationism nor global police responsibility, but he continued to recognize the "sound instinct" in each. Interventionists were correct that life in a world surrendered to communism "would be appallingly bleak and hazardous," while "isolationists" were fair to point out that "this country is not an Atlas, capable of carrying the whole noncommunist world on its shoulders." In the end, Chamberlin provided his own suggestion for how to find the middle way between the extremes of isolationism and interventionism-all-the-time. "Much of the answer," he concluded, "lies in building up elements of regional military strength," such that it would become possible "to leave more and more of the responsibility for defending Europe to Europeans, and . . . Asia to Asians." The task, he was sure, would not be easy. But it had to be attempted, for "nothing less than America's survival as a free nation is at stake."[45]

And so the desired foreign policy stance of center-left liberals was America working with its allies through the UN to defend the free world against communist aggression, while for hawkish liberals like Chamberlin it was to remain involved in the world but to concern itself primarily with its own security while encouraging its allies to do the same. The conservatives at *The Freeman* and the *American Mercury*, however, had little patience for liberal internationalism. If America's allies weren't willing to fight communism as militantly as American conservatives would like, then to hell with 'em! Moreover, such writers balked in principle at international organizations, wary of their potential to somehow limit or subvert American sovereignty. Did US membership in NATO, for example, mean that America's fellow treaty adherents "are to be permitted to decide military policy for this country? In other words, are we surrendering American sovereignty to our allies?"[46] Such a situation was especially troubling for the editors of *The Freeman*, given that votes at the UN regarding Korea had demonstrated, in their view, that "our allies are quite capable of deserting us on questions of crucial importance."[47]

Elsewhere in the pages of *The Freeman*, Lawrence R. Brown, whom we've previously noted for his fears of a Soviet invasion of North America, defended the conservative position by arguing that the epithet "isolationist" had lost all meaning. Isolationists, he thought, ought more properly to be called nationalists, as "their great asset in the present circumstances is that they have never been interested in defending anybody but the U.S."[48] Russian American aviator Alexander P. de Seversky went even further, complaining that under Truman the United States had become the "virtual prisoner" of its allies. It was time, therefore, for the United States "to rely on our own strength" by adopting a strategy independent of the vacillations of other countries. If America were to strike out on its own, he continued, it would not lack allies in any case, since other countries would continue to be attracted to "the reality and prestige of our military might."[49] If his premises, however, were that the United States was weak relative to the Soviet Union and that only strength won allies, then wouldn't the countries of Western Europe have already allied themselves with Moscow?

In any event, it is clear that the conservative contributors to *The Freeman* had little patience for the constraints placed on the United States via its alliances and favored a foreign policy that would be much more focused on the narrow self-interest of the United States as they perceived it. Nor did the various editors of the *American Mercury* feel differently. Washington editor Patrick McMahon complained that America was detested even among its allies, such that "we are undoubtedly the most hated nation in the non-Communist world." In short, allied "unity" was an illusion, and the

United States must "evolve an entirely new approach to the Soviet menace—an approach based on unilateral policy, unilateral objectives and unilateral action."[50]

It is quite clear, then, that writings in the leading conservative opinion journals pre-dating *National Review* were fiercely of an America-first mentality. Whereas most liberals stressed the practical need for allies and the moral importance of international institutions like the UN and NATO, most conservatives were quick to write off America's allies as not only impotent but corrosive of American strength and purpose in the world. If the United States stood a better chance of defeating communism by going-it-alone, which conservatives assumed it did, then international institutions and alliances should be disregarded in the national interest.

CONCLUSION

The "great debates" on foreign policy that animated much of the writing found in America's political opinion journals in late 1950 and early 1951 reveal much about the ideological and intellectual currents that flowed during the Korean War. After Chinese intervention in Korea, a coalition of conservatives and hawkish liberals pushed for the United States to expand the Korean War into China. Most contributors to *The Freeman,* the *American Mercury,* and the *New Leader* explicitly opposed the involvement of American ground troops in such a venture but favored a course of action (bombing, blockade, and material support for a Kuomintang reinvasion of the mainland) that might well have ultimately sucked the United States into a major war on the Asian mainland, if not sparked a Third World War. The liberals at *The Nation,* the *New Republic,* and *Commonweal* could not have opposed the conservative suggestion more forcefully. Not only had the Chinese civil war already been fought and lost by Chiang Kai-shek, but a US intervention to reignite it would cost America allies and bog the United States down in Asia when its primary focus should remain Western Europe. The fact that the hawkish liberal position was diametrically opposed to the left liberal position is indicative that the conception of a liberal consensus during the early Cold War period is significantly flawed. Moreover, that conservative publications laid down such a muscular anticommunist line suggests that the stage had already been set for William F. Buckley Jr.—to say nothing of Barry Goldwater—years prior to the advent of *National Review.*

Similarly, the debate begun by Herbert Hoover revealed interesting ideological fissures. Even some conservatives were cool to Hoover's neo-isolationism regarding American involvement in Western Europe, but as the debate became more about whether the United States should act multilaterally or unilaterally in the world, clear positions developed. Left liberal publications were staunchly internationalist, conservative writings were fiercely nationalistic, and hawkish liberals like William Henry Chamberlin came down somewhere in the middle. This again tells us that there were tensions within the so-called liberal consensus and that conservatism was a much more fully developed ideology in the early 1950s than is typically appreciated. As we move on to examine the emotional debate that surrounded the actions and personality of General Douglas MacArthur, these trends will only become more apparent.

4. The MacArthur Controversy

General Douglas MacArthur began causing problems for President Truman as early as August 1950, when his message to the annual meeting of the VFW in Chicago was leaked to the press. In this message, MacArthur effectively called Truman an appeaser for his Formosa policy. Immediately after the Korean War had begun, Truman had ordered the American Seventh Fleet into the Formosa Strait to prevent any additional fighting from breaking out in East Asia, namely, a rekindling of the Chinese civil war. MacArthur, however, viewed that act as keeping Chiang Kai-shek and the Kuomintang caged up when they should have been utilized to fight the communists in Korea and/or on the Chinese mainland. Although MacArthur later apologized to the president, when they met on Wake Island in October, the stage had been set for further disagreements between the commander-in-chief and his commander in Korea. As MacArthur continued to demand absolute victory over the communists, thereby publicly challenging the administration policy of negotiating a settlement to the war in Korea, Truman and the Joint Chiefs of Staff became increasingly frustrated with the insubordinate general. In late March 1951, MacArthur effectively scuttled US peace plans by issuing a unilateral and belligerent ultimatum to the Chinese, warning them to agree to a ceasefire on UN terms or face the threat of an attack on Chinese territory. This was the last straw for Truman, who then privately decided to relieve the general of his duties, pending concurrence from the Joint Chiefs.[1] Unbeknownst to Truman, MacArthur had also recently penned a letter to the House minority leader, Republican Joe Martin, in which MacArthur denounced Truman in no uncertain terms for his refusal to "unleash" Chiang against the Chinese Reds. On April 11, less than a week after Representative Martin read MacArthur's letter aloud on the House floor, Truman announced that Douglas MacArthur had been relieved of his military duties. The great general would be coming home to the United States for the first time in fourteen years.

The firing of MacArthur raised difficult questions and launched divisive debates in Washington and around the country. Was Truman correct to fire MacArthur? And regardless of the constitutional justification for Truman's action, what about the substance of their policy disagreement? Should Korea be a war of containment, to be brought to an end via negotiated settlement, or should it be a war of liberation, aimed at reuniting Korea under the rule of Syngman Rhee? Perhaps most importantly, should the United States carry the war beyond Korea to China itself, even at the risk of involvement in a potentially endless land war in Asia that would split America from its European allies? Finally, what of MacArthur the man? Was he an honorable and patriotic old soldier or a threat to the very fabric of American democracy? Different ideological camps, as represented in America's leading political opinion journals, would have starkly different answers to these questions. On the whole, left liberals viewed MacArthur as a dangerous and arrogant man whose drive to make war on China threatened world peace, while conservatives praised the general for his opposition to the Truman administration's policy of "appeasement" and his resolve to fight communism with everything he had, come what may. Hawkish liberals, for their part, were self-contradictory in their views about MacArthur and his policy proposals, revealing the tension inherent in their position on the ideological spectrum, to the right of liberals but to the left of conservatives.

MACARTHUR AND INSUBORDINATION

The debates detailed in the previous chapter, whether to launch an offensive war against China and whether to take a more internationalist or unilateral stance in the world, were ultimately subsumed by the debate about the imperial personality and insubordinate actions of General Douglas MacArthur. The debate surrounding MacArthur came in three phases. The first was the debate about his insubordinate actions prior to his dismissal. The second was a continuation and rehashing of the debate about whether to prosecute the Korean War to absolute victory by expanding the fighting into China. And the third was the reaction to President Truman relieving the general of his duties. In all three of these phases of the MacArthur debate, the left-of-center liberals at *The Nation* and the *New Republic* were decidedly anti-MacArthur, while the centrist/hawkish liberals at the *New Leader* and *Commonweal* were more ambivalent about the general and his policies. The conservatives at *The Freeman* and the *American Mercury*, however, voiced their full-throated support for MacArthur from the VFW letter all the way through the general's long fade-away in the months after his dismissal.

Of America's leading political opinion journals, it was perhaps the *New Republic* that waved the anti-MacArthur banner most prominently. Even in the earliest days of the war, before the Inchon landing and subsequent crossing of the thirty-eighth parallel, the editors of that liberal magazine were already wary of MacArthur's potential to derail the Truman administration's larger purposes by making unilateral overtures to Chiang Kai-shek on Formosa. MacArthur had flown to Formosa to meet with Chiang on July 31, 1950, where he proclaimed Chiang an ally, despite the Truman administration's desire to effectively neutralize the island via the presence of the Seventh Fleet in the Formosa Strait. MacArthur was acting, the editors wrote, "without authority" and "without any recognition of his subordination to America's political aims." Put simply, "political decisions are involved which MacArthur is not qualified to make." What's more, General MacArthur's independent political course, they argued, threatened the very existence of world peace. So here were the editors of the *New Republic*, some eight months before Truman fired MacArthur, throwing down the gauntlet: "Truman must decide whether he is president, or whether the White House is occupied by MacArthur."[2]

They followed up this comment two weeks later with another curt observation. General MacArthur, they wrote, "seems not to be aware who is President of the United States." By insisting that anything short of unilateral American action to defend Formosa was appeasement and defeatism, they wrote, MacArthur was showing "an amazing degree of insubordination" toward President Truman. What is more, they were astonished at his remarks in his message to the VFW that "Oriental psychology" was inclined to "respect and follow aggressive, resolute and dynamic leadership." To the editors, this was a throwback to the "naked imperialistic jargon" of Kipling's day. Thus, they wrote, even though MacArthur's thinking ignored decades of growing Asian demands that imperialism be ended, it was nonetheless sure to be supported by right-wing Republicans "who have always wanted a military-imperialist policy in Asia, a policy called strength but actually committed to the weakest and rottenest elements in recent Far Eastern history."[3]

The following week brought yet further condemnation of MacArthur by the editors of the *New Republic*. This time, they explicitly laid out the basic disagreements between Truman and the general, thereby highlighting some of the ways in which the debate surrounding MacArthur was simply the next phase of the "Great Debate." First at issue, they wrote, was whether the United States should act alone or with its allies. They noted that, due to MacArthur's meeting with Chiang, many of America's democratic allies were "alarmed and antagonized by our unilateral stand in Formosa."

As we know, the editors came down firmly on the side of multilateralism. The second big issue at stake, they thought, was whether the United States would rely on force or on law to achieve its foreign policy goals. By "law," the editors here meant UN agreements, including noninterference in other countries' internal affairs. But MacArthur, they said, "advances a military program for U.S. expansion in Asia" that "places us on the same level as the Russians in grabbing parts of China."[4] While MacArthur's plans to unilaterally defend Formosa may not have risen to the level of neocolonialist land-grab, his suggestion that the United States use that island as an "unsinkable aircraft carrier" with which "to dominate with air power every Asiatic port from Vladivostok to Singapore" came close.[5] As such, the editors of the *New Republic* felt it necessary to use some very strong language, comparing the would-be foreign policy of MacArthur's America to that of the Soviet Union. Finally, the third major difference between Truman and MacArthur, they wrote, was whether the United States should re-enter the Chinese civil war. Whereas Truman had promised to withdraw the Seventh Fleet from the Formosa Strait after the fighting stopped in Korea, MacArthur's policy of using Formosa as the base for an invasion of the mainland "must force China and the United States into a war."[6] Thus, all of the major issues raised during the "Great Debate," namely, China policy and the degree to which the United States should act unilaterally in the world, were embodied in the MacArthur controversy. And that controversy would only intensify in the winter and spring of 1950–1951.

It was not just in lead editorials that one could find denunciations of MacArthur in the pages of the *New Republic*. Harold L. Ickes, secretary of the interior under Franklin Roosevelt, had a weekly column in that magazine and often wielded his pen as a weapon against the swaggering general. Ickes called MacArthur "arrogant and willful" and compared him to a "spoiled child" whose antics in challenging the president's authority should be resented by "every real American."[7] After Inchon in particular, he wrote, "MacArthur, saturated with self-esteem, as usual, and exalted by the clacking of political partisans of the miniscule mentality of... Joseph R. McCarthy, saw an opportunity to destroy Communism via China and thus become the greatest military hero that the world had ever seen. Why should "The MacArthur" demean himself by asking for orders or by deferring to inferior men who, by accident, happened to outrank him?"[8] As we shall see, Ickes's condemnations of "The MacArthur" for his arrogance and immaturity would only grow more forceful in the months ahead.

Over at *The Nation*, the editors were similarly critical of MacArthur after the VFW message, calling him "imperious" and pointing out that the whole incident "apparently embarrassed the general not one whit."[9] Washington editor Willard Shelton acknowledged that MacArthur had enjoyed an extraordinary career as an officer, but that "he may ruin himself in history, as Gen. McClellan did in regard to Lincoln, if he persists in expressing political judgments in challenge to the established civil authorities."[10] After MacArthur launched his home-by-Christmas Thanksgiving offensive in Korea, just as the Chinese delegation was arriving at Lake Success to discuss peace, the editors wrote that MacArthur seemed deliberately to be sabotaging peace negotiations. Such action, they continued, offered new evidence of what even our allies are coming to believe: "that the UN commander is a law unto himself, that he does not even bother to consult Washington before he acts, that he either makes American foreign policy or ignores it." What was more, as if MacArthur's behavior weren't bad enough politically and diplomatically, the editors also slammed him on humanitarian grounds. The idea of launching an offensive against an enemy that had avoided contact for weeks suggested "a callous indifference to wholesale slaughter at a moment when peace seemed within reach."[11]

Even the pages of the normally hawkish *New Leader* contained strong criticism of MacArthur's insubordination by the spring of 1951. "The first attribute of the good soldier is that he know how to obey orders," wrote the editors, "but Gen. MacArthur has repeatedly shown that he lacks this attribute. Had any soldier under Gen. MacArthur's command violated *his* orders as often as he has disobeyed those of his superiors," they continued, MacArthur "would long ago have dealt with him summarily." But MacArthur pressed on, they wrote, daunted neither by Truman nor by the UN, convinced that "he, and he alone" understood the Far East and what should be done there. It was no small wonder, then, that America's allies believed that MacArthur was trying to start a Third World War. The editors could only conclude that MacArthur's methods "bespeak a mind not of purest democratic virginity," especially considering the "steady stream of propaganda" flowing from general headquarters (GHQ) in Tokyo, "the messianic tone of every pronouncement," and the "cult of hero-worship and martyrdom that has been assiduously encouraged," all of which "seems expressive of a totalitarian mentality hell-bent on having its way at all costs."[12]

This was striking language from an editorial staff that had previously called for the very same kind of military action against China that MacArthur favored. So if the general couldn't find support even in the *New Leader*, were there any opinion journals that defended his controversial actions? As it turns out, the Catholic writers at *Commonweal* may have had their issues with some of MacArthur's statements and behavior, but they were much friendlier to the old soldier than the editors at the liberal journals discussed above. The views MacArthur expressed in the VFW message, they wrote, "command respect" and "can hardly be summarily swept aside." In particular, they thought he had made a strong case for the strategic importance of Formosa, explaining that it could serve as an "unsinkable aircraft carrier" off the coast of Asia. Most surprising, perhaps, was the editors' agreement with MacArthur's racialist generalization about "Oriental" psychology: "When he refers to Oriental respect for forcefulness and decision as opposed to vacillation and appeasement," they wrote, "he undoubtedly is on solid ground."[13] In the end, the editors of *Commonweal* could not go so far as to support MacArthur's embrace of Chiang nor his emphasis on Asia to the neglect of Europe, but it is notable that they differed so significantly in their treatment of MacArthur from their counterparts at the other leading liberal journals.

So with the partial exception of *Commonweal*, no major liberal opinion journal was willing to stick its neck out for the rogue general. The conservatives at *The Freeman*, however, were a different story altogether. Whereas the liberal journals tended to denounce MacArthur for talking too much, the editors of *The Freeman* lamented that he wasn't talking enough! They encouraged him to speak out more about the Far East, and if doing so compelled him to resign his command, they suggested, with tongue in cheek, "you can become a Chinese citizen under Chiang Kai-shek and really go about the business of defending America."[14] Elsewhere they painted MacArthur as the victim of unprovoked attacks in the press, his only crimes his "military brilliance, his common sense and his sterling patriotism." The "potent anti-MacArthur clique" in the nation's capital, they wrote, continued to slander the general in the press. Half-heartedly trying to remain above the fray, they insisted that the violation of their sense of honor at the personal attacks against MacArthur was the only reason they stooped to write about such nonsense: "We wouldn't bother with the anti-MacArthur campaign if it were not so virulent, insistent, continuous and pervasive."[15] These same editors, however, would hold themselves to quite another standard when it came to virulent, insistent, continuous, and pervasive attacks on Harry Truman, Dean Acheson, and George Marshall.

Indeed, *The Freeman* lashed out at Truman and Acheson just prior to MacArthur being fired, calling them "ignoramuses" for not seeing the obvious truth that MacArthur was preaching: that the communists were, "with a monomaniacal intensity that recalls Hitler to the last degree," trying to take over Asia "as the prelude to conquering the world." To the editors, MacArthur was a "great military leader" who knew exactly what the stakes were, but who was being forced by Truman to carry out, in Korea, the ridiculous policy of limited warfare:

> No doubt General MacArthur stands guilty of having expressed himself as a man who doesn't relish being made the instrument of carrying out a blood sacrifice of American soldiers. Generals ought not to have feelings. If it is U.S. and UN policy to feed a few thousand Americans each month into the jaws of a Moloch, no general should object. The Aztec blood ritual is the will of our politicians.

But was this also the will of the American people, they asked? They didn't think so. "We dare the Administration to fire General MacArthur," they chided. "We dare them to let him come home and speak his mind."[16] Of course, that is precisely what the Truman administration was about to do, kicking the debate about MacArthur into high gear. But before we get to the firing itself, let us first reexamine the primary substantive issue around which the entire debate turned: whether to make war on China.

WAR WITH CHINA REVISITED

The MacArthur controversy was about many things. But the one issue that formed the hard core of the whole debate was whether the United States should launch some form of offensive war against China, using its air and sea power to help Chiang and the mainland anticommunist guerrillas renew the Chinese civil war. Thus, as the MacArthur controversy drew toward its climax, the debate about America's China policy only intensified. Most of the opinion journals profiled here stuck to their guns on the issue, those to the left of center opposing any move to expand the war in Asia and those on the right watering at the mouth at the supposed opportunity to reinstall Chiang on the mainland. The *New Leader*, however, the liberal journal that had previously been virtually indistinguishable from its conservative counterparts on the issue, began to hedge a bit when discussing MacArthur's desired policy toward China.

The liberals at *The Nation*, the *New Republic*, and *Commonweal* continued to oppose making war on China whether it was proposed by MacArthur or not. The editors of the *New Republic*, for example, pointed out that making war on China would likely provoke Soviet retaliation as per the Sino-Soviet defense pact, perhaps in the form of a Soviet attack against Western Europe. They also scoffed, given the difficulty the United States was already having on the relatively small Korean peninsula, at MacArthur's insistence that victory in China would be fairly easy. Finally, they pointed out that Chiang's troops had neither the equipment nor the training necessary for a landing as massive as that required to invade mainland China.[17] In short, MacArthur's policy of making Formosa "the base of a future invasion of the mainland" would lead to "the most costly, useless, unpopular and catastrophic war in our history."[18] Harold Ickes wrote that MacArthur's war against China "will cost America and the world more than we can afford" and would "postpone world peace indefinitely, perhaps finally."[19] What is more, Ickes thought that such a policy would "destroy the unity of the American people" and would waste "half of American strength and resources" in a war "that has already been lost overwhelmingly by Chiang Kai-shek."[20] Over at *The Nation*, Washington editor Willard Shelton wrote that an American-supported invasion of China, as per MacArthur, "would obviously swing all Asia violently against us."[21] A *Nation* editorial asked what would happen if and when Chiang's forces "once again" proved no match for the Red Chinese—"are we then to leave them to their fate? It seems clear that this policy could easily lead step by step into full-scale war with China."[22] *Commonweal* echoed these sentiments, editorializing that MacArthur's idea of carrying the war to China was "futile and foolish" and would be "a sure way to world war."[23]

The liberals who rejected earlier conservative calls to launch an offensive war against China, then, were quite consistent in their position once MacArthur became the face of the war-with-China movement. Just as consistent on the other side of the ledger were the conservatives at *The Freeman*, who favored war with China before, during, and after the MacArthur saga. The administration's denial of MacArthur's request to bomb Manchuria, they wrote, "is worse than appeasement."[24] And why, they asked, did the administration "regard our army in Korea as expendable and refuse to permit General MacArthur to take the obvious measures to relieve the pressure upon them and reduce their losses?" They did not attempt to answer their own question. If they had, they might have come up with some of the answers laid out by the *New Republic* above. In any case, they concluded sanctimoniously that Truman, Acheson, and Marshall owed the fathers and mothers of the GIs in Korea some answers.[25]

So, for the most part, the editors of America's leading political opinion magazines did not change their minds about war with China just because

Douglas MacArthur's booming voice began to dominate the conversation. But there was one publication that was not entirely consistent in the line it took on this issue. The *New Leader*, that hawkish liberal journal whose foreign policy often resembled that of conservatives more than that of its fellow liberals, had beaten the drums for war with China rather loudly in the winter of 1950–1951, as outlined in the previous chapter. But once the issue became joined with the MacArthur controversy in the spring of 1951, the editors of the *New Leader* retreated a bit from some of their more bellicose pronouncements of the preceding months. Was an invasion of China using Nationalist troops, as MacArthur favored, actually feasible? they asked. Their answer was a flat contradiction of their earlier line. "An invasion of China," they wrote, "would produce exactly the political result it was designed militarily to prevent: Asia's fall to Communism." Why? Because Asians would interpret such a move as imperialist aggression and would become all the more sympathetic to the communist defenders of the mainland. "Once and for all," they concluded, "the U.S. and the UN should reject, in as strong language as possible, this crazy policy."[26]

While this was certainly a far cry from their previous calls for "full-scale invasion,"[27] they were not ready to give up the Chinese ghost altogether. They continued to favor American aid for "a stepped-up campaign by the anti-Communist guerrillas on the mainland," as well as "the steady infiltration of Chiang's regulars back to the mainland . . . by twos, threes, tens." Chiang's forces, they said, were more likely to succeed in liberating China "than the greatest invasion force we could muster."[28] Here one puzzles to make sense of the editors' thinking. They were opposed to the "crazy policy" of a US-backed invasion of China by Chiang's forces, but then they proclaimed support for just such an invasion, albeit in slow and steady form—death by a thousand cuts, it would seem, as opposed to a D-day-style assault on the beaches of the China coast. This was a noteworthy distinction, to be sure, but was it not a distinction in mere degree rather than in kind? And were the editors not contradicting their earlier policy now, just because they did not want to seem so illiberal as to support MacArthur in his challenge to the president's constitutional authority?

In any case, this was not just a one-time slip-up by the editorial staff. They continued to articulate their new policy in later issues, trying to strike the right balance between what they viewed as MacArthur's recklessness and Truman's timidity. While they were in "hearty accord" with Truman's rejection of MacArthur's desire for "all-out war," they went on to state that "the U.S. must now adopt as its policy the goal of the overthrow of Chinese

Communism." Again, this should not be done by outright American invasion or even by a full-scale US-backed invasion by Chiang. But who, they asked, "in Asia or elsewhere can object to an attempt made by Chinese in China to recover their country?"[29] This would require, of course, substantial American aid to the guerrillas on the mainland and "the ferrying of selected Nationalist regulars from Formosa to join them," but this did not seem to concern the editors. Surely such intervention in China's internal affairs would not be seen by the rest of Asia as any kind of Western imperialism. And surely the anticommunist forces would acquit themselves better than they had in the 1940s so that the United States would never be faced with the choice of whether to escalate its involvement, as happened in Vietnam in the following decade. No, this would be renewal of the Chinese civil war, but "on a higher plane than before," whatever that meant. In the end, the editors of the *New Leader* wanted to have it both ways on this issue. On the one hand, MacArthur was obviously wrong—the United States most definitely should not help Chiang invade China to restart the Chinese civil war. That would be crazy! On the other hand, the United States should definitely help Chiang invade China to restart the Chinese civil war! A foolish consistency, one can imagine them arguing, is the hobgoblin of little minds

MACARTHUR'S DISMISSAL

Despite all of Truman's frustrations with MacArthur, given his VFW message, his trip to visit Chiang on Formosa, and his various statements—even in the face of a gag order issued by the president—questioning the correctness of US Far Eastern policy, the president had been reluctant to fire him. But the straw that broke the camel's back was when, in late March 1951, MacArthur issued a unilateral and belligerent ultimatum to the Chinese, warning them to agree to peace on UN terms or face the threat of an attack on Chinese territory. Not only was this "peace offer" not authorized in Washington, but it came just as the US government was preparing its own peace proposal to end the war. MacArthur's bellicosity effectively scuttled that larger effort. Thus, in the aftermath of this latest example of the general's gross insubordination, Truman decided to relieve him of his duties once and for all. In the couple of weeks between MacArthur's ultimatum and his firing, the contributors to America's leading political opinion journals weighed in on his offer to the Chinese. Not surprisingly, left-of-center liberals opposed MacArthur, conservatives supported him, and hawkish liberals were divided.

The editorial staff at *The Nation* was unequivocal in its condemnation of MacArthur's ultimatum. If he had genuinely wished to end the fighting in Korea, they editorialized, then he would not have done what he did. By threatening possible attacks on the Chinese mainland and eliminating Formosa and China's seat at the UN from discussion, "he practically invited a rejection by Peking." Despite the administration's subsequent repudiations, they lamented, to repudiate an action was not to undo its effect. MacArthur's intervention, they wrote, had clearly damaged Washington's sincere efforts to end the conflict in Korea.[30] The editors of the *New Republic* echoed *The Nation*'s disgust with MacArthur. "All hope has now vanished of an immediate end to the fighting in Korea," they wrote.[31] Clearly, the two leading liberal weeklies viewed MacArthur's actions as contemptible and demonstrably harmful to the interests of peace.

The hawkish liberals at the *New Leader* seemed to agree with their left-liberal counterparts, editorializing that MacArthur's actions were "improper," "rash," even "unpardonable."[32] But William Henry Chamberlin broke with his fellow editors at the *New Leader* and praised MacArthur, calling his offer "as sensible and well-advised as the whimpering cease-fire appeals issued by the UN in December were foolish and demoralizing." Whereas *The Nation* had castigated MacArthur for leaving Formosa and UN membership off the table, Chamberlin said this was only evidence that MacArthur refused to "pay blackmail of the kind favored by the appeasement-minded."[33] Chamberlin's strong disagreement here not only with the left liberals at *The Nation* and the *New Republic*, but with his fellow editors at the *New Leader*, is further evidence that any talk of a "liberal consensus" during the early Cold War is simplistic at best. Indeed, many nominal liberals, like William Henry Chamberlin, had much more in common with avowed conservatives.

Just as Chamberlin praised MacArthur's peace offer, so did the conservatives at *The Freeman* and the *American Mercury*. The editors of *The Freeman* wrote that the only trouble with MacArthur's "clear and statesmanlike declaration" was that it demonstrated a "clarity and firmness of purpose" that neither Truman nor the UN seemed willing to match.[34]

> For just after General MacArthur . . . had informed Mao Tse-tung that he had better quit or look to be hit from any number of unspecified directions, the

> high-level dumb bunnies back home . . . combined to wigwag the signal to Peiping that MacArthur has no authority to say anything. This denial to the UN Commander of the right to use the methods of psychological warfare must have caused Mao Tse-tung to snicker up his sleeve. He knows that MacArthur has been limited to pitching soft flutterballs over the outside corner.[35]

It was not that Truman and Acheson did not want a ceasefire, they explained. It was that they wanted it in terms of a "virtual sell-out," presumably involving a deal on Formosa and Chinese representation at the UN.[36] In the pages of the *American Mercury*, Alice Widener wrote, "It's difficult for a reasonable mind to quarrel with MacArthur's logic" and insisted that if his ultimatum had become policy the United States could have achieved a favorable peace settlement.[37] Her argument on this point flies in the face of the fact that the Chinese wholly rejected MacArthur's conditions for negotiation, but this was nonetheless the conservative line.

After President Truman finally decided to relieve MacArthur in April 1951, the debate about the general and his proposed policies in East Asia was kicked into high gear, laying bare the country's political and ideological divisions. As manifested in the community of political opinion journals, left liberals heartily applauded the president's decision, hawkish liberals disagreed with one another, and conservatives continued to defend the general and lambaste the president. Perhaps no other issue during the entire Korean War provoked as much emotion on all sides as the end of Douglas MacArthur's storied career.

Even prior to the actual firing, liberal writers were making the case for MacArthur's dismissal. No general should "play politics or try to usurp from the President the conduct of foreign affairs," wrote Harold Ickes. "MacArthur has done both."[38] And those were not Ickes's only harsh words. He also wrote bluntly that MacArthur "has failed in Korea." Thus, the general should be relieved by Truman, as Lincoln relieved McClellan, so that the entire cost of his mistakes would not continue to be borne by the "heroic soldiers and marines who chased the MacArthur *ignis fatuus* to the border of Manchuria." What mistakes in particular? Ickes wrote that MacArthur had been warned about the possibility of Chinese intervention but gave those warnings no heed. "As usual," Ickes sarcastically remarked, "MacArthur was all-knowing." Indeed, the general boasted he would have American soldiers home by Christmas. Instead, they were now barely hanging on in Korea. Yet MacArthur supporters were hysterically demanding that President Truman abandon his authority and "give General MacArthur *carte blanche* to determine foreign and military policy in the Far East," wrote an astonished Ickes. "Could asininity go further?" What such calls amounted to, he thought, was a demand that the president delegate unconstitutional powers to the man who was responsible for "the worst defeat in American military history."[39] This last statement from Ickes seems rather hyperbolic in retrospect but, in fairness, writers of all ideological stripes had concluded by Christmas 1950 that the United States had lost in Korea. In any event, Ickes was clearly one of MacArthur's harshest critics. His passionate desire to see MacArthur fired was almost palpable.

The rest of the staff at the *New Republic* ultimately agreed with Ickes once MacArthur issued his ultimatum to China. MacArthur's "contemptuous insubordination" could not be allowed to continue, they editorialized. The general, "one of the world's supreme egoists," had adopted a pomposity "without parallel in our history." Indeed, his disobedience of direct orders was so brazen that the editors could only conclude that he was purposefully trying to goad Truman into firing him. If so, he was on the brink of success. They simply could not see, they concluded, how Truman could possibly avoid dismissing MacArthur.[40]

The editors of *The Nation* felt similarly. After the ultimatum, they wrote that Truman's patience with MacArthur "has ceased long ago to be a virtue." While they openly disagreed with MacArthur on the substance of his China policy, they insisted this wasn't even germane to whether Truman should fire him—the matter was much more basic than that. The issue was not whether MacArthur was right and the president wrong about launching a war against mainland China. The question was who was legally in charge of America's foreign and military policy. They pointed out that the Constitution was quite clear on this point. High policy was to be made by the commander-in-chief, advised by those with the duty to take a global view of regional matters, as opposed to a field commander with a necessarily narrower scope of vision. Put simply, then, "MacArthur should no longer be allowed to try to run [American foreign policy] from Tokyo."[41]

All of this was prior to MacArthur being relieved. Then came the bombshell that it had actually happened. *The Nation* and the *New Republic* were well pleased. The *New Republic* editorialized that MacArthur had made himself "the head of an open conspiracy against the policy of the government he was sworn to serve." Moreover, on purely military grounds, the MacArthur policy of war against China "would likely be disastrous." But the dismissal was not all good news. What the editors were perhaps most concerned about was the outpouring of emotion from MacArthur's devotees in the aftermath of his firing. The extremist clique of which MacArthur was the figurehead, they feared, would not go gently into its long-overdue goodnight. They described this group as "the people who scream 'Communist' at everyone who disagrees with them." Yes, for the editors of the *New Republic*, the members of this MacArthur-McCarthy clique were "dangerous men, bound together by an evil design which they will be slow to relinquish," namely, suppression of civil liberties at home and the reckless expansion of war abroad. In the end, they could only hope that the American people would reject the "undemocratic philosophy of militarism" for which MacArthur stood. And if nothing else came of the firing, at least MacArthur's removal might permit the resumption of a "resolute course toward peace" in Korea.[42]

Harold Ickes was a bit more jovial in his initial reaction to the firing, writing that MacArthur, "the world's champion talker, has talked himself out of his job." MacArthur was not content to command US/UN forces in the Far East, he continued. "He wanted to exercise the powers of the President himself." Ultimately, MacArthur's "open defiance" of the president left Truman no alternative. Regarding MacArthur's would-be calamitous policy of war with China (and perhaps, by extension, the Soviet Union), Ickes wrote, "Fortunately for the United States and Western civilization, President Truman has brought to an abrupt end the careening career of this man who, totally wanting in self-discipline, was, with sputtering torch in hand while drunk with bootlegged power, weaving in and out among open powder kegs which could have been ignited by a single vagrant spark into an explosion that could have shaken the world." Thus, for Ickes, Truman's action in relieving the general may actually have done nothing less than save the world from the horrors of a Third World War. In any case, Ickes was just as disgusted by the behavior of MacArthur's supporters as were his fellow editors. In trying to paint MacArthur as a martyr to the cause of freedom and in calling for Truman's impeachment, MacArthur's partisans intended to "disturb and disunite." People such as Minority Leader Joe Martin, concluded Ickes, "may ostentatiously clothe their bodies in the hand-me-down garb of patriotism, but, perhaps without realizing it, they have exposed their souls in all of their hideous starkness."[43] Finally, on the one-year anniversary of the beginning of the Korean War, Ickes summed up the whole MacArthur controversy in the following damning terms, especially in light of the conservative hero worship that had been running amok since MacArthur's return to the United States: "No one within my memory has done such a reckless disservice to his country as has MacArthur. He should be pilloried with the just indignation of his countrymen whose position in world affairs he has jeopardized and whose morale he has damaged. A thousand McCarthys were less a threat to the America we love than one military coxcomb! 'Hero' indeed! 'Patriot!' 'Military genius!'"[44]

Over at *The Nation*, Freda Kirchwey was less sardonic and more straightforward. The recall of MacArthur, she wrote, accomplished several urgent things. First and foremost, "it rebuked a flagrant act of military insubordination . . . and thus ended a very present threat of Bonapartism." In addition, it prevented a deepening of the divisions between the United States and its European allies and "assured a doubting world" that American policy still favored settlement of the Korean War by negotiation "rather than expansion of the war into China."[45] Contributor Howard K. Smith also invoked the threat of "Bonapartism" embodied by MacArthur and concluded that "no honest American can do anything but admit that Mr. Truman's decision was right."[46]

Washington editor Willard Shelton, like his counterparts at the *New Republic*, was concerned about the domestic political implications of MacArthur's firing. The Republican Party, he wrote, "in a mass surrender to its lunatic fringe," had lined up with General MacArthur in his disputes with the duly elected commander-in-chief. Moreover, he pointed out, it was not just the McCarthys of the party who were engaging in some rather extreme rhetoric: "It was not surprising that Senator McCarthy . . . said of the President, 'The son of a bitch should be impeached,' and followed this with a public speech implying that Truman fired MacArthur only after his aides had befuddled him with alcohol. But the Republican leader of the House, Joe Martin, also talked wildly of 'impeachments,' and dozens of Republican orators shrieked about 'appeasement,' 'treason,' and a 'Far Eastern Munich.'" The Republican Party, he continued, "will campaign for the Presidency next year on McCarthy and MacArthur." Shelton's fears were not ultimately realized, as Eisenhower won the Republican nomination over Taft in 1952, but from the perspective of 1951, with MacArthur's considerable shadow looming over the whole of the American political landscape, it must have been easy to fear the worst. In fact, powerful senators like Robert Taft and Kenneth Wherry were saying that, with MacArthur gone, the only solution left was an American attack on the Chinese mainland. This, for Shelton, would be a nonstarter for America's allies in both Europe and Asia. Such Republicans, he continued,

> speak glibly of Chiang Kai-shek's "divisions" on Formosa, not facing the fact that American troops would have to form the vanguard of a "second front" offensive. They will not send troops to General Eisenhower in Europe for an allied army created under a treaty ratified by the Senate, but they indorse MacArthur's demand to lead an American army against China. Anyone who disagrees with them must be a drunkard or a traitor.

As for the issues central to the MacArthur controversy, Shelton reminded his readers that, up until MacArthur's ultimatum to China, Truman had stood by his general through a slew of defeats and embarrassments. But there was no indication, he wrote, "that MacArthur acknowledged any debt of comparable loyalty to the civilian commander who thus sustained him." Rather, it had become clear to Shelton that MacArthur had effectively presented Truman with a binary choice: "either to replace him or to yield to his plan to turn the Korean conflict into World War III."[47] In other words, according to Willard Shelton, it was not the communists who had been blackmailing the Truman administration in Asia. It was Douglas MacArthur.

Finally, Alexander Werth and Julio Alvarez del Vayo also praised Truman's decision in the pages of *The Nation*. Werth argued that MacArthur had cavalierly wanted to involve the United States in war against China, which could easily have led to a Third World War. The Europeans, he reported, had no enthusiasm whatever for such an adventure and were thus well pleased when Truman replaced his wayward commander.[48] This sentiment was echoed by del Vayo, who reported from the UN that news of the decision was met with "approval, joy, and praise for the courage and wisdom of the President."[49] In sum, the pages of *The Nation* were filled with condemnation of MacArthur, support for Truman, and alarm at the reaction of the Republican Party.

The editors of the Catholic journal *Commonweal* added their voices to the liberal chorus of praise for Truman's decision. MacArthur's VFW message, unauthorized ultimatum to China, and letter to Minority Leader Martin, they editorialized, were the behavior of a man who thought himself above the law. More substantively, they pointed out that his opinion on Pacific policy—the idea that Asia was the "decisive battlefield against the Communists" and that, therefore, the Korean War should be extended into China—was totally at odds with the judgment of the president, the State Department, the Joint Chiefs of Staff, General Eisenhower, and the majorities in Congress and at the UN. As such, they suggested MacArthur's "will-to-power" was "contemptuous of the prevailing reason of the majority" and was in effect behavior that fit the historical pattern of a dictator. What was more, his desire to expand the war into China was almost certain, they thought, to lead to "the futile and bloody trap of a land war in Asia" and possibly even to atomic warfare between the superpowers. According to the editors, "it is the moral obligation of Christians first to exhaust every possible means of averting this unspeakable massacre, and one of those means right now is to limit the war in Korea." In other words, it was the Christian's moral duty to oppose the MacArthur line. After all, the administration's policy of negotiation offered a far better hope for an honorable peace than did MacArthur's "swaggering belligerency." In the end, they wrote, MacArthur "clearly exceeded his authority" and, in defying the normal democratic process, he had contradicted the very cause the United States was purportedly fighting for against Soviet totalitarianism.[50] Apparently, it was not just the secular editors of *The Nation* who rejoiced in seeing that Truman had nipped MacArthur's turn toward Bonapartism in the bud.

Elsewhere, the editors of *Commonweal*, true to their Catholic roots, quoted Pope Pius XII, who said "nothing is lost by peace, but everything can be lost by war." That, in the final analysis, was what the whole MacArthur business boiled down to. To have followed MacArthur "would have led almost inevitably to World War III," whereas Truman had acted to limit the Korean War and therefore the likelihood of a general global conflict. For this simple reason, they concluded, "we support the President wholeheartedly."[51]

Whereas the left-leaning liberal journals *The Nation*, the *New Republic*, and *Commonweal* supported the firing of MacArthur on both constitutional and policy grounds, the hawkish liberals at the *New Leader* had a more difficult time agreeing on whether Truman had done the right thing. The *New Leader*'s editorials tended to express qualified support for Truman, while the writings of two of that magazine's most hawkish anticommunists, William Henry Chamberlin and David J. Dallin, were much less enthusiastic about the dismissal of the swaggering general.

The *New Leader*'s editorial policy was to be sympathetic to MacArthur regarding his policy aims, but to condemn him for his usurpation of presidential authority. On the one hand, the editors suggested that the root of the problem was not just MacArthur's insubordination but also the Truman administration's failure to develop a sensible foreign policy. Thus, the editors were at least sympathetic to MacArthur's position, if not wholly supportive of him. On the other hand, they agreed completely with their fellow liberals that MacArthur had crossed a constitutional line and, as such, needed to be dismissed. "Historians will agree," wrote the editors, "that the President had no alternative except to dismiss the general who was undoubtedly guilty of trespassing in the civil domain of the making of foreign policy."[52] In short, for the editors, while MacArthur's impatience with the UN's procrastination was "understandable," his rashness in taking the matter into his own hands was "unpardonable."[53]

William Henry Chamberlin was hesitant to join his fellow editors in praising the president's decision. While he grudgingly acknowledged that, "on technical grounds, a plausible case can be made for President Truman's dismissal of General MacArthur," the bulk of his writing on the issue was quite supportive of the fired general. MacArthur's departure, he wrote, "leaves a dangerous void in the Far East," in that MacArthur was the preeminent symbol of militant anticommunism in Asia. Indeed, Chamberlin described MacArthur as "a tower of strength against the forces of weakness and appeasement in the Orient." What was more, Chamberlin noted that the firing seemed to have pleased the wrong people. To wit, the Chinese Nationalists "are gloomy," and the "South Korean victims of Red aggression are depressed." But the Indians, he noted, were "exultant," and "what a help India has been in the Korean crisis, contributing not a single soldier but a vast amount of defeatist backseat driving!" In the end, Chamberlin was concerned that, without MacArthur on the front lines, the United States would be tempted to surrender, to "scuttle-and-run as the unworthy ending of the heroic struggle in Korea."[54]

Chamberlin's fellow hawkish columnist at the *New Leader*, David J. Dallin, was even more critical of Truman's decision to relieve the general of command. MacArthur's dismissal, he wrote, meant a victory for communism and a defeat for the forces of democracy. Moscow, he explained, "can well appraise the event as a major military-diplomatic victory." More specific to the situation on the ground in Korea, MacArthur's dismissal "means that no military force will be employed to regain North Korea for the Korean people," which in turn meant that "the aggressors" could prosecute their war in Korea without fear. Dallin concluded his thoughts with a damning comparison: Truman firing MacArthur was akin to the Western powers sacrificing Czechoslovakia to Hitler on the altar of appeasement at Munich. "'I had to do it,' the President announced, 'to maintain peace,'" wrote Dallin. "His words sound ominously like those of another Western statesman, Neville Chamberlain, who exclaimed: 'I bring you peace in our time,' after his return from Munich. Both were mistaken; retreat before an aggressor never serves the cause of peace."[55] What's odd about this analogy, of course, is that the Sudetenland was not Hitler's until it was given to him at Munich, whereas North Korea started out as a part of the communist empire. Thus, according to Dallin, not actively liberating parts of the communist world was the equivalent of actively adding to the Nazi empire in the 1930s. In other words, for liberal hawks like Dallin, *containment* had apparently come to mean *appeasement*. Wars of containment would simply not do. Only wars of liberation would satisfy their anticommunist sensibilities. While some hawkish liberals equivocated somewhat about the dismissal of MacArthur, the conservatives at *The Freeman* did not. They were quite sure that MacArthur was entirely in the right and Truman in the wrong. Even before the firing took place, the editors of *The Freeman* goaded President Truman, literally daring him to fire MacArthur.[56] For the editors, MacArthur was a "great military leader" who understood the evil designs of world communism—unlike the "ignoramuses" Truman and Acheson, who apparently did not realize that Stalin would stop at nothing until he stood astride the entire globe.[57]

The editors of *The Freeman* quickly brushed aside the issue of the president's constitutional authority, editorializing, "We do not dispute President Truman's right to fire an insubordinate General. . . . But to allow the Administration to reduce the MacArthur question to the issue of insubordination is to confuse the whole question of our effectiveness in the Far East." In other words, for *The Freeman*, the controversy was never really about insubordination but, rather, the fundamentals of foreign policy. And on the latter issue, they were sure, MacArthur was obviously correct and Truman dangerously naive. "Of what does MacArthur stand guilty?" they asked. It could not have been any violation of his orders, for he had "meticulously obeyed" them, according to *The Freeman*. No, he was guilty only of believing it was not in America's interests to allow communism to become dominant in East Asia. They painted an excessively grim picture of what the future would look like—a future in which the Asian dominoes fell one by one—if MacArthur's policy was not followed:

> What MacArthur knows is that if Korea goes, Japan will be next. If Formosa goes, Hong Kong and the Philippines will be next. . . . [T]he truth is that if Communism in Asia cannot be checked, the whole of the Malayan area, with its important rubber, oil and tin, must fall into Stalin's hands. That would isolate Australia and New Zealand; it would cut the world in two. It would enable the Russians to paralyze India, take over the oil of Iran and move up to Suez.[58]

Here, as David J. Dallin had done, the editors equated containment with surrender. In reality, Truman had decided to intervene in Korea in the first place precisely because he feared the consequences of unchecked communist aggression. But for the editors of *The Freeman*, containing communism was not enough. The United States had to go on the offensive, particularly against China, if freedom was to survive in the world. Thus, like MacArthur, the editors concluded that the fate of the world might be decided in the Formosa Strait. Preserving South Korea was insufficient. Liberating China was the only way to avoid communist conquest of the world. And this was what the MacArthur controversy was really about to the editors of *The Freeman*—not some petty squabble about generals following orders. Rather, it was about Truman's weakness in the face of communist plans for global conquest.

After MacArthur's dismissal and return to the United States, he traveled to Washington, DC, to address a joint session of Congress, after which he was treated to a ticker-tape parade in New York City. The outpouring of emotion from MacArthur's supporters, in the streets of New York, in the halls of Congress (primarily from members of the Republican Party), and in the press, was ostentatious. *The Nation* described the raptures experienced by members of the Republican Party following MacArthur's return (including ex-president Herbert Hoover comparing MacArthur to St. Paul) as "a weird spectacle, a kind of voodooism in politics, witch doctors prescribing ritual healing for torn primitive emotions."[59] The editors of the *New Republic* were also taken aback by the hysteria, calling it "one of the gaudiest shows . . . that America has ever witnessed." Among the "more extreme utterances in the first caveman yawp of elemental emotion," they noted, were that Truman should be impeached and that the administration was covertly directed by its communist masters in Moscow![60] They wrote that House Republicans "behaved like children, as they stamped and yelled" during MacArthur's address to Congress. When some in the audience started to cry, they continued, "It illustrated to us the profound truth that words that make one man weep may merely give another man indigestion."[61] Later, they used another digestive analogy, describing MacArthur's oratory as "rich and thick and overwhelming like a double ice cream sundae laced with molasses." A single spoonful, they wrote, "gives some unfortunates intellectual diabetes."[62]

Liberal publications tended to blame the press for building up MacArthur's image to the point that it could be politically exploited upon his return home. According to the *New Republic*, "the blame falls less on MacArthur's bent shoulders than on the men in the U.S. who betrayed the tradition of a free press by raising MacArthur to a pedestal of hero worship and infallibility where no servant of a free society should stand."[63] *Commonweal* echoed these sentiments when commenting on the storm of emotionalism whipped up by MacArthur's dismissal.[64] Even at the *New Leader*, where many on staff supported MacArthur, there was a certain disapproval of the pro-MacArthur press. "Some of our press has been frantically building a MacArthur mystique," ran an editorial. "More saddening, and surprising," it continued, "is that all too many ordinary Americans . . . in their psychological need for strong leadership, have fallen for the self-defeating mirage of the savior on horseback."[65]

The pages of the conservative journal *The Freeman*, as one might expect, told quite another story. Rather than the press creating an image of MacArthur-as-god, *The Freeman* insisted that the press was, in fact, unfair to their beloved general. The editors complained that the "McLiberal press," the *New York Times* in particular, treated MacArthur as its whipping boy.[66] In this debate over media bias, we can of course detect undertones familiar to consumers of twenty-first-century political news: liberals complained about the corrosive influence of the conservative press for straying too far afield from the world of factual reality, while conservatives slammed mainstream press outlets like the *New York Times* for having an excessively liberal bias. And all of this in the early 1950s, the era of the so-called liberal consensus.

THE MACARTHUR HEARINGS

The Senate Armed Services and Foreign Relations Committees held weeks of hearings on the dismissal of MacArthur, from May to June 1951. While the proceedings were in large part political theater, they did ultimately have the effect of dampening the white-hot emotions that initially surrounded the firing. Naturally, however, the editors of America's leading liberal political opinion journals viewed the outcome of the hearings quite differently than their conservative counterparts. Liberals viewed the hearings as vindication for the Truman administration, while conservatives thought the exact opposite—that they vindicated MacArthur.

The *New Republic* was harsh in its criticism of MacArthur's testimony before the Senate panel. The editors were particularly focused on MacArthur's admission that he had little to no knowledge of global strategy, but that he nonetheless insisted that the United States should charge full bore into war with China. MacArthur admitted, they pointed out, "that he is ignorant of Russia's capacity to devastate America with atomic bombs." In short, the editors noted that MacArthur was insisting on a policy (war with China) that had truly global implications but that he disregarded any concerns other than those relating to local conditions in East Asia. MacArthur almost lost his army in Korea when he rolled the dice and crossed the thirty-eighth parallel, they wrote. "Now he proposes to gamble with it again, risking its total loss should we engage China and Russia in an all-out war." When Senator Brien MacMahon (D-CT) challenged his right to thus gamble, MacArthur replied, "Everything that is involved in international relationships amounts to a gamble." In such a blithe spirit, they gasped, "we are to plunge into world war." When MacMahon asked how MacArthur intended to defend the United States in the event of such a world war, the general replied curtly, "That doesn't happen to be my responsibility." The *New Republic* could only conclude that such testimony revealed MacArthur to be "unprincipled, arrogant and reckless," and that Truman had him "over a barrel."[67]

Of course, that the facts laid out at the hearings favored Truman was one thing, but the lingering partisan hatred of Truman for firing MacArthur was another. Truman, editorialized the *New Republic*, "has committed the unpardonable sin of being right. Every reasonable person can see now that MacArthur had to go." The facts clearly showed that MacArthur's military judgment was "unsound," and that the "despised, little Harry Truman was right about it all the time," wrote the editors. Of course, this did not diminish the "mob ovation to the intoxicating MacArthur" on the part of his devotees.[68] That mob, however, perhaps began to diminish once the Joint Chiefs of Staff testified. As the *New Republic* put it, MacArthur had let the GOP down, by leading his partisan supporters to believe that the JCS would support him when, in fact, they were unified against him.[69] The position of the Joint Chiefs was best expressed by General Omar Bradley, who famously testified that going to war with China would have been "the wrong war, at the wrong place, at the wrong time, and with the wrong enemy." As such, crowed the editors, "the Republicans have a slightly soiled general on their hands, another McClellan."[70]

The staff at *The Nation* was more matter-of-fact in its treatment of the hearings, Willard Shelton writing that nothing emerged in the hearings to challenge the justice of Truman's actions in firing MacArthur. The political failure of the hearings for the Republicans, he wrote, was exemplified when one Republican warned the GOP "not to tie itself too firmly to MacArthur's kite." That warning, however, may have come a little late.[71] For not a single military witness, noted Shelton, supported MacArthur's position that the United States should bomb Manchuria, blockade the Chinese coast, and "go it alone" in warfare against China.[72] In the end, the editors of *The Nation* were pleased to conclude that the hearings "will at least help puncture the MacArthurian legend of god-like consistency and infallibility."[73]

The leading liberal weeklies, then, were quite confident that the hearings had resulted in a very clear outcome: MacArthur was wrong, both on constitutional and policy grounds, while Truman was vindicated on both fronts. The conservatives at *The Freeman*, however, saw things—as usual—very differently. Whereas the *New Republic*, for example, saw MacArthur's testimony as internally contradictory, the editors of *The Freeman* called his testimony "deeply impressive" and accused the Truman administration and its allies in Congress and in the press of engaging in "the most unscrupulous efforts at a personal smear." That MacArthur's enemies would stoop to the level of personal attacks, they maintained, was "an implicit confession that the policy of the Administration in Korea cannot be defended on its own merits." As for that policy, the editors argued that Truman's limited war in Korea made no sense at all. Instead, the United States should "untie the hands" of its army in Korea by bombing Manchuria and enlisting Chiang's forces in the fight for East Asia.[74] Only then could appeasement be avoided and victory won.

As for General Bradley's "wrong war" comment, they scoffed: "The Bradley epigram assumed the fantastic notion that we are not *already* fighting the Chinese Communists." And in a stunningly casual dismissal of the possibility of World War III breaking out, they wrote, "If Russia came in as a result of following the MacArthur policy, it would spoil General Bradley's epigram anyway." And that was not all. "Whether it would also be the right war at the right place and at the right time," they continued, "is something that Mr. Truman should have asked himself on the night of June 26 when he made the personal decision, without consulting Congress, to throw American troops into Korea." Thus, all of these conservatives' frustrations that had been building up from the beginning of the war now found their release. Truman had risked a Third World War at the outset of the Korean intervention (and unconstitutionally at that), they insisted, yet he had prevented MacArthur from winning in Korea because he feared a Third World War![75] Thus, the conservative editors of *The Freeman* seemed to disagree with every single decision Truman had made from the word go. He should not have gone into Korea in the first place (at least not without congressional authorization), and once he did order American troops in, apparently, he should not have worried too much about the limited conflict turning into a global one.

In sum, the liberal opinion journals argued that the hearings largely discredited MacArthur and vindicated Harry Truman, both on constitutional and policy grounds. The conservatives at *The Freeman*, however, quite tellingly never even addressed the constitutional question. They based their entire argument on the desirability of MacArthur's favored policy, presumably knowing that they had no leg to stand on when it came to MacArthur's repeated acts of insubordination. In the end, even contributors to *The Freeman* had to acknowledge that the hearings were a defeat for MacArthur and his Republican supporters. Edna Lonigan admitted that the Republicans had "failed dismally" at the hearings, but she was nonetheless defiant until the end, rationalizing the failure by saying it was only because the Joint Chiefs and Secretary Acheson had so skillfully blunted MacArthur's sharp points through doublespeak and confusion. In other words, MacArthur's obviously correct arguments had been "drowned by the Administration in a sea of words," a cynical application of "the Machiavellian arts of confusing the people."[76] Here Lonigan made no attempt to substantively address the military arguments made by the JCS that ran contrary to MacArthur. She simply dismissed them as so many verbal acrobatics.

MACARTHUR FADES AWAY

After the speech before Congress, ticker-tape parade, and Senate hearings, public attention to MacArthur began to fade. He launched a speaking tour of Texas in June 1951, in part to test the waters for a possible run at the presidency in 1952, but it was not the rousing success he had envisioned. The liberal weeklies ridiculed the tour, especially as it began to go badly, while conservatives never wavered in their support for the general, even in the midst of his long fade-away.

As MacArthur prepared for his speaking tour, in the luxury of the Waldorf Towers hotel in Manhattan, the editors of the *New Republic* could not help but mockingly express their anticipation. MacArthur had been "brooding up there in his privileged sanctuary of the Waldorf Towers, and now the American de Gaulle is going to break his moody silence," they wrote, referring to MacArthur's frustration with what he called the Chinese communists' "privileged sanctuary" in Manchuria, where he was not allowed to drop American bombs. In words dripping with sarcasm, the editors said they looked forward to hearing "that rich, mellow . . . voice of omniscience" again, "vibrating the cord of patriotism and dispelling all our little human doubts and uncertainties."[77] They did not have to wait long. The following week they wrote bluntly that "General Douglas MacArthur came, was seen, and didn't conquer." If the general's supporters expected Texan political leaders "to flock to his banner, they were sadly disappointed." Indeed, they noted with satisfaction that, while one million people had turned out for his New York City parade, fewer than 100,000 showed up for his five speeches in the Lone Star state. In Houston, where the stadium could seat nearly 80,000 souls, only 10,000–20,000 were in attendance.[78] *The Nation* published a piece by a reporter from Austin who confirmed the sparse crowds and called the whole tour "a wasted effort." Texans, he wrote, "wanted to see MacArthur, but once they had seen him, 90% were satisfied, and didn't bother to listen to what he had to say."[79]

The editors of *Commonweal* were happy to see that, by midsummer 1951, the hysteria surrounding MacArthur's return, "the tornado of emotionalism and demagoguery," as they called it, had subsided considerably.[80] But MacArthur's underwhelming tour of Texas was not yet his final goodbye. The following summer he was selected, primarily due to lobbying by Senator Robert A. Taft, to deliver the keynote address at the Republican National Convention in Chicago. Douglas MacArthur, editorialized *Commonweal*, "will here reach a high point of his spectacular fifteen-month-old fade-away." MacArthur, that "most eloquent prophet of strict Republican orthodoxy, who assures us that he has 'no politics' in him," wrote the editors, "will find at Chicago the most spot-lighted opportunity yet for his bitter indictment of that Administration which has failed to subscribe to his own version of foreign and domestic wisdom."[81] Here was a picture, then, of a bitter old man lashing out at enemies who had long since moved on—hardly an end befitting a man of MacArthur's once towering stature. The general's speech at the GOP convention, wrote Francis Downing, in language almost as full of pity as it was of scorn, "quickly revealed that here was a splenetic old man who had nothing to say. He stood wholly destitute of ideas, of any even elementary understanding of the world about him. The myth forever died." In the end, "he had, at last, faded away."[82]

While those writing in America's left-of-center liberal opinion journals concluded their long fixation on Douglas MacArthur with a mixture of mockery, satisfaction, and pity, the conservatives who contributed to *The Freeman* continued to hoist high the MacArthur flag, regardless of the countervailing winds blowing in their faces. Radio commentator and reporter Frazier Hunt, who would go on to write several books on MacArthur's military exploits, defended the general's speech at the Republican convention. The editors introduced the piece as being about "the terrible price all America has paid for the Administration's refusal to heed and to act upon the counsel of our foremost soldier." Whereas liberal writers viewed MacArthur's post-dismissal life as almost pathetic, Hunt viewed the year since his dismissal as having provided a "tragic vindication" for the old soldier. Before we get to what, exactly, constituted this vindication for Hunt, it is worth noting that he was as effusive in his praise for MacArthur as Harold Ickes was abounding in his condemnation. Hunt recalled the American reversal of fortune early in the war, after the Inchon landing, writing that MacArthur "made good in his role of a modern King Canute, commanding the human sea to stop." He performed this miracle, wrote Hunt, even though "he was violating every tenet of warfare." Only the true master, he concluded, "dares write his own rules." What made MacArthur's performance all the more miraculous, according to Hunt, was that he was forced to fight his lonely battles in Korea while Formosa, "the great island of free Chinese refuge," was blockaded by a US fleet "as though it were a Pacific pesthouse filled with our enemies." Then, upon Chinese intervention, came the moment to "unwrap his bombers and blast the enemy bases and supply lines, but the UN flunkies forbade him, and forced him to fight against these deadly odds with his best hand tied behind his back." Ultimately, of course, Truman decided to fire MacArthur "with all the subtlety of an official executioner of Henry VIII." Truman had apparently decided that critical military supplies must be set aside for Europe. For Hunt, this meant Korea must take second place: "The 19,000 dead and the 110,000 battle casualties must wait to be avenged."[83]

This was both a spirited defense of MacArthur and a bitter indictment of Truman. But Hunt's primary motivation was to exculpate MacArthur, to demonstrate that events in Korea had provided "a tragic vindication" for his views. He tried to establish this vindication by focusing on what had happened in Korea since MacArthur's dismissal, namely, months of stalemate, both militarily on the ground and at the negotiating table. As he put it, "In the fifteen dreary months since MacArthur's relief, the Administration clique that brought about his recall has continued to drag the national honor through the dust and mud of Korea. The stalemate still persists, to our dismay and bewilderment."[84] Pointing out that truce negotiations had gone frustratingly was one thing, but Hunt here made a clear error in logic.

From the premise that the military and diplomatic stalemate of 1952 was undesirable, he concluded that MacArthur's policy of war against China obviously would have been successful if implemented—a speculative leap that could not be proven one way or the other. In the end, perhaps this was what the whole question of war with China and, therefore, much of the MacArthur controversy, boiled down to. Both sides had no recourse but to speculate what the outcome of such a course might be. Liberals foresaw catastrophe, while conservatives and some hawkish liberals envisioned glorious victory. But war should always be a last resort rather than a strategic gamble, and a war of regime change in China in 1951 was anything but a necessity. Moreover, the subsequent American military experiences in Vietnam and Iraq can perhaps give us an indication that prophecies of easy victory at low cost in wars of choice are usually ill-founded.

CONCLUSION

The debate surrounding the MacArthur controversy, from the VFW message to the dismissal and afterward, exemplified the divisions among ideological camps as represented in America's leading political opinion journals during the Korean War. Left liberals were horrified by MacArthur's words and actions, not to mention those of his supporters at home, and were relieved when President Truman dismissed him from his duties, as it signaled a strongly decreased likelihood that the United States would embark upon an expanded war with China. Conservatives, on the other hand, praised MacArthur for having the backbone they thought Truman lacked and were outraged by the firing and dismayed that Mao Tse-tung would be left unmolested in Peking. Hawkish liberals are harder to pin down, as they supported Truman's actions in firing MacArthur on constitutional grounds but tended to agree with MacArthur that the United States should, in some form or another, launch an offensive war against China. William Henry Chamberlin and David J. Dallin, in particular, were nominally liberal voices using their platform at the *New Leader* to advance ideas that were often difficult to distinguish from those published in conservative journals like *The Freeman*. Thus, not only was there an important left-right schism within the so-called liberal consensus during the Korean War but conservative foreign policy ideas were approaching maturity, if not already fully formed.

After the MacArthur din died down and the Korean War entered its prolonged stalemate phase, during the last two years of the war, the attention that the editors of America's leading political opinion journals gave to Korea declined substantially, especially with the approach of the 1952 presidential campaign. Nevertheless, the truce negotiations that began at Kaesong in July 1951 and moved to Panmunjom, until their long-awaited completion in July 1953, were a topic of ongoing concern. As with everything else related to the war, left liberals, hawkish liberals, and conservatives would each have their own reactions to the ongoing truce negotiations and, finally, to the end of the war. It is to the process that led to the truce, then, that we turn our attention in the final two chapters. Next, however, we will take a brief detour to examine some of the overarching domestic fears that informed much of liberal and conservative thinking about foreign policy. On the home front, as we shall see, liberals lived in nearly constant fear of the McCarthyist threat to democracy, while conservatives prophesied doom as, in their view, the United States careened toward a dystopian socialist future.

5. Dueling Domestic Bogeymen

While the debates chronicled in these pages are primarily about foreign policy, political observers and pundits can hardly have been expected to separate and compartmentalize foreign and domestic issues entirely. Indeed, underlying and overlapping with debates about strategy in Korea, diplomacy with China, and deterrence of the Soviet Union were debates about domestic political culture. In this chapter, then, we will briefly pause our discussion of foreign policy issues to examine the most overarching domestic concerns of liberals and conservatives. While neither liberals nor conservatives denied the threat posed by America's enemies in Moscow and Peking, each had their own sense of what imperiled the Union closer to home. For liberals, the greatest threat to American democracy on the domestic front was McCarthyism run amok. For conservatives, it was what they saw as creeping socialism introduced by the New Deal and perpetuated by the Truman administration.[1]

MCCARTHYISM

In February 1950 in Wheeling, West Virginia, just four months before the outbreak of the Korean War, Senator Joseph McCarthy delivered his infamous "Enemies Within" speech, which vaulted him to national prominence. The writers for and contributors to America's leading political opinion journals certainly had much to say about McCarthy's influence on American politics and culture, but with the "loss" of China in 1949 and the advent of war in Korea in 1950, the battle over communism on the home front dovetailed, for better or worse, with writers' concerns about the direction of American foreign policy. As one might expect, McCarthy was often eviscerated in the flagship liberal journals. When Truman first committed American troops to the fight in Korea, for example, *The Nation* was excited that the administration's newfound anticommunist bona fides might blunt the strength of McCarthyist attacks. Now that the United States was actively engaging communist forces on the battlefield, they wrote, "McCarthyism will have a hollow sound when applied to the government that stood up to the Russians."[2] Of course, their expectations would soon be dashed by reality, as the worst of the McCarthyite persecutions were yet to come. Indeed, in marking the dawn of the new year, 1951, they looked back on the previous year's events with little joy. 1950, they recalled, saw the "big lie" deployed regularly in American politics and was "a year in which fear spread poison on all levels of American life."[3] Elsewhere, they even went so far as to call the Senate Subcommittee on Internal Security "Senator McCarran's little Gestapo," in reference to subcommittee chair and McCarthy ally Patrick McCarran (D-NV).[4]

Once it became clear that McCarthyism's momentum would not die out in the wake of Truman's Korean intervention, the contributors to *The Nation* turned their attention to McCarthyism's stranglehold on the Republican Party. Willard Shelton described the GOP as having been "taken over" by the charismatic personalities of Douglas MacArthur and Joseph McCarthy. He wrote that not a single Senate Republican had found the courage to repudiate McCarthy's "nauseating character assassination," nor MacArthur's "all-out assault on popularly elected civilian government."[5] Indeed, following the Republican sweep in the 1952 elections, the editors saw a clear and present danger to the republic on the horizon. In a poetic, if apocalyptic, turn, they wrote,

> Like sleepwalkers stumbling toward a precipice, the American people are moving toward a hazard which many of them sense but few can clearly see. Watchmen shout diverse warnings, but the mass of the people, stirring uneasily to a new consciousness, are still only vaguely aware of the danger. . . . A thousand Paul Reveres are needed . . . to ride forth and tell the people that their liberties are threatened. The present danger is of course McCarthyism.[6]

Michael Straight, lead editor at the *New Republic*, felt similarly. Just prior to the outbreak of the war, Straight traveled the country to write a special report on the public mood. The dominant theme he came away with was "the prevalence of fear in America today." This was primarily a fear of Soviet communism and potential war therewith, but Straight was sure to detail its domestic political implications as well. "Fear of Communism," he wrote, "is the most effective weapon ever developed by the Right in America." Here he had in mind more than just McCarthy's witch-hunting techniques. Americans were being persuaded to oppose change, he explained, "in the belief that all progress leads eventually to Communism." In other words, the political right was successfully invoking the specter of communism to blunt any and all efforts at structural social reform in the United States. For Straight, this was particularly evident in attempts to advance racial equality in the South. Conservatives, in other words, were attempting to shut down any discourse about racial equality by shouting "communist!" at any proponent of civil rights reform. As such, Straight did not pull any punches in suggesting that the GOP, or at least the McCarthyite wing of the party, was moving dangerously close to the territory once trod by Goebbels and the Nazis. "For the first time in many years," he proclaimed, "a major party has been committed to the fascist technique of the Big Lie."[7]

Harold Ickes had little tolerance for McCarthyism either. Since the late 1940s, he wrote, the Republicans had been attempting to win elections "solely on the basis of having seen more Communists, and seen them sooner, than had the Democrats." And now, McCarthyism, which he called "a cancerous growth in our own body politic," had emerged as the logical conclusion of this trend, causing Americans to turn the cold eyes of suspicion upon one another. With the outbreak of war in Korea, his patience had worn out entirely. "It is time," he wrote, "for Americans to recover their sanity." Unfortunately for Ickes and his fellow liberals, political momentum was trending in the opposite direction. Following Republican gains in the 1950 midterms, the editors grudgingly acknowledged just how politically effective demagoguery could be. Every falsehood and slander, they wrote, "was repeated in the Big Lie with a hypnotic repetitive presentation whose effectiveness cannot be denied." As such, McCarthy had become the most dangerous man in American public life.[8] Returning to Straight's Nazi comparison, the *New Republic* wrote, "Honest men recoil from the repulsive fact that degraded types exist who can repeat and repeat bare-faced lies with the manner and conviction of men proclaiming the truth. This weakness among honest men was of great service to Hitler. It serves our own pocket-sized demagogue, Joe McCarthy."[9]

American Catholics may have been divided over McCarthy and his methods, but the Catholic writers at *Commonweal* took a clear line against their fellow communicant's methods, if not against his ultimate aims. At the beginning of the Korean War, when the United States was "literally fighting for the survival of the world," they editorialized, "McCarthy's methods must be scrapped once and for all."[10] That said, the magazine was not above calling for the Communist Party USA to be banned from the American political landscape. Communism in its then-current form, they wrote, was not merely an idea, but a "conspiracy against this government, this people, this way of life." The continued operation of the party within the United States, then, could mean sabotage, treason, and "fifth-column destruction throughout the U.S." Banning the operations of the party was not a question of people's right to think as they choose, but of protecting America's national security.[11] *Commonweal*, then, stood with one foot on either side of the ideological divide. They may have disapproved of McCarthy's means, but they did not necessarily disagree with his anticommunist ends.[12]

Of course, McCarthyism was not a phenomenon limited solely to the political sphere. America's fear of communist subversion bled into other aspects of the culture as well, including education. Given how our own contemporary Culture Wars have spilled over into American public education in the early 2020s, it is striking to read a *Commonweal* editorial from 1952 regarding McCarthyite attacks on "socialist" teachers and textbooks whose purported transgressions included giving sympathetic treatment to the New Deal and/or the UN. The editorial response is an excellent example of how *Commonweal*, staunchly anticommunist though it was, nonetheless denounced the dangers of McCarthyism.

> It seems time to ask who are the really "subversive" elements in American society. The teacher in America has been loyal to his country in all but an infinitesimally small number of instances. The efforts of those who now denounce him as "un-American" for holding attitudes more liberal than their own narrow definitions must be opposed with great vigor and indignation. Such attacks on legitimate intellectual and cultural freedom in the nation's schools constitute one of the most thoroughly subversive threats operating on the American scene today.[13]

The midcentury culture wars raged not only over public education but media and entertainment as well. While anticommunist blacklisting in the entertainment industry certainly predated McCarthy's paranoiac crusade, the attacks on Hollywood personalities and other pop culture icons only accelerated in the early 1950s. The *New Leader*, as we have seen, generally took a strong anticommunist line in foreign policy that was often indistinguishable from that of avowedly conservative publications. But when it came to McCarthyism, the *New Leader* was not shy about letting its liberal flag fly. In 1950, Hollywood actress Jean Muir was blacklisted for her affiliation with the Congress of American Women, a leftist women's rights organization. At the same time, the popular anti–nuclear war song "Old Man Atom," versions of which were recorded by Sam Hinton and Sons of the Pioneers, was withdrawn from circulation following pressure from the Joint Committee Against Communism, a McCarthyite organization based in New York City. Such blacklisting, warned a *New Leader* editorial, was taking the United States a long way "toward the world of *Nineteen Eighty-Four*." The editorial staff was clear: The locus of the real communist threat was in Moscow, not

New York or Hollywood. "If you shot every Communist and fellow-traveler in America today," they wrote, "you would still not be one step closer to ending the Stalinist threat, which originates in the Kremlin, and not in Radio City."[14]

This is not to say that the *New Leader* did not also have much to say about the political manifestations of McCarthyism. They were particularly distressed by the McCarran Internal Security Act of 1950, which was passed over President Truman's veto and, inter alia, required members of the Communist Party to register with the US government and tightened immigration laws so that suspect individuals could be more easily excluded, detained, or deported.[15] The editorial staff mocked the legislation, pointing out that it had "failed to unearth a single Communist," while the masters of the Kremlin remained "safely ensconced beyond McCarran's reach."[16] William Henry Chamberlin and David J. Dallin, among the most conservative-leaning hawkish liberals in terms of foreign policy, both denounced the act, Chamberlin writing that it was "worthy of the Soviet Union, Red China, Hungary or Bulgaria." For a country with the professed democratic ideals of the United States, it was "nothing short of a national disgrace."[17] The editors found the provision prohibiting refugees from communist countries from entering the United States particularly vexing, leading them to ask, "What manner of democratic champion against Communism is America, when it shows so little compassion for Communism's most tragic victims?"[18] This did not quite rise to the level of the white-hot rhetoric regarding immigration and asylum policy in the late 2010s and in the 2020s but reveals that the status of refugees was a hot-button issue during the early Cold War, as it has been in the early twenty-first century.

While most of the hawkish liberals at the *New Leader* were firmly opposed to McCarthy, there was at least one voice that chided liberals for their obsession with him. Norbert Muhlen, German émigré who had fled the Nazis in 1940, was incredulous that many liberals (such as Freda Kirchwey and her colleagues at *The Nation*) viewed McCarthy as the leader of a movement as dangerous to America as communism itself. It was one thing, he wrote, "to oppose the slap-happy, irresponsible, vulgar and non-factual techniques employed by McCarthy," but quite another to build McCarthyism up "into a phantom danger made to seem greater than the real threat."[19] William Henry Chamberlin also took issue with some of his fellow liberals, especially the left-leaning China experts in the State Department, who, in his view, had become "conscious or unconscious agents of a foreign power." For Chamberlin, "vigilant publicity" was the only remedy for such unwitting communist infiltration—though it would be a fuzzy line indeed between this suggestion and the employment of McCarthy's methods. Chamberlin did not seem particularly troubled by this, concluding that he was willing to "let the chips—in the shape of anguished outcries about 'witch-hunting and redbaiting'—fall where they may."[20] Thus, even as left liberals and hawkish liberals were mostly on the same page in being aghast at McCarthy's methods and influence, there were hawkish liberal voices that had little patience for what they perceived to be the counter-hysteria of the left.

This disagreement within the "liberal consensus" boiled to the surface in 1952 with the *New Leader* taking on criticism from both right and left. First, conservative stalwart Ralph de Toledano wrote to the *New Leader* about his disappointment with their anti-McCarthy tone. Toledano lauded the *New Leader*'s bravery in consistently denouncing communism abroad but lamented that the magazine was no longer at the forefront of fighting this ideological evil at home as well. Instead, he complained, the editors had taken to wasting the publication's potential by too frequently "anguishing" over McCarthyism. The editors' reply attempted to stake out a middle ground between conservatives like Toledano and left liberals like Kirchwey. "We are not only opposed to the opportunist methods of McCarthy," they wrote, "we are equally opposed . . . to those former fellow-travelers who use 'McCarthyism' as an excuse to shirk the fight against Stalinism." They closed by suggesting there was an important difference between their own "responsible anti-communism" and the "noxious headline-hunting" of Toledano, who increasingly and frighteningly saw McCarthy as the "Alpha and Omega of anti-Communism."[21] Second, in response to Bertrand Russell's position that the United States was in the grip of a right-wing McCarthyite "hysteria," the *New Leader* published several rebuttals, perhaps the best example of which was penned by Diana Trilling, prominent New York intellectual and wife of Lionel Trilling. She dismissed Russell's main contention, that America was experiencing a reign of terror and that McCarthyism was leading America toward becoming a police state, as "patent nonsense." Then she summed up her understanding of liberalism, which nicely reflected the position of the editorial staff.

> My opposition to McCarthyism does not mean that I deny the existence of a Communist menace. . . . Quite the contrary, *despite* the fact that McCarthyism has made the fight against Communism its fight, I still consider the fight against Communism my fight. The liberal, that is, has two enemies—Communism *and* McCarthyism—and he must refuse to let either one of them seduce him into even a temporary alliance with the other.[22]

The *New Leader*, then, positioned itself as holding the sensible middle ground between the right-wing emotionalism of McCarthy and the left-wing hyperbole of Kirchwey, del Vayo, and Russell. Indeed, it was not afraid of a verbal dust-up with either side.

On the whole, readers could see the *New Leader* shift in its analysis of McCarthyism over the course of the Korean War. Early on, the magazine published pieces that were chiefly concerned with the dangers of McCarthyism itself. But by 1952–1953, the bulk of articles appearing on the subject were about liberal overreaction to the perceived threat. Richard Rovere, a former staff member at *The Nation*, took his erstwhile publication to task for its exaggerations about the state of the union during the McCarthyite era. Rovere opened with a dutiful statement about the threat posed by McCarthyism but then arrived at his thesis: "There is, I regret to say, a spurious brand of anti-McCarthyism that can be as dangerous as McCarthyism itself because its image of America is as false and, I am inclined to believe, as intellectually and morally disreputable as that of the Yahoos and primitives who have made McCarthy a power in the land." Here he was effectively equating his ex-colleague Freda Kirchwey's "derangement" with that of McCarthy himself! Nor did he spare Kirchwey from further critique. He took issue with her argument that the dangers posed by McCarthyism were "essentially no different" from those facing a soldier in battle. "Essentially no different?" he asked incredulously, "for the Editor of *The Nation* to compare her peril and that of her unenlisted readers to that of a soldier under fire seems to me to betray a grossness of feeling and a willingness to bandy words that dishonors her profession and mine."[23] On those few occasions when McCarthy himself was the main object of an editorial attack, the tone tended to be flippant rather than serious, as when the editors mocked McCarthy's 1952 election eve attack on Adlai Stevenson for its "lack of sincerity and conviction, as though McCarthy himself knew that he was perpetrating a hoax that he did not believe in."[24]

Fortunately for anti-McCarthy liberals, the contributor who had the last major word on the subject before the end of the Korean War in 1953 and McCarthy's downfall in 1954 was none other than the architect of containment policy himself, George F. Kennan. In a lengthy and eloquent essay based on a talk he gave at Notre Dame, Kennan expressed his fear that the conformity demanded by McCarthyism's "semi-religious cult" had begun to draw around the United States "a cultural curtain similar in some respects to the Iron Curtain of our adversaries." Kennan was particularly keen to explore two undertones he detected in McCarthyist ideology: anti-intellectualism and hyper-masculinity. First, he noted McCarthyism's "conscious rejection and ridicule of intellectual effort and distinction." Second, he pointed out that anticommunism's most strident adherents often demonstrated a strange obsession with the need to demonstrate their own virility, "by exhibitions of taciturnity, callousness, and physical aggressiveness—as though there were some anxiety lest, in the absence of these exhibitions, it might be found wanting."[25] Kennan concluded with the warning that the McCarthyite forces of intolerance and political demagoguery were morally unrestrained, incapable of self-control, and able to be stopped only by external forces. Given his audience, Kennan suggested that those external forces were none other than his listeners and readers. To prevent the victory of "violence and suspicion and intolerance" required a collective effort by those willing to stand up for the social value of intellectual pursuit—not to be cowed by bullying and fear.

It would be difficult, perhaps, to find a message from 1953 that is as relevant today as this one. But that is not to say that readers of the *New Leader* agreed with Kennan, especially as his argument cut against the grain of what often appeared in its pages. For example, Alfred Kohlberg (John Bircher, China Lobby champion, and McCarthy ally) responded to Kennan's argument with disdain. He first blamed Kennan for being part of the diplomatic cabal that "threw away" America's victory in World War II (presumably by "appeasing" Stalin at Yalta, etc.). Then came the ad hominem: "Is Mr. Kennan duly humble and apologetic? Not a bit of it." Instead, sneered Kohlberg, "He sets out to lecture the rest of us 'common men,' and not in words of one syllable, either."[26] Apparently, the irony that he was largely making Kennan's point for him was lost on Kohlberg.

This exchange between Kennan and Kohlberg is fascinating for many reasons, not least because it speaks to the wide ideological range of the *New Leader*'s readers and contributors. As a nominally liberal publication, it appealed to and published pieces by the likes of George Kennan. As a hawkishly anticommunist magazine, it was read by and sometimes included the voices of individuals like Ralph de Toledano and Alfred Kohlberg. Perhaps this split personality helps make sense of the journal's evolution regarding McCarthyism, as here chronicled. Whereas *Commonweal* drew a sharp distinction between anticommunist ends and unsavory means in assessing McCarthyism, the most germane difference at the *New Leader* was initially that between foreign and domestic policy: the staff was staunchly anticommunist in its foreign policy, but anti-McCarthy at home. But as the Korean War bogged down and dragged on, the editors focused more criticism on what they viewed as hyperbolic liberal hand-wringing over McCarthyism than on McCarthyism itself. Here the magazine shifted subtly toward the conservative view but, as we shall see, never engaged in full-throated apology for McCarthyism like *The Freeman* and the *American Mercury*.

In the pages of *The Freeman*, readers could often find pro-McCarthy sentiments like those expressed by Forrest Davis, who called for "the elimination on the home front of pods of potential subversion." Whom did Davis have in mind here? His list was broad in scope. A proper anticommunist clampdown, for Davis, would mean "excising Achesonianism as well as ridding the government of all the Communists, crypto-Communists and genuinely suspected persons who have found lodgment there." Davis did not specify what exactly would qualify someone as such, opening the door to a fairly broad McCarthyist reading of those concepts, but what strikes the diplomatic historian is the call to "excise Achesonianism," a reference to the Truman-Acheson foreign policy that set the course of American diplomacy for the better part of the four-decade-long Cold War. While it may seem incredible for Davis to have lumped one of the foremost architects of the Truman Doctrine, Marshall Plan, and NATO into a basket of communists and crypto-communists, his primary reason for opposing Acheson was the Secretary of State's supposed responsibility for inviting the Korean War via "the destruction of the Chinese Nationalist bulwark against Communism in Asia."[27] In other words, this was the familiar conservative criticism that the Truman administration had "lost China," which was, of course, one of the loudest battle cries of the McCarthyite movement.

Elsewhere, the editors denounced the "liberal press" for glibly dismissing as "McCarthyism" the noble and necessary efforts of anticommunists to purge the government of communist influence.[28] Forces on the right, of course, have a long history of criticizing the press for its supposed liberal bias, from cries of "Lugenpresse!" to "fake news!" The pro-McCarthy voices at *The Freeman* were simply the 1950s version of this trope, further laying the groundwork that would be built upon in the late twentieth and early twenty-first centuries by the likes of Rush Limbaugh and Fox News.

William F. Buckley Jr. took a related but slightly different tack in articulating his support for McCarthy. For Buckley, McCarthy deserved support not because of the means he employed, but because he was the only one capable of dealing with the crisis at hand. Given the existential threat posed by communism, wrote Buckley, conservatives had no alternative but to support McCarthy. What mattered was not McCarthy's manners, but "treason in the State Department." Whereas the Catholic liberals at *Commonweal* opposed McCarthy's methods even while endorsing his anticommunist ends, Catholic conservatives like Buckley were willing to tolerate his sometimes uncouth conduct in the greater service of rooting out communists in the government.[29]

Speaking of Buckley, *The Freeman*'s editors used his story, as told in *God and Man at Yale*, to defend McCarthy while also decrying American higher education. The fact that Buckley, "a real historical conservative," was such a rare bird on the campus of an elite institution was proof enough that, contrary to the tormented cries of liberals, "McCarthyism" had done nothing to numb free speech on campus. "In fact," they editorialized, "he was so much out of the ordinary that people in New Haven haven't yet got over a sense of bewildered surprise that Mr. Buckley could actually exist." After all, during his time on campus he was able to challenge and briefly disturb the "Keynesian-cum-Fabian status quo." For this, they lament, he was naturally called a fascist—a predictable but damning indictment of how American higher education was supposedly dominated by left-wing ideology. Sounding much like Buckley himself, they wrote:

> Such is the pabulum that is the orthodoxy of the moment in the American university world. It is an orthodoxy that Joe McCarthy has done nothing whatsoever to disturb. Nobody is being "persecuted" for teaching it, nobody is being forbidden to read, write or mouth the junk that passes for economic and political thought in the modern university world. Indeed, "liberalism," far from being scared of anybody, reigns smugly and contentedly over an intellectual world that is just about as placid and uninvigorating as the Sargasso Sea.[30]

The conservatives at *The Freeman*, then, consistently downplayed the deleterious effects of McCarthyism, instead playing up the supposed liberal indoctrination being insidiously carried out by America's media and academic elite. While the Culture Wars are typically thought to have begun in earnest in the 1990s, here is proof that Buckley and his fellow conservatives helped sow the seeds decades earlier.

The editors of *The Freeman* later tied their critique of academia even more directly to their defense of McCarthyism, complaining about "the irrationality of the college-educated mob that has descended upon Joseph R. McCarthy." Such was Senator McCarthy's personal constitution, they wrote, that he must possess "a sort of animal negative-pole magnetism which repels alumni of Harvard, Princeton and Yale." Indeed, they concluded that well-educated liberals were primed to react to anything that came out of McCarthy's mouth like Pavlov's dog to a bell.[31] They also reacted snidely to a 1952 ranking by political scientists of sitting US Senators, which placed

McCarthy and McCarran very near the bottom of the list. In other words, they objected, to be rated highly by these "political scientists," a senator must be a Roosevelt-Truman New-Fair Dealer. If, by contrast, a senator is "for the principles of the original American Republic, or if he is at all concerned with Communist infiltration, he is automatically rated a dope." This, concluded the editors, revealed less about the composition of the US Senate than about "the state of the academic mind."[32] Again, the implication here is that there was some kind of vast left-wing conspiracy at work in the ivory towers of America's colleges and universities. Taken together, these conservative critiques of America's intellectual elite reveal a deep and long-held resentment toward the credentialed and the beginnings of a smoldering culture war, to boot.

Following Republican Dwight D. Eisenhower's victory in 1952, there was a brief moment when conservatives threatened to back away from their unwavering support for McCarthy. After all, he no longer had relatively easy Democratic targets like Dean Acheson to pick on. Even so, he kept up his attacks on the State Department, now under the leadership of John Foster Dulles. At this point, *The Freeman* was given pause by McCarthy's increasingly "wild" rhetoric, which they likened to that of a "one-eyed bull in the political china shop." Their main concern, of course, was not that honorable men might be falsely accused on the basis of little to no evidence, but that his latest actions "made things more difficult for his defenders and easier for his detractors." It would be tragic, they wrote, "if the country became diverted from the problem of Communists in government because of any personal shortcoming of a junior senator from Wisconsin."[33] Even as the editors began to distance themselves from McCarthy himself, then, they maintained belief in the righteousness of his cause. Nor did this momentary bout of conscience last very long. Within a month they were back to defending McCarthy, at least indirectly, by denouncing as ridiculous the idea that the United States was under some "reign of terror" (a la Bertrand Russell) where "Grand Inquisitor McCarthy" lords over "helpless victims."[34] Their rebuttal, in this case a reasonably fair one, was that criticism of McCarthy continued to flow from those who disagreed with him, which could obviously not occur if America were living under some right-wing totalitarian nightmare.

The Freeman's conservative cousins at the *American Mercury* did not disagree. In reflecting on the McCarthy-era cultural and political environment, former *Mercury* editor Eugene Lyons wrote that if liberals were to be believed, America was then in the midst of "anti-Red hysteria amounting to a reign of terror, marked by black fear, witch hunts, character assassination, and thought control." In his view, however, if anyone was guilty of imposing such an Orwellian regime on the American people, it was liberals themselves. The idea that the United States was "in the throes of unlimited hysteria, trampling wildly on customary freedoms," he wrote, was naught but a liberal article of faith, unsupported by any real evidence. More to the point, Lyons argued that liberal opposition to McCarthyism was all part of the same anti-American propaganda campaign that originated in Moscow. To wit, "the choral cries of hysteria amount to a smear-America campaign, and the fact that smearing America is the top assignment for Communists the world over is scarcely coincidental." Indeed, he charged, it was not without significance that the worst such smears could be found in the pages of *The Nation*, "the house organ of totalitarian liberalism."[35]

Not coincidentally, the debate about whether McCarthyism was the appropriate domestic response to the communist threat largely coincided with the debates about whether US policy in Korea constituted the appropriate actions abroad. Left liberals saw in McCarthyism a threat to American democracy perhaps as great or greater than that posed by communism itself. Hawkish liberals took a more nuanced position, generally decrying McCarthy's methods even as they sometimes expressed sympathy with his anticommunist aims. What's more, many hawkish liberals took issue with what they viewed as left liberal "counter-hysteria" about McCarthy, while conservative commentators were as unqualified in their support for McCarthy as they were in their disdain for anti-McCarthy liberals.

"CREEPING SOCIALISM"

Just as McCarthyism represented all that was threatening and vile about the world to liberals, so did the specter of socialism strike terror into the heart of every conservative. In *The Freeman*'s inaugural issue, the editors laid out their conservative worldview. Dating their political discontent to the dawn of the New Deal twenty years earlier, they wrote that the definition of freedom in the Roosevelt-Truman era was too often tied to "some cloudy collectivist concept," marked by the error "that the individual is entitled only to the particular freedoms that the state is gracious enough to permit him." Zeroing in on FDR's freedom from want and freedom from fear, they retorted that these were in fact "not liberties at all," but rather, "commonly possessed by prisoners and slaves." FDR's spurious freedoms were, for the editors, the false promises of the socialist/welfare state. Indeed, economic freedom was the new publication's bedrock principle: where there is no economic freedom, they declared, "there can be no freedom of any other kind."[36] Although they didn't credit him by name, this assumption was clearly adapted from Friedrich Hayek's 1944 thesis in *The Road to Serfdom*. Indeed, such was the influence of Hayek's argument—that too much government intervention in the free market would necessarily lead to a totalitarian political system—that the idea was regularly taken for granted by conservatives, almost as an article of faith. No wonder, then, that this lead editorial was titled "The Faith of *The Freeman*."

Conservative fears that America was drifting toward socialism continued to appear in the new magazine. One editorial proclaimed that "only a Republican victory can reverse the trend toward all-powerful Government."[37] Another chided the Truman administration for its "extreme left wing policies,"[38] then made an unabashed appeal to the slippery slope. Socialism, it read, is "an advanced form of statism. And in our modern order there is no stopping place along that road save Russian socialism."[39] Literary giant William Faulkner even lent his voice to the discussion, prophesying that the greatest threat to America was no longer located abroad, but at home in the halls of government. "The enemy of our freedom," he wrote, "faces us now from beneath the eagle-perched domes of our capitals and from behind the alphabetical splatters on the doors of welfare regimentation."[40] George Schuyler, future John Bircher and author of the autobiography *Black and Conservative*, put it even more forcefully. He wrote that America's intellectual and journalistic elite had "boarded the bandwagon of totalitarianism, eloquently advocating a goose-stepping society" that could end only in "dictatorial control of the entire economy."[41]

Even *The Freeman*'s ads were revealing of conservative fears. On the back cover of an issue in January 1951, for example, the magazine sought more subscribers with the following text: "When traditional American freedom flourishes once more, we shall halt the progress of 'creeping socialism' which seeks to transfer more and more volition from the private citizen to the bureaucrat. *The Freeman* is dedicated to the cause of freedom. It is the outspoken voice protesting against the Trojan horse of communism and socialism within our walls."[42] Specifically, what this likely meant was nicely summarized by Garet Garrett, longtime America-Firster and opponent of the New Deal. Garrett suggested that the welfare state was a betrayal of the nation's founding principles, writing, "The founders who wrote the Constitution could no more have imagined a Welfare State . . . than they could have imagined a monarchy."[43] Neil Carothers also sounded the alarm bell, writing that thoughtful Americans were right to be concerned about the trend toward socialism. In complaining chiefly that corporate taxes were too high, he advanced an argument that would depress any good conservative: "Any reader who is worried about a future socialism should stop worrying. It is already here."[44] Elsewhere, sounding like Ronald Reagan lamenting how Medicare destroyed American liberty, the editors wrote of the "spacious days of freedom" prior to the New Deal. From our perspective in the twenty-first century, the conservative propensity to issue such breathless warnings about socialism's impending takeover of America are cast in a new light when we consider that they have been ongoing since at least the implementation of the New Deal, now almost one hundred years ago.

Continuing this thread, John L. Beckley more explicitly previewed the conservative supply-side justifications for tax cuts in the late twentieth and early twenty-first centuries, arguing that the burden of any tax increases necessary to pay for Cold War rearmament should not fall on "business and people with large incomes," as this would "stifle the expansion of production" and could "collapse the profit system and force us into socialism." He warned that Americans should be wary of the imposition of socialism not all at once, but slowly and in stages. Should that occur, it would mean the slow death of everything that had made America great. In other words, if the government continued to destroy the profit incentive through excessive taxation, America would "wake up to find ourselves as weak as Samson shorn of his hair" and "would ultimately gravitate to our assigned orbit around the great Red Star."[45] High taxes would lead inexorably to the communization of the once great United States and its consequent subordination to new masters in the Kremlin. Such catastrophizing was not uncommon among conservative writers. In criticizing Truman's 1951 decision to impose temporary price controls to curb wartime inflation, Towner Phelan wrote that the "permanent Washington bureaucracy" (which conservatives in more recent years have taken to calling "the deep state") constituted a totalitarian threat more dangerous than communism.[46] No doubt there are those on the right to whom this does not sound unreasonable, but if we reflect on Cold War emergencies such as the Cuban Missile Crisis, it is difficult to entertain this argument with a straight face.

Editor Henry Hazlitt summarized the crux of this recurring argument quite nicely in a piece with an appropriately pithy title, "Welfare to Socialism to Communism." Despite the title, he declined to detail how, exactly, welfarism would inevitably lead to communist dictatorship, except to remind his readers that this had already been done by Ludwig von Mises.[47] In this view, there was little meaningful distinction between "partial" socialism, as it was practiced in countries like England, France, Norway, and Sweden, on the one hand, and full-fledged Soviet communism on the other. Indeed, for Hazlitt, "What has happened in Russia . . . is not some hideous betrayal of socialism; it is its consummation and inevitable end-product."[48] Thus, according to Hazlitt, some of America's closest European allies were already sleepwalking toward socialist serfdom—a treacherous path that the United States had, knowingly or otherwise, begun to travel as well.

The Freeman's Henry Hazlitt may not have laid out precisely why welfarism must lead to totalitarianism, but William Bradford Huie of the *American Mercury* was willing to take a stab at an explanation. Huie explained that the government largesse brought into vogue via New Deal programs like Social Security had infantilized the American people. In other words, it created a culture marked by individuals abdicating responsibility for their own welfare, instead relying on the government to fulfill all their needs. How did this threaten democracy? Because, according to Huie, democracy was impossible to sustain without a mature citizenry. Indeed, he argued, totalitarianism preyed precisely on people of juvenile capabilities.[49] In short, government centralization via the welfare state created a citizenry that was more ovine than human, which in turn facilitated greater bureaucratic sprawl, leading to more infantilization, and so on. Elsewhere, Huie ranted vulgarly against the "sanctimonious, socialistic, tax-exempt-security sonsofbitches" who had exchanged their god in Heaven for one in Moscow, London, or Washington, and who armed themselves not with the Bible but with Marx, Bevan, and Roosevelt.[50]

Excessively hyperbolic or not, this Hayekian slippery-slope argument that conservatives so embraced dovetailed with the emergence of William F. Buckley Jr., via the success of *God and Man at Yale*. A *Freeman* review of Buckley's opus hailed the young author for exposing Yale's "collectivist teaching" and for establishing that liberals were "guiding us toward the slave state." Buckley's book, wrote Felix Wittmer, demonstrated that

> government controls inevitably kill the spirit of private enterprise and lead to mediocrity, fearfulness, sterility, and the end of that great civilization which has blossomed in the West since . . . the Middle Ages. By hammering relentlessly and powerfully at the wall of socialist superstition which has beclouded the vision of thousands of well-meaning intellectuals for the past two decades, Buckley, the self-proclaimed conservative, has established himself as a solid pioneer of a new radicalism.[51]

While the United States has not become a slave state in the years since 1951, given the future evolution of the conservative movement—from Barry Goldwater and the Reagan Revolution to Newt Gingrich, the Bush Doctrine, and Trumpism—Wittmer's prediction of a "new radicalism" was prescient, indeed.

While Buckley would ultimately succeed in bringing together the various strands of conservatism—anticommunist, religious, and economic—he did not operate in a vacuum. Other groups were already at work uniting the diverse manifestations of the conservative worldview. For instance, a group of Christian conservatives based in Cincinnati, Ohio, who called themselves the Circuit Riders, were praised in *The Freeman* for having established a vigorous movement "to combat the socialism and crypto-communism that finds such widespread refuge under the benevolent cloak of the social gospel."[52] In a lengthier piece, contributor Edward A. Keller called socialism "irreconcilable with true Christianity." Among Keller's arguments was his contention that any socialist state necessarily aimed to become a substitute for God, thus violating the first commandment. And this, he continued, would lead to the divine dominoes falling in a way that could end only in apocalypse: "The First Commandment having been outlawed, the next logical step is the discarding of all God's Commandments."[53] Christian conservatives such as The Circuit Riders and Edward Keller were thus at the leading edge of forging an alliance between religious and economic conservatives in the early 1950s, a relationship that would come to full flower in the Reagan era and beyond.

Of course, Buckley's *God and Man* dealt not just with American Christianity but with his experiences in the halls of one of America's elite universities. We have already chronicled how conservatives often criticized American higher education for its supposed collectivist leanings, but libertarian author Jack Schwartzman took this critique to an entirely different level. Schwartzman was concerned that the leftist ideology being spewed in college classrooms not only was self-perpetuating but endangered the very fabric of democracy in the United States. He warned his readers that the "Statist" college-educated youth of today "will be the professor and the businessman of tomorrow; he will fit into the totalitarian pattern of the Coming Order." For Schwartzman, the modern collegian "is the servant of the coming Super-State." But this was not all. America's colleges were not only preparing their students to be bureaucratic automatons but also something much darker. In chillingly Orwellian language, Schwartzman concluded, "If you send your son to the colleges of today, you will create the Executioner of tomorrow."[54] More recent right-wing personalities like Glenn Beck, it turns out, did not emerge ex nihilo, but stand on the shoulders of earlier merchants of doom.

Towner Phelan wove many of these threads of conservative concern—the welfare state, liberal control of the media and education—into a single tapestry of warning to Western civilization. The "counterfeit liberalism of the Welfare State," he wrote, was grounded in "an immoral totalitarianism that worships naked power." To drive home just how threatening welfarism was to American tradition, Phelan emphasized its foreign beginnings, asserting that the concept was "Germanic in origin and based on the philosophy of Hegel and Karl Marx." What was more, it was also "closely akin to the philosophy of Hitler." This might sound nonsensical at first blush, as Marx and Hitler were on opposite ends of the ideological spectrum, but Phelan's argument points to an assumption shared by many conservatives in the postwar era, namely, that communism and fascism were two sides of the same statist coin. The welfare state, in this view, was a necessary step on the path to an all-powerful state. Whether that state would best be considered fascist or communist was ultimately immaterial, as either outcome would sound the death-knell of individual freedom. In any case, Phelan then pivoted to an even more fraught argument by equating the plight of those living under the welfare state to that of the four million enslaved people in America's antebellum South. "Before our Civil War," he explained, "the Negro slaves in the South had social security. They had no worries about their livelihood or their old age, but they were slaves." As such, "social security and slavery are natural bedfellows. The Welfare State can be achieved only at the expense of individual liberty." Phelan then set his sights on the elite liberal molders of public opinion. "The Welfare-State philosophy which has corrupted our society is spread primarily by those who regard themselves as the 'intelligentsia,'" he wrote. "They are the dominant left-wing majority among the thousands of university professors, teachers, writers, book publishers, book critics, newspaper editors, columnists, radio commentators, lecturers, clergymen and Hollywood script writers." According to Phelan, these high priests of liberalism were, in turn, influenced by left-wing journals such as *The Nation* and the *New Republic*. "It is a sad commentary," he lamented, "that in our great country *The Freeman* is the only important journal of opinion upholding the American tradition." As American conventional wisdom was thus forged in a leftist furnace, it was no accident that America's youth were being "indoctrinated in favor of totalitarian socialism." While most American teachers, one suspects, would have been surprised to hear that they were serving as instruments of totalitarian indoctrination, Phelan was nonetheless clear that America stood on the brink. Unless the "shapers of public opinion turn away from worship of Welfare-State socialism and embrace the philosophy of freedom," he warned, "it is only a question of time until the creeping socialism of today creates the totalitarian state of tomorrow, and man's last hope of freedom is gone."[55]

While the hawkish liberals at the *New Leader* were typically not far removed from conservatives when it came to their foreign policy positions, this was not necessarily the case when it came to the threat of creeping domestic socialism. Rather, hawkish liberals were just as likely to mock conservative fears as to share them. After making a passing reference to the British prime minister's refusal to roll back the National Health Service, for example, a *New Leader* editorial took sarcastic aim at conservative slippery-slope arguments by blithely commenting, "We assume that the American Medical Association and John T. Flynn will now train their biggest guns on that dangerous socialistic long-hair, Winston Churchill."[56] In other words, as staunchly anti-Stalinist as hawkish liberals were, they had not forfeited their ability to distinguish between European social democracy and Soviet communism in the same way that conservatives had. To wit, the *New Leader* published an article that described Sweden as the "model welfare state." Such a description would have been unthinkable in the pages of *The Freeman* or *American Mercury*, which took as an article of faith that any implementation of social welfare programs whatsoever would necessarily lead to political tyranny. Even William Henry Chamberlin, whose writings so frequently appeared in *The Freeman*, came out quite explicitly against conservative conflation of socialism and communism, which he called "an unfair practice of some conservative controversialists."[57] Should we really, he asked incredulously, put Clement Attlee under the same political umbrella as Joseph Stalin?[58] While Soviet communism, Chamberlin pointed out, was marked by political dictatorship, European socialism was dedicated to free elections and civil liberties. What's more, the United States was then rearming against the threat emanating from Moscow, not from London, Paris, or Stockholm. Even the most hawkish of the hawkish liberals, then, did not buy the Hayekian argument peddled by conservatives that there was no meaningful distinction between welfarism, socialism, and communism.

This is not to say that there was not robust debate among contributors to the *New Leader*. Influential anticommunist writer Max Eastman set off a lengthy debate in 1952 with a piece that argued the familiar Hayekian thesis: that government economic planning inevitably leads to despotism. In the American context, however, he did not see this happening via a Bolshevik-style coup, but through the less obvious, if more insidious, methods of liberal reformers, or "bureaucratic socialists." Such liberals, he suggested, would justify economic planning in the name of a freer and more equal society, but one that would ultimately turn out to be anything but. For Eastman, a state apparatus with too much control over a nation's economy must possess the authority to coerce individual actions. In other words, authoritarianism was "intrinsic" to a state-planned economy, whether ushered into being by "hard-headed Bolsheviks, soft-headed Social Democrats, or genteel liberals." Of course, to Eastman, a violent Bolshevik overthrow of the American political and economic order seemed fanciful. In sum, it was neither communists nor fellow travelers who posed the greatest threat to freedom in the West, but "piously aspiring" liberal reformers.[59] In letting fly his arrows, Eastman repeatedly aimed at one particular liberal by name: Arthur M. Schlesinger Jr. Schlesinger's scathing response appeared in the *New Leader* three weeks later.

Schlesinger characterized Eastman's criticism of American liberals as shrill, impetuous, and dogmatic. Schlesinger wrote that he had not recently read an article so deliberately misleading "outside the Stalinist press itself." Far from being at the head of a sinister socialist conspiracy, Schlesinger defended himself as a center-of-the-road New/Fair Dealer who supported a free market with guaranteed standards in wages, hours, working conditions, education, housing, and health care. More to the point, Schlesinger rejected out of hand the idea that one had to choose between pure laissez-faire and pure communism, with no room for anything in between. For Schlesinger, Eastman's implication "that those who do not accept the gospel according to Hayek" were "crypto-socialist or proto-Stalinist" was utter nonsense. Finally, after criticizing Eastman for praising Joseph McCarthy as a "clear-headed patriot of freedom," Schlesinger turned his ire against the entire emerging conservative establishment. He pointed out the hypocrisy of conservatives who opposed statism when statism meant regulating the economy in the public interest, but seemed to embrace a more sinister form of statism that sought to regulate political speech and thought. "I must confess frankly," he concluded, "that I am tired of those who rave against compensatory fiscal policy or public hydroelectric projects or the graduated income tax as horrendous invasions of personal freedom, but see nothing wrong with the McCarran subcommittee or with *God and Man at Yale* or with the persecution of a teacher in West Virginia because she is an agnostic."[60] We still hear echoes of this argument in the ongoing Culture Wars of the twenty-first century, as liberals often accuse conservatives of demanding "small government" when it comes to taxes and social programs but not when it comes to cultural issues like marriage equality or reproductive rights.

In any case, this feud between Eastman and Schlesinger did not end with Schlesinger's rebuttal. William F. Buckley Jr. penned a letter to the editors to argue that Schlesinger had failed to satisfactorily address Eastman's central contention: that political freedom rests on economic freedom.[61] Meanwhile, economist Abba P. Lerner chimed in by agreeing with Schlesinger that there was a clear distinction between economic policy and the democratic process itself. There was no reason, he argued, why limited economic planning could not coexist with a healthy democratic process. Under such a system, government policy would respond with more or less planning as voting preferences shifted. Here, for Lerner, was the difference between totalitarianism, marked by the destruction of the democratic process, and social democracy, where elections determined policy outcomes within the boundaries of a mixed economy.[62] Labor leader Mark Starr also opposed Eastman's position, writing that his proposed dichotomy between collectivism and individual freedom was a false one. According to Starr, a degree of collectivism was indispensable in modern society. After all, neither the armed forces nor grade schools, to name but two examples, were under private control, yet this state of affairs had not snuffed out all vestiges of American freedom.[63] This series of articles concluded with sociologist Daniel Bell and economist Carl Landauer also contributing pieces that criticized Eastman for his simplistic analysis.[64] In toto, while the *New Leader* did publish Eastman's piece, the editors and contributors thoroughly rejected his argument, which was largely a restated version of Hayek's thesis. In this case, then, rather than aligning with conservatives as they so often did in matters of foreign policy, hawkish liberals broke with them decidedly.

In the pages of *Commonweal*, there was a similar tension between the editorial line, on the one hand, and the editors' responsibility to include multiple perspectives on the other. The editors, for example, wrote of their desire to see the US economic, political, and social system move away from the pure laissez-faire capitalism of the conservative imagination. Using language that would horrify conservatives, they expressed their support for "regulation and subordination of the profit motive, increasing co-determination in American industry, [and] more extensive social security."[65] Elsewhere, they defended New Deal reforms and dismissed Hayekian fears that FDR had ushered in an era of creeping socialism that could lead only to totalitarianism.[66] On economic policy, then, the editors clearly gravitated more toward the social justice wing of Catholicism than the conservative one.

William F. Buckley Jr., by contrast, authored an essay in the Catholic magazine that laid out exactly the opposite view. Indeed, Buckley openly worried that statism during the Truman years had advanced so far that the gap between American and Soviet political and economic life had virtually disappeared. In comparing the possibility of Stalin winning the Cold War to that of Truman winning it via "a totalitarian bureaucracy within our shores," Buckley wondered, "does it make much difference if we lose our freedom to a Georgian bandit or to a Missouri ignoramus?" Although Buckley ultimately decided that Truman posed less of a threat to American liberties than did Stalin, that he posed the question at all was provocative and telling enough. Nor did Buckley's worries end with the Democratic administration. He also warned that the "ideology of the Leviathan State" had infected American political culture so thoroughly that even the Republican Party was vulnerable to its siren call. He cited Republican support for "managed currency, egalitarian tax policies, minimum wage laws, civil rights legislation, labor monopolies, and social security."[67] In Buckley's view, then, there actually *was* something of a liberal consensus, and it was empowering America's "domestic enemy, the State." If these trend lines continued, he predicted, then democracy in the United States may well disappear within several decades. Looking ahead to future election years, Buckley prophesied that "the Big Issue of 1984 might center on whether there shall be an election in 1988."[68] This prediction clearly did not come to pass. Instead, 1984 turned out in many ways to be the electoral culmination of everything Buckley had worked for his entire life, as his friend and ideological bedfellow Ronald Reagan was reelected to a second term in a historic landslide victory.

While *Commonweal* did not shy away from giving Buckley a platform from which to broadcast his views, most contributors to the Catholic journal disagreed with the young conservative upstart. Catholic priest and Notre Dame philosophy professor Leo R. Ward, for example, criticized Buckley for conflating Christianity and capitalism.[69] A later editorial pointed out that Buckley continued to peddle his "anti-papal economics" even though Catholic teaching overtly repudiated his "socio-political heresies."[70] In sum, while readers could find conservative perspectives on "socialism" from the likes of Max Eastman and William F. Buckley in the pages of the *New Leader* and *Commonweal*, the bulk of opinion published in these magazines was on the side of mainstream liberal thinking on economic policy. To wit, most contributors rejected the Eastman/Buckley/Hayek thesis that there was no middle ground between individualism and collectivism and embraced New Dealism: that pragmatic government intervention in and regulation of the free market best served the interests of a democratic people.

The left liberals at *The Nation* and the *New Republic* scarcely bothered to engage in a philosophical debate regarding "socialism" like that which pitted Eastman against Schlesinger, or Buckley against social justice Catholics. Instead, when they discussed the issue at all, it was generally in the context of concrete political issues like Truman's proposal for a universal health care system. Both flagship liberal journals supported Truman's doomed proposal and breezily dismissed conservative and American Medical Association complaints about "socialized medicine."

CONCLUSION

The debates about domestic political culture both overlapped and contrasted with the debates about foreign policy during the years of the Korean War. On the conservative side in particular, support for McCarthyism and opposition to Roosevelt-Truman social welfarism at home coincided almost perfectly with support for MacArthurism and opposition to Truman-Achesonian containment abroad. On the liberal side, by contrast, domestic issues tended to jumble up what we have seen in terms of ideological leanings on foreign policy. Yes, left liberals predictably opposed McCarthyism and supported Truman's universal health care proposal, but hawkish liberal positions were much more of a mixed bag. While the contributors to the *New Leader* in particular were largely indistinguishable from conservative writers when it came to foreign policy, their views on domestic matters were a different animal entirely. On McCarthyism, they opposed both McCarthy *and* their fellow liberals who thought him as much of a threat as Stalin. Regarding the idea of creeping socialism, they entertained both sides of the debate but ultimately rejected conservative fears by emphasizing the very real distinction between social democracy and communist totalitarianism. Next, we shall turn our attention back to the foreign policy debates that were so prevalent during the Korean War: those that emerged from the peace negotiations at Kaesong and Panmunjom.

6. Negotiations

With MacArthur gone and the Truman administration more determined than ever to end the war by negotiated settlement, the United States responded favorably to Soviet UN ambassador Jacob Malik's proposal to begin ceasefire negotiations in late June 1951. China agreed and the talks began in July in Kaesong, Korea, a site deemed "neutral" though in communist-controlled territory. Almost immediately, the talks were bogged down as neither side was willing to budge on the location of a ceasefire line. The communists (a delegation made up of Chinese and North Korean officials) demanded a return to the antebellum status quo at the thirty-eighth parallel, while the United States insisted on present battle lines, which would be much more easily defensible than the prewar boundary. By the end of August, communist negotiators had walked away from the talks, and the stalemated war continued with no end in sight until October, when negotiations resumed at Panmunjom, just a few miles east of Kaesong but a more properly neutral location. By November 1951, communist negotiators had effectively agreed to the US demand that the ceasefire line run along present battle lines, but then a new and more intractable problem became the sticking point: repatriation of prisoners of war. The United States had polled its communist prisoners and determined that a shockingly high number, roughly 100,000 out of 170,000, did not wish to return to communist China or North Korea.[1] As such, American negotiators proposed that prisoners be repatriated on a purely voluntary basis. The communists balked at this suggestion, demanding that *all* prisoners be returned to their country of origin, and once again, in April 1952, talks were suspended. The negotiations would resume on an on-again, off-again basis for the better part of a year, while soldiers on both sides of the conflict continued to kill and die.

A STILL-DIVIDED KOREA

After the war entered its final, prolonged phase of stalemate and negotiation, America's political opinion journals were filled with arguments for or against a settlement that would leave Korea divided. Some explored the nuances of what it might mean for Korea to be divided at various locations, whether the thirty-eighth parallel, the present battle line, or Korea's "narrow waist," approximately ninety miles north of the prewar boundary. But mainly, the debate was either-or. Left liberals favored a divided Korea as the most practical means of ending the war and the threat it posed to the larger peace of the world, while conservatives and hawkish liberals tended to oppose any settlement that left Korea divided in any way.

While the *New Republic* opposed division of Korea at the thirty-eighth parallel, and instead argued for the "narrow waist," citing the superior defensibility of the latter line, that magazine's editors nonetheless accepted the ultimate division of Korea as a practical necessity.[2] Their liberal brethren at *The Nation*, however, were much more willing to accept a peace premised on a Korea divided at the thirty-eighth parallel. While *The Nation* agreed with the *New Republic* that the current battle line was "a considerably better defense position," its editors said the thirty-eighth parallel was "politically the only logical line," as the communists were apparently unwilling to accept any line that meandered north of that boundary.[3] As we shall see, this was not the only time *The Nation*'s editors were relatively sympathetic to the positions staked out by the communist negotiators. Indeed, even after the communists dropped their "stubborn demand" that the truce line be drawn at the thirty-eighth parallel, *The Nation* suggested that it was a perfectly valid proposal. The editors acknowledged that the parallel was an "artificial" dividing line between the two Koreas but ultimately insisted that it was "the only logical dividing line once the shooting stops."[4]

Whether a truce line was drawn along the thirty-eighth parallel or somewhere else, both *The Nation* and the *New Republic* agreed that the forced unification of Korea should no longer be on the table. On this point, the Catholic liberals at *Commonweal* reluctantly agreed, writing that the United States must ultimately resist the temptation to demand unconditional surrender in Korea.[5] Settling for a divided Korea meant that the United States would not have achieved what it had hoped but had fought the war "to the point of diminishing returns," such that it had become expedient to negotiate a settlement.[6] They added finally that the only alternative to accepting a divided Korea was "full-scale war against China," which they thought was both impractical and dangerous. Thus, the armistice, for all the frustration it may have caused anticommunists, was "simply a practical expression of the realities of power."[7]

For mainly pragmatic reasons, then, left liberals endorsed plans to end the fighting in Korea by leaving that country divided, half-communist and half-free (or half-communist and half-Rhee, as it were). Division was anathema, however, to the conservatives at *The Freeman*. That journal was adamantly opposed to any settlement leaving Korea divided. Only rarely, and with evident reluctance, did contributors to the magazine bow to practical reality.

A good example of conservative ideological insistence that the war in Korea would be useless unless it resulted in the decisive defeat or overthrow of communist China can be found in a *Freeman* editorial from July 1951. "If all that a year of bitter fighting in Asia is to produce is the *status quo ante* division of Korea along the 38th parallel," asked the editors at the onset of negotiations at Kaesong, "can it be truthfully said that 'aggression' has been punished?" Their answer was a blunt "obviously not," since, in their view, it was not enough to merely check aggression and contain communism. What was required was to destroy the aggressors, in this case North Korea and China. US acceptance of a peace agreement allowing North Korea and China to exist as before the war, then, would be "cumulatively disastrous." Not only would such a peace effectively recognize the communists' right to rule in Peking and Pyongyang; it would also likely lead to communist China eventually being seated at the UN while Formosa was bargained away to the communists. Worse, they concluded, leaving Korea divided would demoralize Western Europe, "where the Germans, observing our weakness for Yalta-inspired divisions, would be put on notice that East and West Germany are to be permanently surrendered."[8] While it makes sense that the continued existence of communist North Korea might make the *East* German government feel more secure, why the editors thought the outcome of the Korean War would imperil the existence of *West* Germany is unclear. Presumably they were implying that the lack of punishment inflicted on North Korea for its aggression could only encourage East Germany to attack its Western neighbor. In any case, it was their grim assessment that such an outcome in Korea would have profoundly dangerous consequences both in Asia and around the world.

As the truce talks and the inconclusive war dragged on, *The Freeman*'s editors returned to one of their favorite themes: the inconsistencies of President Harry Truman. "President Truman is himself authority," they wrote, "for the statement that an agreement with the Communists is not worth the paper it is written on, yet at his orders our negotiators have been trying desperately to get such an agreement." What was worse, any truce in Korea could free up communist Chinese forces to aid their allies in Indochina or even launch an attack on Formosa. Meanwhile, Korea would remain divided as before the war. "The only real difference, as compared with the situation prior to June 25, 1950," they concluded, "is that South Korea would have been laid waste, and that UN forces, consisting overwhelmingly of Americans, would have suffered 100,000 casualties."[9] Frustrated with Truman's handling of the war from beginning to end, they viewed a truce in Korea as a worthless end to a worthless war.

Nor did the passage of time ease their objections to the long-awaited truce. Korea, they wrote, was the first war in American history fought "without a firm will to win." And the results were an indictment of the Truman administration's lack of resolve to fight the war to a definitive conclusion. That the United States would have easily defeated China, they wrote, "is scarcely open to reasonable doubt," as evidenced by "the direct firsthand testimony of one of America's greatest soldiers, General Douglas MacArthur." Although MacArthur's ideas had been thoroughly discredited during the Senate hearings on his dismissal, the editors stood by their man. Had MacArthur been permitted to wage war as he saw fit and defeat China, they wrote, "the Chinese invasion of Korea might not have ended in one of the greatest military debacles in history." Indeed, Mao's prestige would have been much diminished "and a favorable condition would have been created for Nationalist landings on the mainland." But, as it happened, American power, especially air power, had been made impotent by the Truman administration's infirmity of purpose. Consequently, "the prestige of Red China has been enhanced."[10] In sum, the editorial staff at *The Freeman* objected to a truce leaving Korea divided primarily because such a truce would stand as the most obvious symbol of the path not taken—the path of general war with China.

Even once the truce's terms were all but concluded and the end of the killing was in sight, there was, according to *The Freeman*, "no cause for jubilation." After all, the best that the United States had been able to achieve was a draw "with two economically backward Asiatic satellites of the Soviet Union." More to the point, the truce would leave in place "an unnatural, unhistorical, and uneconomic partition of Korea." Moreover, the truce left a huge Chinese army in North Korea and represented "a retreat from the position taken by the UN Assembly in October 1950, when that body authorized the forces of Gen MacArthur to drive to the Yalu."[11] In short, then, signing off on a divided Korea meant the United States and UN had broken their solemn promise to the people of Korea, who would thereafter remain under the constant threat of a communist sword of Damocles.

All of this said, the editors of *The Freeman* were not so ideologically driven that they could not see which way the winds were blowing as the truce talks wound tortuously toward their conclusion. Although critical of Truman for failing to reunite Korea or reignite the Chinese civil war, they preferred a settlement leaving Korea divided to indefinite limited warfare waged as a "substitute for victory." "With the possibility of winning a dynamic victory in the Far East gone," they wrote, "truce at the 38th parallel is far more to be desired than a continuation of random and aimless slaughter."[12] A few months later, they modified this argument slightly, indicating that only a truce line drawn according to present battle lines would be acceptable.[13] But by June 1953, the editors were willing to call the expected armistice in Korea "an honorable peace."[14] Their change in tone here is perhaps best explained by the fact that it was no longer Truman, Acheson, and Marshall who were the authors of America's Far Eastern policy, but Eisenhower and Dulles.

The hawkish liberals at the *New Leader* generally agreed with the position staked out by the conservatives at *The Freeman* regarding a Korean settlement that would leave the country disunited. While William Henry Chamberlin, one of the two most hawkish on the editorial staff, actually argued in favor of ending the war by a negotiated settlement that would bisect Korea, he did so only grudgingly. It was Chamberlin's hawkish compatriot David J. Dallin who argued most forcefully against any course of action that would leave Korea divided.

When truce negotiations began in the summer of 1951, David J. Dallin encouraged his readers to keep in mind who the real enemy was. Actual battle conditions notwithstanding, Dallin insisted that America's real enemy in Korea was neither North Korean nor Chinese. Rather, the real enemy was of quite another sort. Behind Kim and Mao, he explained, "we see other faces with other, non-Korean and non-Chinese names. We face a group of relentless, ruthless men, who are ready to fight to the last drop of Chinese or Korean blood." For Dallin, that enemy, of course, was the Soviet Union—the puppet master making the North Koreans and Chinese dance across the Korean battlefield like so many marionettes. As such, he warned, American policymakers needed to keep their wits about them, for they faced an enemy "who is always on the watch for our weaknesses, failures and hesitancies." And for Dallin, heading into negotiations with the express purpose of making peace in Korea was playing directly into Moscow's hands. Of course everyone wanted peace, he wrote, but wasn't the United States a bit too publicly eager for it? Entering into peace talks in Korea thus amounted to telegraphing to the enemy "that we will be glad to settle for the shabby old status quo embodied in the absurd and unstable 38th Parallel!" The enemy in the Kremlin "hears our peace slogans" and concludes that the United States would settle for "peace *at any price*." From this, he insisted, the Soviet enemy could draw only one conclusion: "That it will pay him to redouble his efforts and be more intransigent than ever."[15]

The following week, Dallin laid out what he thought would be the dire consequences if the war in Korea ended with that country still divided. Mere restoration of the status quo in Korea, he wrote, "would be fatal and would be fraught with dangers far greater than any we have encountered thus far." The Korean War, in Dallin's view, was launched by Stalin as the first small step in a campaign of global domination. Thus, the war was not started simply to conquer South Korea, and it would not end with an armistice. Stalin would not be so easily discouraged—"he will never scrap his sweeping plans because of a few military setbacks. If he does consent to a truce in Korea, it will only be to obtain a breathing-spell in which to regroup, retrain, and re-equip." For Dallin, then, the issue was not peace in Korea per se, but whether to proceed with strength or weakness against Stalinist expansionism. He painted those who could not see this as either willfully blind or dangerously naive:

> Those who seriously believe that a Korean truce would inaugurate a period of stable peace in the Far East should be sent to the foot of the class. Their prototypes are men like Henry Wallace, Owen Lattimore and Julio Alvarez del Vayo. They ignore the paramount factor in contemporary history—[Soviet communism's] aggressiveness, expansionism, tenacity and ruthlessness. Communism will never become peaceful; once it launches an attack—as in the case of Korea—it must be smashed or it will finally triumph.

The operative phrase here is the conclusory one: *it must be smashed or it will finally triumph*. For Dallin, making peace via a divided Korea was tantamount to surrender, and "Surrender never means peace—least of all surrender to tyranny." That was why, he concluded, the United States needed to go on fighting in Korea until the elimination of communism from that country was fully attained.[16]

Dallin was not alone in his views among the editorial staff of the *New Leader*. That magazine editorialized in July 1951 that the United States should not settle for "half a loaf" in Korea. After all, to imagine that Stalin and Mao had abandoned their program for conquest of all Asia would be the "sheerest self-delusion." Korea must be reunified under democratic auspices, or else "peace will become a mockery of our dead." The editors closed the piece by moving beyond Korea to discuss US Cold War policy more generally: "We are dealing, above all, with men who have a global plan and will stop at nothing to realize it; we must hammer out a global strategy of our own . . . with a view to taking the offensive against [them]." If there remained any doubt that they were advocating a liberation/rollback strategy, they quickly laid it to rest. "Our ultimate objective," they wrote, "must be nothing less than to free the entire world—not only Korea—from tyranny."[17] Clearly, there was no room in this vision for peaceful coexistence with the Soviet Union, much less for a still-divided Korea.

After nearly two years of diplomatic wrangling at Panmunjom, the editors of the *New Leader* continued to oppose any settlement that would leave Korea divided at or near the thirty-eighth parallel. They took pains to remind their readers that a UN General Assembly resolution from October 1950 explicitly called for an independent, democratic, and united Korea. As such, that the United States was apparently willing to accept a divided Korea amounted to "a dramatic demonstration of UN impotence in the face of Stalinist power." Thus, they argued, "the principle result of the war would have to be summarized, by almost any historian, as the deflation of the international prestige of the U.S."[18] Even with the new life breathed into hopes for peace that came with the death of Joseph Stalin in March 1953, the *New Leader* maintained its hawkishness, editorializing that new Soviet premier Georgy Malenkov's grip on power was tenuous at best and, as such, Soviet Russia was more vulnerable than it had been since before Stalingrad in 1942. Thus, the confusion resulting from Stalin's death had delivered to the United States a momentous opportunity. And the most immediate thing the United States could do to further destabilize the communist world was to achieve victory in Korea. Indeed, wrote the editors, "A UN march to the 39th Parallel would have profound effects in every corner of the Kremlin's empire."[19]

Given this sustained bellicosity, it is no surprise that the editors were disappointed with the new Eisenhower administration when Secretary of State John Foster Dulles, who had talked so often of the need for a strategy of liberation/rollback during the 1952 campaign, proposed a settlement in the Far East that would leave Korea divided at its "narrow waist." Even though such a division would be ninety miles north of the thirty-eighth parallel and would constitute a comparatively easy line of defense, the editors called Dulles's suggestion "appeasement" and a "Far Eastern Munich" that "would mean world war." *Any* settlement that left Korea divided, they wrote, "would betray one of the main principles motivating our intervention there," namely, "the unification of Korea under an independent, democratic government." If communism maintained even a toehold on the Korean peninsula, it would remain in position to launch a new aggression against the Republic of Korea, likely leading to an even bloodier conflict. Under such a scenario, the United States would have effectively fought a small war "in order to fight a bigger one."[20] Why the editors felt the Republic of Korea would remain vulnerable if bordered by North Korea at the thirty-eighth parallel or Korea's waistline, but could rest secure if bordered by China at the Yalu, is not entirely clear. The point here is simply that they continued to oppose any division of Korea whatsoever, regardless of the practical benefits of ending the stalemated war at the soonest possible opportunity.

Surprisingly, the one partial exception to the *New Leader*'s line was the normally bellicose William Henry Chamberlin. Chamberlin was certainly not happy about the prospect of an indefinitely divided Korea but, given the Truman administration's decision to reject what Chamberlin considered to be the obviously superior MacArthur program of total victory, he recognized that a settlement premised on the status quo ante was "probably the best obtainable" remaining solution.[21] Thus, among both conservatives and hawkish liberals, the overwhelming weight of opinion opposed any negotiated settlement that would leave Korea divided in any way. A divided Korea gained grudging acceptance only once it became clear that Truman's perceived timidity had eliminated any possibility of a MacArthur-type "victory" in Korea.

WERE THE COMMUNISTS NEGOTIATING IN GOOD FAITH?

Lying just below the surface of the debate detailed in this chapter was the question of whether the Chinese and North Korean communists were ever actually trustworthy negotiating partners at Kaesong and Panmunjom. Not surprisingly, the conservatives at *The Freeman* and the hawkish liberals at the *New Leader* routinely dismissed the communist role in the negotiations as nothing more than diplomatic chicanery, while the left liberals at *The Nation* tended to give the communist negotiators the benefit of the doubt. Interestingly, the liberals at the *New Republic* and *Commonweal* were not sure what to make of communist intentions, vacillating in their assessments with the ups and downs of the tortuous talks.

From the beginning of the negotiations, the hawkish liberals at the *New*

Leader were the loudest and most persistent critics of the very idea of negotiating with communists. For these liberals, a communist diplomat was necessarily a wolf in sheep's clothing and could never be trusted or taken at his word. According to this view, grounded equally in experience and paranoia, communist diplomacy was simply warfare by other means, the ulterior motive of world conquest never lurking too far behind the veil of compromise. For this reason, any truce agreement in Korea was not likely to be worth the paper on which it was signed, and the sooner American negotiators realized this, the better.

Communist actions at Kaesong, according to a *New Leader* editorial, were "designed to cover the brutal face of Communism with a friendly mask." Indeed, the editors suggested that the communists' goal was simply to prolong the ceasefire negotiations, "to sap as much UN will, energy and patience in the process as they can." Having been bested on the battlefield, they argued, "the Communists are resorting to the most devastating of all weapons: psychology." The path toward a ceasefire, then, was being made deliberately difficult, and Americans would need "all our moral and mental resources to negotiate it without mishap."[22] The editors defined what exactly they meant by this warning in a follow-up piece a few weeks later, writing that the communist strategy in the peace talks was "the employment of wearing-down tactics" such that the United States might, in exasperation, commit some irrational error that would benefit the communist cause. In this sense, the communist negotiators were trying to gain through psychological warfare what they had failed to win on the battlefield. Again they reminded their readers of their view that the Korean War "is only one aspect of an all-Asia war—indeed of a world war—in which a variety of weapons is used." Thus, though the United States might have been honor-bound to explore any avenue, however slim, that might result in peace, it would be "excessively foolish" to put too much stock in the truce talks.[23]

The editors later ascribed an additional motivation to the communist negotiators for dragging their feet, this time at Panmunjom: to tie down US forces in Korea while they escalated military action in Indochina. "After seven months of negotiations—surely the most protracted on record—there is no sign that the Communists are willing to conclude a truce," they wrote. "All we have discovered is that the Communists are willing to talk and talk," and meanwhile the warfare in Indochina "continues on a large scale." Thus, they concluded, "we see the classic Communist tactic of talking peace in one place while conducting war in another." The Panmunjom deadlock, then, was for the editors of the *New Leader* "a dangerous trap in the making."[24]

And the communist use of such apparently diversionary tactics fit nicely with the editors' overarching theory of communist strategy in the Cold War. The Korean talks had plainly revealed, they wrote, that the communists were manipulating American good faith to turn military defeat into political victory. Indeed, the West's political surrender "remains their objective, to be achieved through psychological attrition"[25]—most immediately at Panmunjom, but ultimately on a global scale.

It wasn't just *New Leader* editorials that denounced the communists for negotiating in bad faith. Readers could find occasional pieces written by various individual contributors as well. Contributing editor David J. Dallin, for example, was incredulous at Moscow's demand that the Soviet Union be included as a "neutral" observer of any would-be truce, writing that this was "one of the most hilariously grotesque incidents of the monotonous Panmunjom parleys."[26] Bruno Shaw, a longtime Asia correspondent for the Associated Press, wrote that the negotiations had been quite frustrating for the American people: for months on end, he wrote, American representatives at Panmunjom "have been subjected by Communist military spokesmen to nauseating doses of arrogance, contempt and vituperation."[27] Finally, Edward Hunter, on the editorial staff at the conservative *American Mercury* and frequent contributor to the *New Leader*, wrote that, in attempting to negotiate with the Chinese communists, America was painting itself into the same corner that it had forced Chiang Kai-shek into years before when it encouraged the generalissimo to form a coalition government with Mao. "We Americans and the rest of the free world," he wrote, "are now being given at Panmunjom a taste of what we helped give the Nationalist Government not so many years ago." The United States, he continued, had insisted that Chiang try to negotiate a mutually agreeable end to the Chinese civil war, ending in a nearly complete victory for the communists. Now it was the Americans who were trying to bargain with Peking. Thus, "The shoe is now on the other foot. How successful are *we* in reaching an agreement with a group which considers negotiation only an opportunity for stalling tactics or for permitting the other side to give in completely?"[28]

The pages of the hawkish *New Leader*, then, were consistently filled with pessimism about prospects for reaching a reasonable agreement with the communist negotiators at Panmunjom. These sentiments were just as prevalent in the pages of the conservative journal *The Freeman*. In September 1951 *The Freeman* complained that, after two months and "more than a score of meetings," the talks had gone "exactly nowhere." Why? Because of communist disingenuousness. "If there were any real sincerity in the Chinese Communists' desire for peace," wrote the editors, "a cease-fire could have been arranged in a single day."[29] What was more, the editors faulted American negotiators for enabling such insincerity, writing in astonishment, in December 1951, that it had taken them four months to reach the conclusion that the communists were not trustworthy partners in peace. America's newfound distrust of the Chinese and North Koreans "was of course completely justified. But why did it take four months to occur to our negotiators? They would have started with it, if somebody had given five minutes of real thought to the matter."[30] In other words, only stupidity could explain America's "incredible fumbling" of the truce talks. According to *The Freeman*, that's precisely what the Truman administration had in spades.

While the *New Leader* and *The Freeman* were unceasingly consistent in their view that the negotiations to end the war in Korea were a waste of time, the liberals at the *New Republic* and *Commonweal* moved back and forth along the spectrum of trust as the negotiations ebbed and flowed. At the very beginning of truce talks, in the summer of 1951, the *New Republic* answered the question of whether Russia wanted peace in Korea with, "There is good reason to believe that she does." As for the Chinese, the editors thought they might be "more stubborn than the Russians," but that ultimately it was in their interests to negotiate a good-faith ceasefire.[31] Within a few weeks, however, as the Kaesong talks broke down, they wrote, "We are forced to the reluctant conclusion that the Russian peace maneuver is not genuine, and represents no real change in policy." And so the *New Republic* reversed course every so often for the remainder of the war, as circumstances warranted. In November 1951 the exasperated editors wrote that the Korean truce talks were dragging along with just enough halting progress to suggest that the Chinese were genuinely torn between resuming hostilities and signing an agreement.[32] And much later in the war, once peace in Korea was actually within reach, they threw their hands up, concluding that it was "a toss-up" whether Moscow sincerely wanted peace.[33] Such was the degree of their bewilderment that the editors of the *New Republic* suggested, at various times, that the *Russians* were the decisive party in whether there would be peace in Korea, and at other times that the critical party was the *Chinese*. In any case, by the time the truce was all but concluded, in the summer of 1953, they finally came down on the side of regarding the communists as at least occasionally genuine partners in peace. "The longest truce talks in history," they wrote, "have taught us again that the Communist nations share common ground with us in opposing warfare in which no military decision can be reached."[34]

The Catholic liberals at *Commonweal* were similarly undecided regarding the communists' trustworthiness as negotiating partners. By agreeing to negotiate at all, they argued, the communists proved that they could actually be reasonable—so long as you were negotiating with them from a position of superior strength. Thus, while the editors thought it wise for the United States to remain skeptical about Soviet intentions, they felt strongly that every possible means of preventing further bloodshed should be exhausted before the world was thrust into "the black night of atomic war."[35] Once the Chinese and North Koreans broke off the talks at Kaesong, however, the editors concluded that the communists had become "incapable of any real negotiation" and that their "only talent in the present diplomatic sphere is for bluster and obstruction."[36] As the talks started and stopped and started again, they lamented that men were dying every day while communist intentions remained obscure. The negotiations, they acknowledged resignedly, "will go on and on."[37]

We have seen that conservatives and hawkish liberals did not trust the communists one whit when it came to negotiating in good faith to end the Korean War. The liberals at the *New Republic* and *Commonweal*, for their part, had mixed feelings about whether negotiating with communists was worthwhile. The left liberals at *The Nation*, however, were consistently willing to give the communists the benefit of the doubt. In fact, the staff at *The Nation* occasionally went so far as to suggest that if anyone could be justifiably accused of not negotiating in good faith, it was the United States!

When Jacob Malik, Soviet ambassador to the UN, proposed ceasefire discussions in June 1951, Freda Kirchwey granted that his speech was "dressed in the conventional Soviet language of self-righteousness and abuse." She was convinced, however, that the purpose of his speech was "not merely to let out a new propaganda blast." Rather, she believed, "his basic purpose was peace."[38] Even when the talks began to hit their long series of snags, *The Nation* persisted in its optimism, chiding the "gloom-mongers" who predicted failure and doubted communist intentions. A "dispassionate observer," ran the editorial, should understand that the communists "quite evidently" wanted to end the war.[39] Whereas those at the *New Leader*, for example, tended to focus on the numerous breakdowns in the talks, to support their pessimistic assessment of negotiating with the enemy, the staff at *The Nation* regularly highlighted the resumptions of the talks to bolster their optimism. Instead of viewing the periodic walkouts and breakdowns as heralding the futility of dealing with communists, the staff at *The Nation* viewed the repeated resumption of the talks as evidence of the communists' "eagerness to keep the talks going."[40]

Editor Freda Kirchwey bemoaned the breezy dismissals in Washington of the Soviets' peace gestures. It was, after all, Moscow that proposed ceasefire negotiations, she pointed out—not Washington. Yet time after time Soviet concessions were "denounced as fakes, as propaganda."[41] When it came to whether the Soviets really wanted peace, she suggested, the proof was in the pudding. Indeed, *The Nation* pointed out, the biggest sticking point at Kaesong had been the location of the would-be ceasefire line. The United States had insisted on battle lines, the Soviets on the thirty-eighth parallel. But as the talks resumed at Panmunjom, it was the Soviets who gave up their demand, agreeing to negotiate on the basis of current battle positions. This amounted to a major concession on the part of the communists.[42]

By 1953, the Panmunjom talks had ground to a halt over the POW issue. When the breakthrough finally came, *The Nation* credited the Chinese. "As we go to press," the editors excitedly wrote, "China has announced its readiness to cooperate in hurdling the last barrier to the long-sought truce in Korea." China had "made its bid; it is up to the West to meet it."[43] This was a curious manipulation of events. In reality, the United States had "made its bid" when it proposed voluntary repatriation. Now China was meeting it. The editors of *The Nation*, however, seemed to see things the other way around, viewing China as the initiator of this final push toward peace.

In any case, as peace in Korea edged ever closer, the editors expressed their astonishment that officials in Washington were still so skeptical of the communists' apparent willingness to end the war, even in the face of overwhelming evidence that Moscow was "ready to go to almost fantastic lengths to settle outstanding feuds." They suggested that US officials were going out of their way to find fault with otherwise sensible communist proposals—"feverishly hunting booby traps," as they put it. Why? America's "psychological warfare chiefs," they wrote, had "devoted themselves so assiduously to cold war propaganda that they are practically dumbfounded by the prospect of peace." While Eisenhower and Dulles, they admitted, were exercising an obvious duty in taking precautions against would-be communist tricks, America should also guard against a mentality "so immersed in the search for Red shenanigans" that it let the opportunity for peace slip away.[44] According to *The Nation*, then, if the promise of peace failed to materialize, American paranoia, not communist skulduggery, would be to blame.[45]

With the end of the war in view, in June 1953, the editors first made the point that the war could have ended on similar terms two years earlier had MacArthur not started his "ill-fated drive" into North Korea, which brought China into the conflict. But all of that was in the past now:

> These considerations, as well as the acrimonious, seemingly endless truce talks, the months of stalling and haggling, will be shoved into the background by the overwhelming facts that men are no longer killing and dying and that the agreement when it came was one of compromise—a precedent of immense value to show that settlements with the Communists *can* be reached through negotiation and mutual concession. Skeptics should not forget that the final decision on POWs required the sacrifice by the Chinese and North Koreans of one of their most stubbornly held positions.[46]

According to *The Nation*, the burgeoning peace was due mainly to the communists' willingness to compromise. This proved once and for all that hard-line American anticommunists were mistaken in their belief that nothing could be gained by negotiating with the enemy. Moreover, America had long demanded that the Soviet Union go beyond mere rhetoric and demonstrate its commitment to peace through its actions. With the concession on POWs, which allowed for the consummation of the armistice in Korea, wrote the editors, "We asked for deeds and now we are getting them."[47]

STALEMATE AT PANMUNJOM

The truce talks at Panmunjom were deadlocked for nearly two years until an agreement on the POW issue was finally reached. During that time, the discussion in America's leading political opinion journals often turned to the question of what the United States should do given the frustrating standstill. As was so often the case, conservatives and hawkish liberals aligned on one side of the issue, arguing that renewed and expanded military action was the only way to break the stalemate, while left and center-left liberals took the less provocative, but perhaps less satisfying, position that the only sensible way forward was to press on with a limited war and hope for the best from Panmunjom.

By the beginning of 1952, once negotiations had already dragged on for more than half a year, the editorial staff at the *New Leader* had had enough. In their view, the indefinite diplomatic stalemate only served the purposes of Asian communism, as it kept American military power tied down in

Korea while it freed Chinese military resources to be diverted to other theaters of war, namely Indochina. In their own words, "we must force the issue, and either hasten the truce talks to their desired conclusion or break them off and divert Communist military power back to the point where our own is greatest: the Korean battlefield." The mechanism for this course of action would be an ultimatum specifying a time limit for concluding a settlement, after which hostilities would escalate. They acknowledged that their proposal, if adopted, would risk the resumption of the war on a large scale "and perhaps even of extending it to the Chinese mainland." But they thought these risks worth taking, in view of the "greater danger that, if we remain passive, Southeast Asia may fall."[48]

They repeated this same line of reasoning several months later, writing that because the communists would sign a truce "only under severe duress," the time had come for a "decisive and bold" ultimatum.[49] By June 1952 their patience had worn yet thinner. The talks had "conclusively broken down," they wrote, and "since Peking and Moscow obstinately refuse to make peace through suasion, there is only one course left: to use compulsion." Whereas in the past they had neglected to suggest a specific amount of time for their proposed ultimatum, here they recommended that the United States adopt a policy whereby the war would be resumed on a large scale unless an agreement was reached within one week. A short amount of time to resolve such complex issues, to be sure, but they were confident it would work: "We are convinced that an ultimatum will succeed where talk failed."[50]

They made this same argument over and over for the following year, culminating in their call, on the eve of the armistice agreement, for US/UN forces to drive north to the Yalu and reunify Korea if the communists rejected the latest UN offer.[51] Adding a darker overtone for the first time, they concluded that the "recent atomic-artillery tests in Nevada plainly indicate new possibilities for a rapid and victorious termination of that tragic conflict."[52] Nor was the *New Leader* the only journal to call for the potential use of atomic weapons as a means to end the fighting in Korea. After suggesting in an editorial that American negotiators should simply walk out of the Panmunjom talks,[53] the conservative monthly *American Mercury* published a piece by Senate Minority Leader Styles Bridges (R-NH) in which he coldly concluded, "There should be no political restrictions on weapons used in the field against armed Communists. We didn't hesitate to employ atomic weapons against the Japanese in 1945; if they can be used in 1953 to save American and South Korean lives, as well as to disarm the Communists, then why shouldn't we use them?"[54]

To the liberals at the *New Republic* and *Commonweal*, such loose talk was horrifying. *Commonweal* editorialized that if the United States were to resort to atomic weapons, "it will be misfortune for all mankind," regardless of the immediate results in Korea.[55] Similarly, the *New Republic* warned against the snake oil that American use of the bomb in Korea would turn out to be. "No proposal could be more unsound," wrote the editors. "Strategically, atom bombs would be almost useless against the scattered Chinese forces. Politically, the wanton suffering inflicted on civilians would destroy all that sacrifice has accomplished for the UN." Indeed, the editors of the *New Republic* counseled staying the course in Korea. Continuing with limited warfare while there was no end in sight to the diplomatic wrangling at Panmunjom would "be tested by tremendous pressures" and would take discipline, restraint, and maturity, but they were sure that this was the only way peace could be forged in embattled Korea.

Regarding the *New Leader*'s primary argument that the truce talks should be abandoned for a renewed military offensive, the *New Republic* editorialized as follows:

> If we drive forward 60 miles in a limited offensive we will open the way to a new stalemate. If we set the Yalu River as our goal, we will be choosing to defend from now on a frontier four times as long as the 140 mile line we now hold. We will be pushing our troops within range of Communist planes based in Manchuria. As we widen the war, we will narrow our base of support in the UN.[56]

In other words, pushing north to Korea's "waist" or yet further to the Yalu would, at best, exchange one stalemate for another or, at worst, make US troops more vulnerable along a less defensible line while alienating critical allies. In fairness, the *New Republic* did not address what psychological and diplomatic impact such a course of action might have on the Chinese, which was the whole point of the *New Leader*'s proposals, but in any case this was their objection to renewing the war on a large scale. The least bad of all the options facing the United States, they concluded, was simply to continue negotiating and hope for the best. "There is nothing dramatic or noble in the act of waiting," they wrote. But compared to all the risks and uncertainties that were sure to come with a renewed war, waiting for a diplomatic breakthrough was clearly the lesser of two evils.

The Catholic liberals at *Commonweal* took a similar position. They acknowledged America's "legitimate impatience" with the truce talks but wrote that the United States needed to guard against being goaded into the "fatal move" of carrying the war to China. Like the *New Republic*, they favored "a policy based on cool thinking, patience and resoluteness."[57] They later elaborated that expanding the war to China, out of frustration with the lack of progress at Panmunjom, would not only risk World War III but require a tremendous expense of American strength "without striking even one blow at the prime enemy." After this echo of Omar Bradley's famous "wrong war" comment, they concluded that Korea, while confounding to Americans who were used to absolute victory, was a "vital military holding operation" that must not be allowed to become something much more dangerous, even if much more satisfying, to the American psyche.[58] "Limiting and localizing the war as far as possible," they wrote, "seems the only practical course open to us."[59]

The only real contribution to this topic from the editorial staff at *The Nation* was their idea that the negotiations be transferred from Panmunjom to the UN. This would require that the United States give up sole negotiating authority in favor of the full assembly at Lake Success. This plan, they wrote, offered "the only hope of an armistice," as neither military action nor continued diplomatic stalemate pointed toward a way out. The way to peace, for the editors, was to "end the dictatorship of the American command" by allowing the UN General Assembly to decide the terms of the truce.[60] This would have been an unruly process, to say the least, and it is unclear what they envisioned the role of communist China and North Korea to be in these negotiations, but *The Nation* was otherwise silent on the subject of how to proceed from Panmunjom.

In all, the debate over what to do given the prolonged deadlock at the conference table broke down as follows: conservatives (at the *American Mercury* and *The Freeman*) and hawkish liberals (at the *New Leader*) favored giving the communists an ultimatum consisting of a date by which an agreement must be reached, after which the war would be resumed on a large scale, possibly including the use of atomic weapons. The liberals at the *New Republic* and *Commonweal*, on the other hand, rejected the talk of an expanded war as irresponsible and unpractical. As unsatisfying a position as it might have been in the short-term, those two journals favored patient adherence to the path of diplomacy and limited war.

CONCLUSION

Whether the issue was settling for a still-divided Korea, the communists' sincerity in negotiating for peace, or what to do given the diplomatic deadlock at Panmunjom, conservatives and hawkish liberals tended to take hard-line positions that were largely indistinguishable from one another as the truce negotiations progressed. That the hawkish liberals at the *New Leader* would split from left and center-left liberals and align themselves more closely with conservatives on the issues raised by the Korean War was, by the time of the truce talks, not surprising. But as the truce talks wore on, liberal journals were divided in other ways as well. The left liberals at *The Nation* were much more eager to accept a Korea divided at or near the thirty-eighth parallel than their center-left counterparts at the *New Republic* and *Commonweal.* They were also optimistic about the communist capacity to negotiate in good faith, whereas the *New Republic* and *Commonweal* were ambivalent at best. On a variety of issues raised by the truce talks, then, liberal opinion journals were hardly in the kind of harmony that "consensus" would imply, while conservatives and hawkish liberals once again made common cause.

7. The Armistice

The one issue that proved more intractable than any other during the truce negotiations was whether prisoners of war would be returned to their countries of origin forcibly or voluntarily. Of particular concern was that approximately 100,000 of the 170,000 North Korean and Chinese prisoners held by the United States indicated that they did not wish to return home. Given the possibility, if not probability, that those 100,000 Chinese and Korean prisoners, who had publicly expressed their anticommunist sentiments, would be "reeducated," tortured, or executed upon their return to their countries, the Truman administration, for reasons both moral and propaganda-related, refused to be an accomplice to such crimes. The United States, then, insisted that prisoners be repatriated on a purely voluntary basis. The communists angrily rejected this proposal, knowing that to accept it would amount to a major propaganda defeat. And so the fighting continued.

In January 1953, Dwight Eisenhower became the new president of the United States. He and his secretary of state, John Foster Dulles, engaged in a fair amount of saber-rattling regarding the Korean stalemate, threatening to "unleash" Chiang Kai-shek against Mao's regime on the Chinese mainland and even to use nuclear weapons against North Korea to break the diplomatic deadlock. Then, in March 1953, Soviet dictator Joseph Stalin died. New Soviet premier Georgi Malenkov wanted to extend an olive branch to the United States, and within weeks communist negotiators at Panmunjom agreed to an exchange of sick and wounded POWs. Thereafter, the Chinese and North Koreans softened their position on voluntary repatriation, signaling that they might accept a deal whereby prisoners who did not wish to return to China or North Korea would be sent to a neutral country rather than to Formosa or South Korea, respectively. By June 1953, after three years of war, only one holdout refused to go along with the agreed-upon framework: South Korean president Syngman Rhee. President Eisenhower used all of the diplomatic pressure he could muster to convince Rhee to accept the deal, and on July 27, 1953, an armistice was finally signed, ending the Korean War. In the end, the United States turned over approximately 76,000 prisoners to the communists. The original offer, which the communists had angrily rejected almost two years earlier, had been 70,000.

THE POW ISSUE

The contributors to America's leading political opinion journals viewed the impasse over the repatriation issue in different ways, though the divisions here were not nearly as stark as those regarding other issues. Conservatives and hawkish liberals argued fiercely that the United States must not abandon the anticommunist prisoners. At times, they advocated that the United States simply release the prisoners unilaterally, thereby circumventing the talks altogether. Conservatives in particular occasionally raked the Truman administration over the coals for its lack of resolve in failing to take such action. On the other side of the spectrum, the liberals at *The Nation*, the *New Republic*, and *Commonweal* were split on the prisoner issue. While never advocating a unilateral release, *Commonweal* joined the *New Leader* in its strong support for the rights of the prisoners. The *New Republic* started out non-committal on the issue but gradually moved toward the position taken in the pages of *Commonweal* and the *New Leader*. Only the left liberals at *The Nation* declined to take a strong position on how best to balance the interests of 100,000 prisoners, on the one hand, and ending a war on the other.

In the pages of the *New Leader*, David J. Dallin wrote sympathetically of the thousands of Chinese prisoners who tattooed themselves with anticommunist slogans, wrote "petitions in their blood declaring that they would rather die than return to Communist China," and erected a makeshift Statue of Liberty in the prisoner camp at Koje. By all of these actions, he pointed out to his readers, these prisoners were knowingly condemning themselves to death if they were ever returned to the mainland.[1] For the duration of the war, Dallin remained forcefully opposed to any compromise agreement that would return even a fraction of the anticommunist prisoners.[2] But the *New Leader*'s position was most clearly articulated in an editorial appropriately titled, "Don't Betray the Korea POWs!" Even as the truce talks dragged on, the editors wrote that the greatest issue in Korea was no longer peace or war itself. Rather, "we are confronted by the greater problem of sustaining the moral basis of our whole position in the world, without which neither peace nor freedom is possible." The prisoner issue, then, transcended the Korean War. To the editors, it was a symbol of what the entire Cold War was about—the moral superiority of the American system to that of the Soviet system. Thus, they wrote despairingly of rumors that the United States was about to give in and turn over all the prisoners to China and North Korea. If the United States were to abandon the prisoners to this cruel fate, it would be an act "as dishonorable and perhaps more disastrous than Munich." Such an "unholy secret compact" would generate "a tidal wave of revulsion" and would condemn the Truman administration to go down in history as "one of the most treacherous ever conceived." Putting the issue in blunt life-and-death terms, they asked, "Shall we be responsible for the murder of these men? Shall we consciously offer them up as sacrifices to the Soviet Moloch?" What was more, in addition to "revolting the consciences of all decent men," sending thousands of declared anticommunists to their deaths would be regarded by the peoples of Asia as final proof of the "perfidy of a Western imperialism for which human sacrifice, particularly the sacrifice of Asian lives, means nothing." Thus, not only were tens of thousands of lives at stake—so was the place of America in the hearts and minds of people around the world, particularly in Asia. If the United States proved willing to cooperate in the deaths of so many thousands at the hands of communist totalitarianism, then what would be the point of continuing "our crusade for a better world"? If the United States betrayed the POWs, it would also betray "the whole cause of freedom."[3]

The conservatives at *The Freeman* took a similar position, writing that, at Panmunjom, "U.S. honor and humanity face a critical test. Both are deeply involved in the proposition that no unwilling prisoner in our hands shall be sent back to concentration camp, torture, and death." The United States, they urged, must not break faith with honor and humanity again, as it had at Yalta, by failing to protect its prisoners in Korea.[4] They concluded simply, "There must be no Far Eastern Yalta."[5] And in the pages of the *American Mercury,* Alice Widener wrote that for America to abandon its insistence on voluntary repatriation would be a betrayal of the prisoners to whom the United States had offered its protection and would dissuade potential allies around the world from ever believing American promises again.[6]

As usual, then, the positions taken in conservative publications and in the hawkish *New Leader* aligned quite nicely. What was unusual was that these positions seemed to align with those taken in the pages of the liberal Catholic weekly *Commonweal.* The editors of *Commonweal* wrote that the prisoner issue was not one of those typical international issues where a certain amount of give-and-take was a practical necessity. Rather, because it was an issue of fundamental moral integrity, there could be no compromise. "In the name of the UN," they wrote, "we have repeatedly called for individuals serving with the Communist forces to cross into our lines, pledging our protection to those who sought sanctuary in this fashion." Not only had many such surrenderers openly repudiated the communist leaders of their countries, pointed out the editors, but many had also become Christian converts. In any case, to the larger point of moral integrity, they concluded, it was clear what would become of these individuals "if we surrender them against their will to the Communist police power." To do so would amount to "a gross betrayal of our own moral position in the struggle between freedom and slavery."[7] This was precisely the position taken by the *New Leader*: that the prisoner issue was symbolic of the moral foundations of the entire Cold War. Indeed, the editors wrote that, by so many prisoners refusing repatriation to their communist countries, the United States had won "a great moral victory" that was worthy of celebrating even more than a major victory on the battlefield. Their conclusion further indicates that they viewed the military aspect of containment as but one means to victory in a larger contest that was primarily moral in nature: "The defections in Korea should give us renewed hope. They indicate in a very dramatic fashion that we are on the right track. If we can continue to contain Communist armed aggression, we can look forward with increasing confidence to victory in the struggle for men's allegiance, freely given."[8] Finally, the staff at *Commonweal* was committed to holding firm on the prisoner issue even if it meant the prolongation of the war. "In the name of justice and humanity," they wrote, "the U.S. has no choice but to hold its ground."[9]

Even the left liberals at the *New Republic* slowly gravitated toward the strongly anticommunist position of the *New Leader* on the prisoner issue. Initially, the editors of the *New Republic* did not take a decisive position, writing only that there would be "grist to fill the mills of demagogues" no matter what the United States did about this "agonizing problem."[10] But by mid-1952, the editors were singing a much more definitive tune. The only thing that made continued fighting in Korea worthwhile, they wrote, was that the United States was fighting to uphold the right to political asylum for those seeking refuge from the oppression of communist totalitarianism. This principle, they continued, was symbolically important to America's entire cause, not to mention public image, in Asia. Many Asians, after all, had come to suspect America of harboring an "unconscious contempt for non-whites," a notion that would be strengthened if the United States cut a deal to turn over unwilling Asians to communist torture in order to win the freedom of a much smaller group of American prisoners.[11] Where the *New Republic* had been non-committal in the past, its editors now concluded that protecting the rights and safety of the prisoners was sufficiently important to continue the stalemated war indefinitely. "If patience is needed to move from a stalemate to a truce," they wrote, "then patience is worth it for peace."[12]

On the prisoner issue, then, representatives of virtually every camp across the political spectrum were in agreement. The United States was right to refuse to turn over tens of thousands of men to nearly certain torture or death, even if it meant prolonging the war in the short term. Sacrificing those lives and the principle behind them was simply too great a price to pay for peace. This broad consensus, however, only went so far. The liberals at the *New Republic* and *Commonweal* suggested that the best course of action was to continue the limited war and the negotiations until the communists gave in on the repatriation issue. The hawkish liberals at the *New Leader* and the conservatives at *The Freeman*, by contrast, were not satisfied to stay the course and hope for the best. They advocated bold and immediate action. They wanted the United States to render voluntary repatriation a fait accompli by simply releasing the appropriate prisoners unilaterally.

The *New Leader* first came out cautiously, supporting only the South Korean proposal that the anticommunist prisoners of Korean origin be released. "There is no earthly reason," wrote the editors, "why POWs of Korean ancestry, to whom Seoul is willing to grant full citizenship, should suffer a moment longer in POW compounds." Once these former communist soldiers were made free men, "the UN would become in fact as well as in name the champion of all who are enslaved by Communism throughout the world." And as an added bonus, these 30,000 Koreans could add to the pool of labor and military manpower in South Korea.[13] It was not long, however, before they included the release of Chinese prisoners in their proposals as well, urging in the spring of 1953 the immediate release of "the freedom-loving Koreans and Chinese in our stockades." After all, their liberation would have great motivational significance for those still fighting against their will in communist armies.[14] They later made an even more explicit appeal for the anticommunist Chinese prisoners to be released and sent to Formosa, where they could potentially take up arms against their erstwhile oppressors on the mainland. Indeed, even in defiance of the final agreement, which would send the anticommunist Chinese to a neutral country rather than to Formosa, they urged that "the escape of the freedom-loving Chinese soldiers to Formosa should be expedited as rapidly as possible."[15]

The conservative *Freeman* agreed, editorializing that there was a "simple remedy" to the truce deadlock: to release "immediately and unconditionally" all anticommunist Chinese and North Korean prisoners. The North Koreans could melt into the population of South Korea, while the Chinese could do the same on Formosa. "Humanity and common sense should long ago have dictated this simple procedure," wrote the editors. "It is inconceivable that a further dragging out of this issue should be permitted."[16] Indeed, the editors of *The Freeman* went much further in expressing their disgust at the lack of US/UN resolve on the prisoner issue than their counterparts at the *New Leader*, who actually praised American negotiators for their determination to protect the prisoners.[17] By contrast, *The Freeman* wrote that the negotiators had given away too much by agreeing that prisoners would be repatriated by default unless they indicated explicitly that they would forcibly resist. "Is there anyone who can still contend, in the face of such infamy," they sneered, "that the UN is a great moral force?"[18]

A similar anger at the lack of fortitude exhibited by the American negotiators could be found in the pages of the *American Mercury*. Contributing editor Edward Hunter wrote, in reference to General Ridgway's suggestion that the number of prisoners willing to be repatriated could be increased by a revised screening process, that one would have to search "far and wide to find anything so detrimental to Asian morale as the whole disgraceful POW scandal in Korea." What else could Ridgway's proposal mean, he scoffed, "than that the Americans didn't want these people to be on our side" and were trying to persuade them "to please go back to their Communist masters and take their punishment?"[19] In short, the conservatives at *The Freeman* and *Mercury* generally agreed with the hawkish liberals at the *New Leader* on the prisoner issue, but they were willing to go a step further by expressing their disgust at any and all American attempts to assuage communist embarrassment in the hopes of drawing the war to a speedier conclusion.

Hawkish preference for a unilateral prisoner release and conservative anger at any hint of compromise notwithstanding, there was broad agreement in the pages of America's political opinion journals about the need to protect the rights of the anticommunist prisoners in US/UN facilities. The left liberals at *The Nation*, however, never jumped aboard the bandwagon of this unusual consensus. Their view of the prisoner issue was not as black and white as that of their contemporaries. If anything, they saw justice as being on the communist side of the prisoner divide. They first addressed what they viewed as American hypocrisy in claiming the moral high ground in the prisoner debate.

> During the prolonged debate on the question of voluntary vs. forced repatriation of prisoners, we have been wearing a mantle of nobility which, in our hurry to buy, we grabbed from the oversize rack. We have been asserting, for instance, that it would be inhuman to return to the Communists some 100,000 prisoners whom we claim to be anti-Communists. But the sincerity of our concern

> for them must be judged in light of the passage last week of the McCarran act, which—unless vetoed by President Truman—will effectively see to it that wherever these poor prisoners go once they are freed, it won't be to this country.[20]

President Truman did veto McCarran's bill, but his veto was overridden by Congress and the act became law. The relevant provision here was that members or former members of the Communist Party were barred from entry into the United States. Thus, the prisoners in question, even once they had publicly denounced communism, would not be welcome in the United States by virtue of their former status in the North Korean People's Army or People's Liberation Army of China. As for the idea that the anticommunist Chinese prisoners should be released to Formosa, *The Nation* incredulously asked, "Can anyone deny that it is a threat to Communist China's national security to permit the transfer of Chinese soldiers to the Nationalists in Formosa?" *The Nation* stood alone, then, in arguing that communist China had legitimate security interests at stake in the prisoner negotiations. Lest we think that *The Nation* was wholly on the side of the communists, however, the editorial continued, "But to say we have overstated our case on the war prisoners issue is not to say that we have no case at all." They argued that UN forces should refuse to hand over South Koreans who had been pressed into service in the North Korean army, communist soldiers who had deserted their ranks due to American promises of safety, and any prisoners who had actively aided the United States in the war effort. As for the other prisoners who might not wish to return to communist China or North Korea, they rather coldly concluded, "The rest, it would appear, should be repatriated."[21]

Elsewhere, Freda Kirchwey placed equal blame on both sides for the truce talk stalemate, writing that the impasse over prisoner repatriation was produced by "Communist intransigence on the one hand and on the other by the determination of the U.S. to prevent even the discussion of compromise proposals aimed at breaking the POW deadlock."[22] And finally, when the editors of *The Nation* turned to the American treatment of communist POWs in Korea, they were not altogether flattering. At issue was the alleged massacre of some two hundred communist prisoners by guards acting under American orders at Koje. "Even if they were 'fanatical,' even if their eyes were 'glazed,' even if they were acting under orders and planning a mass escape," they wrote, "it is difficult to accept the military view that they could be subdued only by being killed." First alluding to Soviet deputy foreign minister Andrei Gromyko's attempts to blow the incident out of proportion and concluding with another charge of American hypocrisy, they wrote, "One need not accept Mr. Gromyko's preposterous charge that the U.S. is engaged in the 'systematic extermination' of Communist prisoners, to admit that this second major killing within a year is a poor way of demonstrating our tender concern over the fate of Communist POWs who might be repatriated against their will."[23]

THE TRUCE

As the truce talks at long last approached their resolution, the contributors to America's leading political opinion journals began to reflect upon what exactly peace in Korea would mean for the larger Cold War. On this point there was perhaps greater consensus than on any other issue raised during the three-year course of the war. In short, representatives from each of the major ideological camps agreed that peace in Korea would not herald a broader peace between the superpowers and, thus, excessive joy or optimism about the truce was naive. Whereas writers like David J. Dallin had greeted news of the outbreak of the war in 1950 with almost childlike anticipation of all its epochal possibilities, there was no one in 1953 who thought the Korean War had lived up to such expectations. Instead, left liberals, hawkish liberals, and conservatives alike agreed that the Cold War would simply go on and on, with all its dangers in both Europe and Asia, whether men were killing each other in Korea or not.

Starting from the left side of the political spectrum, *The Nation* editorialized that the coming truce "will bring with it a flock of problems more important and far more difficult to resolve than those now being discussed at Panmunjom."[24] The *New Republic* echoed this sentiment, writing, "A lot of people think that when and if the Korean truce is signed they can breathe freely and relax." Unfortunately, they continued, "already signs contradict this." Communism, directed by Moscow, was already developing a post–Korean War strategy, which they thought would include the prospect of renewed focus on wresting Indochina from the French.[25] The editors of *Commonweal* perhaps captured the national mood best upon the signing of the armistice, reporting that "the only cheers in Times Square armistice night were muted and self-conscious, prompted by the newsreel cameraman. The city streets," they continued, "were otherwise silent." In short, they wrote, the Korean War ended as emotionlessly as it had been fought for the previous year. This did not mean that people were indifferent to the ending of the conflict; it just meant that Americans had simply "learned to live with war" and were skeptical about the armistice. But that was probably for the best, they concluded, because the Cold War implied "many more years of inconclusive struggle, and there will be few occasions to cheer or parade."[26] Fittingly, given the lack of national enthusiasm, they reported, "Peace in Korea" was not even the lead editorial in that week's issue.

More specific to the problems that would remain in Asia after the armistice, *Commonweal* wrote of the need for the United States to contain China as it had already committed itself to containing the Soviet Union. After all, they wrote, "China is now the major power in Asia. It is rigidly unified and growing in industrial and military strength." While this may have been a considerable exaggeration of Chinese strength at the time, the editors thought it conceivable that China would next project its newfound power in Indochina, Burma, Thailand, or Formosa. If it did, "she will have to be met again with power." And even if China remained outwardly peaceful, there would remain the difficult diplomatic issues of recognition and admittance to the UN. In short, "we have stopped warring with Communist China," they wrote. "We now have the infinitely more difficult problem of living in the same world with her."[27]

According to the *New Leader*, the Korean War was, from its beginning, "but one phase of an all-Asia war and of a world war, in which both hot and cold weapons are being used." That war, continued the editors, would not magically end when negotiators signed a paper in Panmunjom. Rather, it would end only "when Communist totalitarianism is forever banished from the earth."[28] The Cold War would indeed last until Soviet totalitarianism imploded under the weight of its own contradictions, but not before the superpowers would fight more and deadlier proxy wars than Korea. This cold assessment of the significance (or lack thereof) of the Korean truce, then, proved to be quite accurate. William Henry Chamberlin added, in the midst of the negotiations, that even if the communists were to drop their "insolent and preposterous demands," there was "little reason to believe that an armistice would be followed by a genuine peace." Just as likely, thought Chamberlin, was "some new act of aggression elsewhere in Asia."[29] In other words, the guns falling silent in Korea would mean little in the larger context of the Cold War.

The conservatives at *The Freeman* agreed. The dream of lasting peace, they argued, was out of reach due to the "continuing nightmare" that was communist global strategy. Marxism, according to the editors, simply did not allow for what Khrushchev would later call peaceful coexistence.

"Peace" to a communist, they continued, "is merely the continuation of war by other means"—war that "cannot possibly end for any committed Marxist until the last bourgeois has surrendered or died." Thus, they concluded, even though they would be glad when the killing of Americans stopped in Korea, they could not bring themselves to believe an armistice would amount to much in the grand scheme of the Cold War. Indeed, if the United States maintained a strong military presence in Formosa and Japan to deter future Chinese aggressions, they thought, that would do "far more to keep the peace in the Far East than a whole dictionary of words poured out on paper."[30]

THE SIGNIFICANCE OF THE WAR

There was broad agreement, then, that the end of the Korean War would not bring with it the end of the frightening standoff between communism and the West. But what larger effects *did* the war have? And how would the truce impact those developments? Interestingly, the motley collection of liberals at the *New Republic, Commonweal*, and *New Leader* all had similar answers to these questions. At times, these three journals all claimed that the Korean War awoke the United States from its post–World War II slumber, as though Korea was a splash of Cold-War reality to the face, prompting a dramatic rearmament program not only at home but also via its allies overseas. At the same time, the contributors to all three publications worried that the end of the war would bring with it the tendency for the West to breathe easily, lower its guard, and relax as though the Red threat had dissipated.

As early as the summer of 1951, just as truce talks were beginning at Kaesong, the *New Republic* was proclaiming that "Korea has helped to waken the democratic world from its slumbers," in that "it has accelerated the tempo of preparedness in Europe and the U.S."[31] By 1952, they were no less grandiose in their pronouncements about the lasting significance of the war.

> It is not too early to calculate the historical consequences of Korea; there are three in particular whose importance can't be exaggerated: It has removed the doubt that the West would tolerate further Russian aggression. *We* won't. It has put America in a posture of defense so that, for the first time in history, American strength will be available immediately if war breaks out without any two-year wait—a condition that might have averted World Wars I and II. Thirdly, we and Russia now know almost certainly, that any similar act of aggression will precipitate full-scale war.[32]

In other words, Korea had changed everything. Both sides now understood the full import of their actions. Before Korea, all of this was guesswork. Thus, "Truman's intervention in Korea gives him an important place in history despite all his faults," wrote the editors. "A major precedent is set." The world now knew that the United States would simply not tolerate further communist aggression on the Korean model. More importantly, the Soviets now knew that another Korea would spark World War III, and that this war would involve the use of America's "new small-type A-bombs, and maybe big ones as well." The Korean episode, then, "probably rules out a big war occurring through accident or misunderstanding."[33] Since the United States had drawn such a bright line in the sand, ran their argument, if the Soviets started a new war, it would be because they purposefully chose to do so. Korea had simplified the rules of the game.

In the pages of *Commonweal*, readers could find expressions of pride and satisfaction at how the United States had responded to the Korean crisis. Even as the truce talks seemed mired in the muck of 1952, the editors proclaimed the following about the significance of the Korean War:

> In the meantime we should not discount what has been accomplished in Korea. At the very least the challenge successfully met there wakened the nation to the extent of its peril. Our soldiers have fought to a standstill enemy forces which were numerically vastly superior, and by our stand we have served effective notice on the Soviet that in the future there will be no Munichs, no Czechoslovakias, no cheap victories. All this adds up to a major accomplishment, regardless of the ultimate outcome of the Korean truce negotiations.[34]

For the editors of *Commonweal*, Korea was a turning point in the Cold War because it demonstrated American willingness to stand up to aggression in a way that the Western powers could not or would not do in the 1930s. No matter what happened around the conference table, they were sure this alone would modify communist behavior. Once agreement was finally reached on the repatriation issue, more than a year later, they looked back over the three years of war, suggesting that Korea "may go down in history as one of the great Communist mistakes of the post-war period," since its effect was to awaken the free world to the reality of the communist danger.[35]

David J. Dallin, contributing editor and weekly columnist in the *New Leader*, we should recall, could scarcely contain his excitement at the outset of the war. He saw Korea as the beginning of a new chapter in history. Communist expansion would stop, and a Western crusade of liberation would begin. Though events did not play out quite as he might have liked, he nonetheless expressed satisfaction toward the end of the war. "Three years ago," he wrote, "the U.S. policy of containment was in its infancy and, prosecuted half-heartedly, could not challenge Soviet military superiority." But now, he crowed, "the military power of the U.S. is much greater than it was, and is allied with the military forces of other nations." He was especially pleased that America had taken steps to rearm Germany and Japan as bulwarks against communist expansion. Soon, Western power would be "so formidable that no sane enemy would dare challenge it." In conclusion, he wrote, communism's "days of easy expansion are over."[36] As the United States started down the path of permanent military readiness, history had begun a new chapter, indeed.

Even as the liberals at the *New Republic*, *Commonweal*, and *New Leader* were assessing the significance of the war as that of a grand awakening, they also worried deeply about the possibility of the truce ushering in a new period of drowsiness. "Peace in Korea," editorialized the *New Republic*, "could be a disaster for the entire democratic world. This could happen if we went back to sleep, once the fighting had stopped." The communists, after all, would not suddenly abandon their long-term struggle to advance their system through means other than open warfare. Thus, if Congress reacted to peace by slashing defense and foreign aid spending, wrote the editors, "victory in Korea would amount to worldwide defeat."[37] Two years later, as the prospect of peace in Korea drew near, they echoed this sentiment, writing, "We sigh at the prospect" of the United States taking its foot off the gas of preparedness. "Europeans who six months ago feared we would precipitate a third world war may soon be aghast at Congressional demands to cut taxes and bring the boys home."[38] The liberals at the *New Republic* were obviously committed to the maintenance of a robust global line of containment.

As were the Catholic liberals at *Commonweal*. In the run-up to the 1952 presidential election, they warned that a promise to slash military expenditures might lead to electoral victory. If this occurred, they continued, "In this way the Soviet could gain with soft words what it has been unable to accomplish with arms." However tempting it may be, the United States must not forget that "having the Soviet as a determined adversary is like wrestling an octopus; you can never lower your guard because you never know where the next blow is coming from." Put more directly, for the United States to let down its guard in the aftermath of a truce in Korea would be folly. Weakness, they warned, "is the road, not to peace, but to war. Failure to arm would simply invite further Soviet aggression."[39] The editors of the

New Leader agreed. The armistice, they wrote, was almost certain to lead America to ease up on its determination to rearm against the communist threat. Korea, they reminded their readers, occurred when Americans least expected it. Who could say that Stalin—then still drawing breath—wouldn't strike elsewhere the moment the United States let its guard down again? "The armistice," they concluded boldly, "will impose greater demands upon our intelligence, patience and will than has the war."[40]

As soon as MacArthur was fired and it became clear that the United States would seek a negotiated settlement to the war based on a divided Korea, the contributors to America's political opinion journals began to take up the question of what the war had accomplished. At the end of the day, would the ambiguous outcome of the war be a victory or a defeat for the United States? On this question emerged one of the sharpest divides between liberals and conservatives concerning the ultimate significance of the war. Quite simply, liberals considered the outcome a victory for collective security and containment. Conservatives, on the other hand, considered the war a humiliating defeat for the United States and a demonstration of the futility of collective action. Indeed, one of the lessons of Korea, for conservatives, was that the United States should thenceforward "go it alone" on the world stage.

Early on in the truce talks, the *New Republic* editorialized that, once a truce agreement was realized, "The UN would have won the first great test of a collective attempt to halt aggression." Elsewhere, the editors wrote that the UN "had thrashed the first big effort at organized aggression since it was founded." This reality, they wrote, stood in contrast to the conclusions of those like General MacArthur and Senator Taft, who insisted that there could be no satisfactory outcome except a complete military victory over the entire communist world, that the Korean War was a defeat for America, and that the UN was, in Taft's words, "a total failure."[41] Merely preserving the Republic of Korea, for the liberals at the *New Republic*, "will realize the aims of the UN which set out to repel the aggression." On the other side of the coin, they continued, it was a "major defeat" for the Chinese and Korean communists.[42] They held to this view as the war drew to its close in the summer of 1953, writing that the final outcome of the war would be a "victory for the UN."[43] This was not merely the view of the *New Republic*, but of every major liberal political opinion journal. Even *The Nation* and the *New Leader* found common ground on this point! *The Nation* editorialized that a truce that preserved South Korea would be "incontrovertible evidence that collective resistance to aggression does work." Where the League of Nations had failed, the American-led UN had succeeded.[44] The *New Leader* agreed, editorializing that, "for the UN, the armistice will represent a victory." An act of "calculated aggression was," they continued, "for the first time in modern history, halted in its tracks by swift and united action."[45]

Over at *Commonweal*, collective security was also the theme. The West's response to Korea in 1950, wrote the editors, was the exact opposite of that to Ethiopia in 1935. Korea had given the free world "some real measure of promise that as it grows stronger, it need not again flee in fright from another Ethiopia to another Munich and on to another ultimate reckoning." Korea, then, was a symbol of the new hope that the UN represented. "We did not fight in Korea a war to end all wars," they wrote. Rather, Korea represented merely the first engagement "fought in behalf of a world community whose faint contours" could only begin to be glimpsed.[46] Indeed, Korea marked "a turning point in the concept of the free world's unity." Probably no soldiers in history, they grandly proclaimed, "have had a more significant role than the UN troops in Korea." After all, they were fighting for "the peaceful ideal that is incarnated in the United Nations organization—and their sufferings will bear fruit for the world. . . . By their sacrifices—it is not beyond belief—the world has been spared the horror of a third world war."[47] The Korean War was not just a victory for collective security. It was a victory for world peace.

The editors of *Commonweal* continued to pursue these themes as the truce talks progressed, writing in 1952 of the "high principles" and "noble cause" for which American boys were fighting in Korea. The cause had for its object, they wrote, "nothing less than the ending of aggression in the world. To suffer wounds, maltreatment or death for such a cause is worthy of America's greatest war heroes." Adding a human touch to the otherwise abstract political debate surrounding the war, they hoped such a reminder "can provide an answer to those soldiers' families that are on the wrack these anxious days."[48] And in their final editorial about the war, they paid further tribute to those who fought it—the men who "proved that collective security is more than a slogan, and that honor lives. For that reason, this war may prove, in the eyes of history, to have been the most crucial event of the mid-century." In the end, they concluded, "our soldiers held not only the four hundred mile line in Korea, but the line around the world which divides the military power of Communism from the non-Communist world. It was a worthy cause. It was fought with bravery, surely, and with decency."[49]

To liberals across the board, then, Korea was regarded as a victory—a victory for collective security and against aggression; a victory for the maintenance of peace in the world instead of the kind of appeasement that led to the slaughter of tens of millions in the Second World War; and a victory for the UN in fulfilling its general purposes and specific resolutions, especially in light of the League of Nations' earlier failings. The conservatives at *The Freeman* and the *American Mercury*, on the other hand, did not hold back when it came to proclaiming Korea an ignominious defeat for both the United States and the UN. Whereas liberals, even of the hawkish variety, hailed the outcome of the Korean War as a shining example of collective security in action, conservatives scoffed at such notions, arguing that the failure of UN intervention in Korea was undeniably self-evident.

Korea, editorialized *The Freeman*, "has been as discouraging a performance for the UN as Manchuria and Abyssinia were for the League of Nations." Future historians, posited the editors, might well look back on Korea as the beginning of the end of the world's illusions about the collective security capabilities of the UN. The editors complained that only a few UN members other than the United States contributed anything to the fight, and those that did gave only a token amount of support. What was most infuriating to the editors, though, was that those nations that failed to contribute to the war effort were often the very same who consistently blocked and frustrated American attempts to take decisive action, such as unleashing the Chinese Nationalists, that they thought could have ended the military stalemate. Nations like India, for example, which, they complained, had failed to put a single man or gun on the front, "were most vociferous . . . in their pressure for appeasement." The editors breezily dismissed the concerns of such nations as nothing more than "wild talk about the danger of unloosing a third world war." They could only conclude that it was high time that internationalism stopped meaning "that other nations are always right." Put another way, since the UN had "little if any value as an instrument for opposing aggression," perhaps the "soundest lesson from the whole unhappy Korean experience is that American security depends first on its own strength."[50]

The Freeman's attack on the UN continued right up to the eve of the truce signing, when the editors wrote, "The very title United Nations has become for some well-meaning Americans a mystical fetish, blinding their eyes to the utter impotence of the UN." During the three years of war in Korea, they continued, the position of the UN was one of "confusion, of divided counsels, of almost grotesque helplessness." Again they singled out India for contributing nothing to the fight against aggression "except an ambulance corps and an infinite amount of defeatist backseat driving." Instead of having fought under the auspices of the UN, they wrote, the United States would have been much better off partnering with those actually committed to the fight, namely, the South Koreans, Japanese, and Chinese Nationalists. In conclusion, wrote the editors,

> The fiasco in Korea should be the last. Never again should Americans be asked to give their lives as part of an unequal bargain in which the Americans do the fighting and dying and the UN does the appeasing and capitulating. Let the next war, if Communist aggression makes such a war necessary, be fought by the U.S. on straightforward grounds of national security and self-defense, with as many allies as we can persuade to join in a common cause, but without the silly pretense and serious practical disadvantages of posing as champions of an organization that was hopelessly divided from the moment when it was set up.[51]

Yes, the Soviet veto posed a major problem for future collective action against another communist aggression, but saying that the UN was an abject failure on the scale of the League of Nations was an incredible statement at the end of the Korean War. This argument, made by conservatives, reflected their predisposition to oppose categorically any foreign policy based on multilateralism. As such, while these conservatives cannot rightly be labeled "isolationists," as their liberal contemporaries often tried to portray them, they were most certainly *unilateralist* in their foreign policy.

The success or failure of collective security via the UN aside, conservative journals also summed up the Korean War as a defeat specific to the United States. At the conclusion of the war, the editors of *The Freeman* asked, "What have we gained as the result of more than three years of war, of the expenditure of billions, of 140,000 American casualties?" Would Americans in 1953, if they had to do it all over again, support taking the same course of action that Truman had led them down in 1950, only to have Korea remain divided and Mao still in power? "The question," they wrote, "answers itself." After all, they argued, the United States had failed to halt communist aggression. Indeed, South Korea seemed no more secure than it was prior to the North Korean invasion. As a result of the American failure to unify Korea by force, in other words, "the threat hanging over the independence of Korea is greater than ever." What was worse, *Chinese* aggression was neither stopped nor adequately punished. To the contrary, they asserted, Mao had every right to feel that he had won a big victory. What was more, "the front is some two hundred miles [further] south than it was when the Chinese swarmed over the Yalu and attacked in force in Nov 1950. And not a bomb has fallen in anger on Chinese air bases in nearby Manchuria or on military and industrial targets in China proper." *The Freeman*'s final word on the Korean War was as follows:

> As one looks back on the tangled Korean story and forward into the dark and uncertain prospect in the Far East one feels that there is a very strong case for General MacArthur's crisp epigram: "There is no substitute for victory"—at least when one is fighting against barbarians. The wrong turn was taken when the U.S., under the pressure of timid and wavering so-called allies, failed to respond to the challenge of the Chinese Communist attack by hitting back at every proper military target in Manchuria and China proper with all the air power at our command.

In looking back over the three years of war in Korea, they concluded, "Americans have no reason to feel proud or happy."[52]

The *American Mercury* was even harsher in its assessment, if more poetic and thoroughly steeped in the mythos of American exceptionalism. As early as the beginning of the peace talks in 1951, the editors of the *Mercury* were ready to proclaim Korea a historic defeat for the once-great United States. "Some future [G]ibbon, reflecting on the decline of the United States of America," they prophesied, may write:[53]

> The eighth of July, 1951, was a pivotal date in the history of the republic. Up to that date, for one-hundred seventy-five years, America had known grandeur and victory. In all its wars the nation had forced its enemies—the enemies of mankind—to sue for peace. A white flag had never been substituted for the Stars-and-Stripes. . . .
>
> Yet, in a scant six years after 1945, so vitiated had been the nation by Communist propaganda, and so inept had its leadership become, that the republic was willing to accept its first defeat. After an expenditure of twenty thousand lives and twenty billion dollars, after reducing Korea to dust, Americans were willing to send white-flag-carrying emissaries into an enemy-held city seeking peace terms. The nation which had become the responsible custodian of the Western heritage, the nation whose cause had become the cause of mankind, this nation was now willing to withdraw before the barbarians.
>
> . . . And from that date on . . . America, like Carthage after Hannibal had failed to sack Rome, knew nothing else but defeat.[54]

CONCLUSION

No one can pretend to know with any certainty, of course, what "some future Gibbon" will write about the United States in the twentieth century. But at least from our perspective in the early twenty-first century, the beginning of the truce talks in Korea in 1951 do not seem to have been as historic—or as portending of imperial decline—as the editors of the *American Mercury* foresaw. The Korean War, as it turned out, was neither a harbinger of a glorious future of world unity in the face of aggression, as liberals might have hoped, nor the sign of weakness, decline, and defeat that conservatives feared. In terms of checking overt military aggression and containing communism, however, the war was an unmistakable success. It is true, as conservatives loved to point out, that the United States failed to unify Korea by force, but this was never the *primary* purpose of the American or UN intervention. A unified, independent, and pro-Western Korea would have been icing on the containment cake, as it were, but once the Chinese intervened, this short-lived secondary goal was rightly dropped due to the Truman administration's fear of being sucked into, in General Bradley's words, "the wrong war."

In any case, the debate outlined here sheds light on the divisions of political opinion in America in the early 1950s. For left liberals, containing communism was the proper course of action, even if it meant more "little wars" like Korea. The prospect of "rollback," or a liberation crusade, say, in China, however, was horrifying to such thinkers. Hawkish liberals, on the other hand, were much more willing to entertain the notion of rolling back the communist tide and were therefore much more critical of what they took to be the Truman administration's timidity in prosecuting the Korean War. Still, at the end of the day, such liberal hawks were pleased with the outcome of the war, noting that communist aggression had indeed been checked. Finally, conservatives were insistent that the United States take the lead in liberating the mass of humanity then suffering under the communist yoke—especially in China. For them, the outcome of the war in Korea was not a success by any measure. In failing to destroy North Korea *and* communist China, the United States had essentially capitulated to aggression. Korea had become, in their view, nothing less than an Asian Munich.

What this reveals poses a twofold challenge to much of the historiography of the political and intellectual landscape of the early Cold War period in America. The consistent divisions between groups of liberals, especially on points as fundamental to Cold War policy as that of containment vs. liberation, suggest that the notion that there existed a "liberal consensus" needs to be rethought, or at least properly qualified. Moreover, the idea that there was little in the way of a coherent intellectual conservatism prior to the emergence of *National Review* in 1955 needs to be revisited as well.

Just as taking a fresh look at the Korean War can reveal much that has been overlooked about American foreign policy in the mid-twentieth century, so putting the microscope on the debate surrounding the war, as revealed in America's political opinion journals, can reveal fresh truths about the American political-intellectual tradition of the recent past.

Conclusion

The debates that took place in the pages of America's leading political opinion journals during and about the Korean War were both robust and revealing. What those debates revealed is that there was significant and consistent disagreement among liberals on a variety of issues raised by the war. The sharpest dividing line was that between left liberals, like the editorial staffs at *The Nation* and the *New Republic*, and hawkish liberals, especially those at the *New Leader*. The liberals at *Commonweal* ranged back and forth over this dividing line, but more often than not came down closer to the left. In any case, the hawkish liberals at the *New Leader* often favored foreign policy positions that bore a greater resemblance to those of the hard-line conservatives at *The Freeman* than to those of their fellow liberals. This division further complicates the idea of a coherent "liberal consensus" among American opinion-makers during the early Cold War.

Yes, most liberals thought that Soviet-style communism was a threat to American interests, but beyond this general principle, there was little about which left liberals and hawkish liberals agreed. Left liberals, for example, generally supported the strategy of containment as defined by George Kennan and implemented by Harry Truman, while hawkish liberals tended to hold such a passive strategy of combating communism in contempt. Such liberal hawks instead favored a strategic posture that more closely resembled a liberation crusade. This split manifested itself during the Korean War in two primary ways: the debate over whether to unify Korea by force or accept that country's indefinite division, and the debate over whether to carry the Korean War to China with the aim of overthrowing the regime of Mao Tse-tung and replacing it with that of Chiang Kai-shek. Left liberals and hawkish liberals did not even agree, moreover, about whether American anticommunism should be universal or case-by-case. On this point, the most striking example is once again liberals' divergent views of Chinese communism. To hawkish liberals, a communist was a communist, and the Chinese "aggression" in Korea was all the proof that was required. Left liberals, however, were more sympathetic to the view that Chinese communism represented, to some degree, the legitimate aspirations of the impoverished Asian masses, and that communist China was not necessarily a natural and permanent ally of the Soviet Union. As such, they argued—to the horror of liberal hawks—that the United States ought to be willing to make certain concessions to China, including diplomatic recognition, which would carry with it the Chinese seat at the UN.

In addition to shedding new light upon the divisions within the so-called liberal consensus, an examination of the "forgotten debate" about the Korean War in America's political opinion journals also leads us to a fresh appreciation of the position of the conservative movement in the early 1950s. Far from being disorganized and fragmented, the conservative movement, as represented in *The Freeman* and the *American Mercury*, was already blending together the various strands of conservatism: libertarianism, anticommunism, and traditionalism. Of course, our examination has focused primarily on conservative anticommunism, but, even so, we have seen that there was a uniquely conservative brand of anticommunism that often went beyond the hawkishness of the liberal *New Leader*. Specifically, conservative writers were much more willing to contemplate general war against the communist world, including a war of liberation against communist China. In the aftermath of the MacArthur firing, for example, even hawkish liberals retreated a bit from their most bellicose anti-Chinese pronouncements. Conservatives, by contrast, doubled down on MacArthurism, arguing as forcefully as ever that any policy aims other than the unification of Korea and an offensive war against China would amount to the most cowardly kind of appeasement.

This analysis has focused on the debates that played out in America's leading political opinion journals during and about the Korean War. There are some interesting and important issues it does not address, however, which would be fertile areas for future study. For example, while the New Left did not emerge until the 1960s, could its roots be traced back to the Korean War? As the war was winding down, I. F. Stone published *The Hidden History of the Korean War* in 1952 and also began producing a leftist newsletter, *I. F. Stone's Weekly*, in 1953. At the time, Stone's work was either ignored by mainstream liberals or, in the case of the *New Republic*'s Michael Straight, summarily dismissed as conspiratorial to the point of unreasoned paranoia.[1] By the end of the war, William Appleman Williams, another eventual hero of the New Left, had published his doctoral dissertation, *American-Russian Relations, 1781–1947*, and also began contributing to publications such as *The Nation*, in which he began making his now familiar argument that it was the United States, not Stalinist Russia, that was primarily to blame for the Cold War.[2] Neither Stone nor Williams enjoyed much attention or support in the early to mid-1950s, yet both would provide inspiration for the New Left in the 1960s. While the emergence, during the latter stages of the Korean War, of these two mavericks of the left provides further evidence for the fragmented nature of liberalism during the early Cold War, it also points us toward the need for further exploration of the 1950s roots of the leftist movements of the 1960s.[3]

Just as the roots of the New Left can, to some degree, be traced back to the Korean War, so too can the roots of another movement that took even longer to emerge: neoconservatism. Intellectual historians John Ehrman and Richard Pells have each argued that the Cold War liberalism of the 1950s and early 1960s introduced the attitudes that informed the rhetoric of neoconservatism in the 1970s and 1980s. As such, some of the more hawkish liberal writers profiled in this book, such as William Henry Chamberlin and David J. Dallin, can perhaps be viewed as direct forebears of the foreign policy neoconservatives that first coalesced under the Reagan administration and reached their zenith during the presidency of George W. Bush. More generally, it could be argued that the divisions between left liberals and hawkish liberals during the Korean War prefigured the liberal-neoconservative split that took place in the 1970s. Thus, Ehrman and Pells's argument—that the true significance of the intellectuals of the 1950s "lies as much in their legacy to their successors as in the issues they raised in their own era"[4]—points the way toward further research that could more directly tie the personalities and thinking of the hawkish liberals of the 1950s to the neocons of the 1970s and beyond.

In addition to future research that would seek to connect the debates detailed in this book to the social, political, and intellectual movements of the 1960s, 1970s, and beyond, there are other areas of inquiry that could provide further evidence for my conclusions by elaborating on some of the themes raised herein. One area ripe for elaboration is that of the liberation vs. containment debate. While issues raised by the Korean War, such as whether Korea ought to be reunified by force and whether the United States should launch an offensive war against China, formed a significant part of this debate, much of the discourse concerning such grand Cold War strategy was too abstract and general to fall under the conceptual umbrella of the Korean War. Issues such as what, exactly, conservatives and hawkish liberals meant by a "strategy of liberation" would be worth exploring, for example. Did this necessarily mean that the United States should go on the offensive militarily? Or did it mean simply that the United States should launch some vague diplomatic, political, and/or propaganda offensive? And if the latter, was this necessarily inconsistent with the Point Four–style development assistance strategy favored even by left liberals? Moreover, what can we learn about the states of liberalism and conservatism by more closely examining the personal attacks launched by conservatives and hawkish liberals against such personalities as President Truman and Secretaries of State Marshall and Acheson for their "softness" and "appeasement"?

There are also several important debates that arose tangentially to the war in Korea that would be worthy of further investigation. One of these involves the differing attitudes toward America's international relationships, both with individual countries and with institutions like the UN. Countries like Britain and India, for instance, were some of the favorite whipping boys of conservatives and hawkish liberals. This included leaders like Clement Attlee and Aneurin Bevan of Great Britain, as well as Jawaharlal Nehru of India. For publications like *The Freeman* and the *New Leader*, such countries and such leaders were dangerously sympathetic to Stalin and, what was worse, exerted far too much influence over American policymakers. Left liberals, on the other hand, especially those at *The Nation*, often came to the defense of British and Indian foreign policy, arguing that those countries provided an essential restraint on a sometimes overzealous and immature American statesmanship. As for the UN, most liberals tended to view the international organization as the last best hope of humanity, while conservatives sneeringly dismissed such notions as the pathetic talk of half-redeemed former communists who had never given up their naive dreams of one-worldism.

The Korean War stands as one of the least remembered yet most significant events of twentieth-century American history. And the debates that raged in the pages of America's leading opinion journals during and about that war reveal much that has been similarly overlooked by many historians of American intellectual and political culture. Not only do these debates help us further explore the nuances of the "liberal consensus" during the early Cold War, but they also help us understand more deeply the roots of the modern conservative movement. All of that said, I think it is important to remember not only this "forgotten debate" but also what that debate was ultimately about. It is all too easy to look back on wars of the past and draw academic conclusions far removed from the killing and dying that occurred on the battlefield. I am glad, then, that I received a personal reminder about this when I first began working on this project.

About ten years ago, while visiting family near Punta Gorda, Florida, I accidentally stumbled upon an inconspicuous little place called the Military Heritage Museum. I decided to step inside to see what it might have to offer a young scholar such as myself, then a doctoral student and adjunct professor. As I paid my entry fee, I noticed the elderly man behind the counter wore a hat indicating that he was a Korean War veteran. I quickly struck up a conversation with him, eager to find out during what part of the war he had served and what his experience had been. He had served, he told me, at Pork Chop Hill. As our conversation turned to the subject of my research, I did my best to explain that I was interested in examining the various aspects of the public debate about the war. He seemed a bit puzzled by this and exclaimed, "What was there to debate? Men were dying over there!" I gave him the example of the debate about the Truman-MacArthur controversy, and he seemed to understand more clearly. But his initial reaction stuck with me. The subject of this work is, after all, at the end of the day, war. More than 30,000 Americans, nearly 140,000 South Koreans, more than 200,000 North Koreans, and hundreds of thousands of Chinese were killed in action during the three years of war in Korea. As many as 2.5 million civilians may have lost their lives as well. And then there are the millions more who were either wounded in action or who served and returned home after the war with the emotional and psychological scars that only war can provide. It is to all those American GIs, war-weary Chinese "volunteers," and countless Korean men, women, and children who suffered or died as a result of this "forgotten war" that I dedicate this analysis. I hope it serves as one small contribution through which the Korean War can become more readily remembered.

Notes

INTRODUCTION

1. Among historians, the idea of a postwar liberal consensus was first popularized in Godfrey Hodgson's 1976 work, *America in Our Time: From World War II to Nixon: What Happened and Why* (Princeton, NJ: Princeton University Press, 1976). Since then, the idea has been debated, qualified, and challenged. Still, as Robert Mason and Iwan Morgan have recently pointed out, the idea stubbornly retains its utility, especially as we contrast the relatively centrist politics of the postwar era with today's hyperpolarized landscape. See Mason and Morgan, eds., *The Liberal Consensus Reconsidered: American Politics and Society in the Postwar Era* (Gainesville: University Press of Florida, 2017).

2. Andrew Preston has argued that the liberal consensus in foreign policy, more precisely the "Cold War consensus," actually only lasted 1946–1949, after which the Chinese Revolution and Korean War left Americans divided on how best to confront global communism. In short, Preston argues that Korea, not Vietnam a decade and a half later, marked the end of the consensus era. The present analysis, while not explicitly making the same argument, can be seen as adding a bit more fuel to its fire. See Andrew Preston, "Containment: A Consensual or Contested Foreign Policy?" in Mason and Morgan, *The Liberal Consensus Reconsidered.*

3. Robert Tomes, *Apocalypse Then: American Intellectuals and the Vietnam War, 1954–1975* (New York: New York University Press, 1998), 4–5.

4. Tomes, *Apocalypse Then*, 12–13.

5. Tomes, *Apocalypse Then*, 11.

6. The seminal work on postwar conservatism remains George Nash's *The Conservative Intellectual Movement in America Since 1945* (New York: Basic Books, 1976), in which he argues that the three strands of conservatism—libertarianism, anticommunism, and traditionalism—were not ultimately unified into a coherent whole until the emergence of the *National Review.* John Moser has recently pointed out that little work has since been done to build upon the foundations laid by Nash regarding the immediate postwar period. See John Moser, *Right Turn: John T. Flynn and the Transformation of American Liberalism* (New York: New York University Press, 2005).

7. John Diggins, *Up from Communism: Conservative Odysseys in American Intellectual Development* (New York: Columbia University Press, 1994), 13, 326.

8. Diggins, *Up from Communism*, 386.

9. Of course, we now know that, while Stalin supported Kim Il-sung's adventure so long as it would be the Chinese and not the Soviets who would intervene should things go poorly for the North Koreans, the Soviet premier was not the original spring from which the invasion flowed. Nevertheless, that Stalin was the puppet master behind

the invasion was a widely shared assumption among both liberals and conservatives at the time. See Sergei Goncharov, *Uncertain Partners: Stalin, Mao, and the Korean War* (Redwood City, CA: Stanford University Press, 1993), and Jian Chen, *China's Road to the Korean War: The Making of the Sino-American Confrontation* (New York: Columbia University Press, 1996).

10. William O'Neill, *A Better World: The Great Schism: Stalinism and the American Intellectuals* (New York: Simon and Schuster, 1982), 201–202.

11. O'Neill, *A Better World*, 197.

12. See also Julian Zelizer, *Arsenal of Democracy: The Politics of National Security—From World War II to the War on Terrorism* (New York: Basic Books, 2010).

13. For an in-depth analysis of the Truman administration's public relations efforts during the war, as well as the evolution of the political establishment's complex relationship with the press as the war ebbed and flowed, readers should consult Steven Casey, *Selling the Korean War: Propaganda, Politics, and Public Opinion* (New York: Oxford University Press, 2008).

14. Under Maguire's ownership, the *Mercury* flirted with overt antisemitism, profascism, and White supremacy.

15. Suzanne was Senator Robert "Fighting Bob" LaFollette's second cousin. Her father, William, though not as famous as his cousin, served as a congressman from Washington from 1911 to 1919. As a young woman, Suzanne had the opportunity to work in the Capitol Hill offices of both men.

16. Some recent works have downplayed the importance of *The Freeman* in molding the modern conservative movement. See, for example, Jerome Himmelstein, *To the Right: The Transformation of American Conservatism* (Berkeley: University of California Press, 1990) and Kevin Mattson, *Rebels All!: A Short History of the Conservative Mind in Postwar America* (New Brunswick, NJ: Rutgers University Press, 2008). Other works have argued that, while *The Freeman* was small, peaking at a circulation of about 20,000—as compared to the *New Republic*'s 50,000—it was nonetheless profoundly influential. George Nash, in *The Conservative Intellectual Movement in America since 1945*, pays much attention to *The Freeman* as a forerunner to *National Review* as does William Rusher in *The Rise of the Right* (New York: W. Morrow, 1984), a memoir of his time at *National Review*. Rusher calls the founding of *The Freeman* one of the most important, if overlooked, developments of modern conservatism, suggesting that it was the "John the Baptist" to *National Review*'s Jesus. See also Alfred Regnery, *Upstream: The Ascendance of American Conservatism* (New York: Threshold Editions, 2008). Circulation figures taken from Merrill Peterson, *Coming of Age with The New Republic* (Columbia: University of Missouri Press, 1999) and Theodore Peterson, *Magazines in the Twentieth Century* (Urbana: University of Illinois Press, 1964).

CHAPTER 1. THE OUTBREAK OF THE WAR

1. As noted in the Introduction, we now know that Stalin was hardly the mastermind behind the attack. Rather, the Soviet leader only reluctantly gave Kim Il-Sung permission to launch the invasion.

2. William Costello, "Improvisation in Korea," *New Republic*, July 10, 1950, 13–15.

3. "Korea: Two Kinds of Defeatism," *New Republic*, August 7, 1950, 5; "Peace Aims for Korea," *New Republic*, September 25, 1950, 3–4.

4. Harold Ickes, "Once More We Fight for Time," *New Republic*, July 31, 1950, 17.

5. Percy Winner, "Why Europe Hangs Back," *New Republic*, December 11, 1950, 12–14.

6. Julio Alvarez del Vayo, "Storm over Africa," *The Nation*, July 8, 1950, 29–32. The issues raised by del Vayo's allusion to China and Chiang Kai-shek will be explored in full detail in chapter 4.

7. Del Vayo, "Political War," *The Nation*, July 22, 1950, 73–74.

8. "The Shape of Things," *The Nation*, July 1, 1950, 1–3.

9. "The Shape of Things," *The Nation*, July 22, 1950, 69–71.

10. Freda Kirchwey, "A Plan for Korean Peace," *The Nation*, August 26, 1950, 177–178; Vera Micheles Dean, "No War—but Civil Strife," *The Nation*, September 16, 1950, 242–244; "The Shape of Things," *The Nation*, September 23, 1950, 257–259.

11. Alexander Werth, "Notes from Paris," *The Nation*, September 30, 1950, 287–288.

12. Freda Kirchwey, "Democracy's Way Out," *The Nation*, December 16, 1950, 622–625, 645.

13. "Behind Korea," *New Leader*, July 8, 1950, 2, 30.

14. Robert T. Oliver, "Behind the War in Korea," *New Leader*, July 15, 1950, 6–7. Again, it should be recalled that, contrary to the conventional wisdom of 1950, Stalin did not directly order the attack on South Korea but only reluctantly gave permission to Kim Il-Sung to launch the invasion.

15. Jonathan Stout, "Korean Sell-Out After Victory?" *New Leader*, October 21, 1950, 15.

16. "Chiang Kai-Rhee," *The Freeman*, November 13, 1950, 102–103.

17. "The Fortnight," *The Freeman*, December 11, 1950, 163–165.

18. David J. Dallin, "Unite the Two Koreas," *New Leader*, July 8, 1950, 2–4.

19. See Robert T. Oliver, "Behind the War in Korea," *New Leader*, July 15, 1950, 6–7; Hans Kohn, "Korea and After," *New Leader*, September 2, 1950, 8–10; Harold Lavine, "South Korea's GIs—How Good Are They?" *New Leader*, April 16, 1951, 2–5; and "For a New Far Eastern Policy," *New Leader*, April 23, 1951, 2–3, 30.

20. William Henry Chamberlin, "We Must Learn from Korea," September 30, 1950, 19; Chamberlin, "June 25: Crucial Anniversary," *New Leader*, July 2, 1951, 21; Chamberlin, "Some Lessons of Korea," *New Leader*, July 7, 1952, 7.

21. William Henry Chamberlin, "Korea Must Set the Pattern," *New Leader*, October 30, 1950, 19.

22. William Henry Chamberlin, "Germany: Another Korea?" *The Freeman*, October 16, 1950, 41–44.

23. William Henry Chamberlin, "Korea Stalemate Can't Bring Peace," *New Leader*, November 24, 1952, 19.

24. Isaac Don Levine, "Plain Talk and Amerasia," *The Freeman*, October 2, 1950, 20–22.

25. Isaac Don Levine, "Plain Talk and Amerasia," *The Freeman*, October 2, 1950, 20–22.

26. Samuel J. Kornhauser, "Harvest of Folly," *The Freeman*, October 16, 1950, 48–51.

27. Alice Widener, "Second Anniversary in Korea: 1. War of Appeasement," *The Freeman*, June 30, 1952, 657–659.

28. Alice Widener, "The Korean Failure," *American Mercury*, May 1952, 12–24.

29. "Issues for 1952," *American Mercury*, October 1951, 12–13; Styles Bridges, "Korea: A Positive Proposal," *American Mercury*, November 1952, 11–19.

30. Max Eastman, "Can Truman Be Educated?" *American Mercury*, December 1950, 726–732.

31. For a detailed discussion of the Chinese intervention, see chapter 2.

32. Alice Widener, "The Korean Failure," *American Mercury*, May 1952, 12–24.

33. "Gamble in Korea," *The Nation*, July 8, 1950, 23–25.

34. "Washington Wire," *New Republic*, July 10, 1950, 3–4.

35. Daniel James, "Is This It?" *New Leader*, August 5, 1950, 12–14.

36. Daniel James, "What Are the Alternatives?" *New Leader*, August 19, 1950, 16–19.

37. "Survival of the Fittest," *New Leader*, August 19, 1950, 30.

38. "Korea's Birthday," *New Leader*, August 13, 1951, 22–23.

39. Erik von Kuehnelt-Leddihn, "The Constant Shadow," *Commonweal*, July 7, 1950, 311–312.

40. "Fiddling?" *Commonweal*, July 14, 1950, 333.

41. "Politics as Usual," *Commonweal*, July 21, 1950, 355–356.

42. David J. Dallin, "Unite the Two Koreas," *New Leader*, July 8, 1950, 2–4.

43. David J. Dallin, "Unite the Two Koreas," *New Leader*, July 8, 1950, 2–4.

44. William Henry Chamberlin, "Korea Has Rid Us of Illusions About the Kremlin's Real Aims," *New Leader*, July 8, 1950, 21.

45. David J. Dallin, "Unite the Two Koreas," *New Leader*, July 8, 1950, 2–4.

46. David J. Dallin, "Stalin Takes a Breather," *The New Leader*, September 9, 1950, 4–5.

47. David J. Dallin, "Communism Means War," *American Mercury*, October 1950, 400–409.

48. David J. Dallin, "Korea Deflates Soviet Prestige," *The New Leader*, October 30, 1950, 10.

49. Freda Kirchwey, "Democracy's Way Out," *The Nation*, December 16, 1950, 622–625, 645.

50. Freda Kirchwey, "Democracy's Way Out," *The Nation*, December 16, 1950, 622–625, 645.

51. Freda Kirchwey, "Democracy's Way Out," *The Nation*, December 16, 1950, 622–625, 645.

52. Freda Kirchwey, "America's Asian Policy," *The Nation*, July 22, 1950, 72–73.

53. "Politics as Usual," *Commonweal*, July 21, 1950, 355–356.

54. "Gamble in Korea," *The Nation*, July 8, 1950, 23–25.

55. Julio Alvarez del Vayo, "Storm Over Africa," 29–32.

56. "The Shape of Things," *The Nation*, July 22, 1950, 69–71.

57. "Behind Korea," *New Leader*, July 8, 1950, 2, 30.

58. Daniel James, "What Are the Alternatives?" *New Leader*, August 19, 1950, 16–19.

59. "Gamble in Korea," *The Nation*, July 8, 1950, 21–23.

60. "Washington Wire," *New Republic*, July 10, 1950, 3–4.

61. Henry Hazlitt, "Our Political Paralysis," *The Freeman*, December 25, 1950, 198–200.

62. "Why Truman Should Resign," *The Freeman*, January 22, 1951, 261–262.

63. Walter Trohan, "The Tragedy of George Marshall," *American Mercury*, March 1951, 267–275.

64. "Mistake Number One: Ground War in Korea," *The American Mercury*, September 1951, 17–18.

65. Samuel J. Kornhauser, "Harvest of Folly," *The Freeman*, October 16, 1950, 48–51.

66. Samuel J. Kornhauser, "Harvest of Folly," *The Freeman*, October 16, 1950, 48–51.

67. "A Vital Reform," *The Freeman*, November 27, 1950, 135–136. See also "The Fortnight," *The Freeman*, January 22, 1951, 259–260.

68. "The Fortnight," *The Freeman*, December 11, 1950, 163–165. See also Henry Hazlitt, "Our Political Paralysis," *The Freeman*, December 25, 1950, 198–200.

69. "A Vital Reform," *The Freeman*, November 27, 1950, 135–136.

70. "The Fortnight," *The Freeman*, December 11, 1950, 163–165.

71. "The Fortnight," *The Freeman*, May 21, 1951, 515–516.

72. Garet Garrett, "Decline of the American Republic," *The Freeman*, February 25, 1952, 331–333.

73. "Eight Senators Are to Be Commended," *The American Mercury*, November 1951, 18–25.

74. Clinton Rossiter, "The Constitution and Troops to Europe," *New Leader*, March 26, 1951, 12–13.

75. "The Shape of Things," *The Nation*, January 13, 1951, 21–24.

76. "Who Makes War?" *The Nation*, January 20, 1951, 52.

77. "Who Makes War?" *The Nation*, January 20, 1951, 52.

CHAPTER 2. CHINESE INTERVENTION

1. I don't include conservative voices in the debate over the thirty-eighth parallel because *The Freeman* didn't begin publication until October 1950, once that line had already been crossed, and the *American Mercury*, published monthly rather than weekly, was unable to comment in a timely fashion upon such fast-moving events.

2. Although Shelton, Kirchwey, and others at *The Nation* consistently opposed unification of Korea by force, they did at times advocate for unification by peaceful means,

namely, a ceasefire to be followed by a UN Trusteeship and nationwide elections—essentially the same as the original plan for Korea following World War II. See Freda Kirchwey, "A Plan for Korean Peace," *The Nation*, August 26, 1950, 177–178; Willard Shelton, "The President's Policy," *The Nation*, September 9, 1950, 221–222; and "The Shape of Things," *The Nation*, September 23, 1950, 257–259.

3. Willard Shelton, "Mr. Truman Takes Over," *The Nation*, July 8, 1950, 27–28.

4. Willard Shelton, "Notes from Capitol Hill," *The Nation*, August 19, 1950, 162.

5. "The Shape of Things," *The Nation*, October 7, 1950, 297–300.

6. Freda Kirchwey, "Deadly Parallel," *The Nation*, October 14, 1950, 327–329.

7. Freda Kirchwey, "Unanswered Questions," *The Nation*, October 28, 1950, 376–377.

8. "Washington Wire," *New Republic*, August 28, 1950, 3–4.

9. "Washington Wire," *New Republic*, September 25, 1950, 3–4.

10. "Peter Kihss, "The United Nations—in Korea and Later," *New Republic*, July 31, 1950, 11–14.

11. "Peace Aims for Korea," *New Republic*, September 25, 1950, 5–7.

12. Waldemar Gurian, "After Korea, What? The Time of 'Containing' the Soviets Is Gone," *Commonweal*, July 21, 1950, 359–362.

13. "Trusteeship for Korea," *Commonweal*, September 1, 1950, 501.

14. "Double Talk," *Commonweal*, September 29, 1950, 598.

15. "The Great Divide," *Commonweal*, October 6, 1950, 621.

16. David J. Dallin, "Unite the Two Koreas," *The New Leader*, July 8, 1950, 2–4.

17. Robert T. Oliver, "Behind the War in Korea," *The New Leader*, July 15, 1950, 6–7.

18. "Nehru's Peace Mission," *The New Leader*, July 29, 1950, 30–31.

19. "Unite Korea!" *The New Leader*, September 30, 1950, 30.

20. "No Yalta in Korea," *The New Leader*, October 7, 1950, 30.

21. Julio Alvarez del Vayo, "Mao Is Invited," *The Nation*, November 18, 1950, 452–453.

22. Freda Kirchwey, "Attlee vs. Truman," *The Nation*, December 9, 1950, 519–520.

23. Willard Shelton, "Gloom in Washington," *The Nation*, December 9, 1950, 523–524.

24. Archibald MacLeish, "War or Peace: The Undebated Issue," *The Nation*, December 16, 1950, 595–597.

25. "Not by Arms Alone," *The Nation*, December 23, 1950, 667–668.

26. "Spectre of World War," *New Republic*, November 27, 1950, 6.

27. "Washington Wire," *New Republic*, November 20, 1950, 3–4.

28. "The New War in Korea," *New Republic*, December 11, 1950, 5–6.

29. "Washington Wire," *New Republic*, December 25, 1950, 3–4.

30. "Blood, Sweat, and Tears," *Commonweal*, December 15, 1950, 243–245.

31. "Through the Asian Crystal Ball," *Commonweal*, December 22, 1950, 269–270.

32. "Huffing and Puffing," *Commonweal*, December 8, 1950, 222.

33. "Blood, Sweat, and Tears," *Commonweal*, December 15, 1950, 243–245.

34. "Huffing and Puffing," *Commonweal*, December 8, 1950, 222; "Stampede," *Commonweal*, December 15, 1950, 246.

35. "The Bomb," *Commonweal*, December 15, 1950, 245.

36. "Blood, Sweat, and Tears," *Commonweal*, December 15, 1950, 243–245.

37. "Are We at War?" *The New Leader*, November 13, 1950, 30–31.

38. David J. Dallin, "Asia or Europe?" *The New Leader*, November 27, 1950, 14–15.

39. William E. Bohn, "The Communist Enemy Within," *The New Leader*, December 11, 1950, 5. Just as the writers profiled here had erred in their assessment that Stalin ordered the North Korean invasion in the first place, so too were they mistaken that Stalin was directly behind the intervention of the Chinese "volunteers" in Korea.

40. See "The 'New War,'" *New Leader*, December 4, 1950, 30; "The World Situation," *New Leader*, December 11, 1950, 30–31.

41. Ralph de Toledano, "Lament for a Generation," *The Freeman*, December 25, 1950, 214–216.

42. Lawrence R. Brown, "Why Stalin Needs Asia," *The Freeman*, January 22, 1951, 271–274.

43. William Henry Chamberlin, "Appeasement is Suicide," *The New Leader*, December 25, 1950, 20.

44. William Henry Chamberlin, "Appeasement is Suicide," *The New Leader*, December 25, 1950, 20.

45. William Henry Chamberlin, "The Thing to Fear Is Fear Itself," *The New Leader*, February 12, 1951, 19.

46. William Henry Chamberlin, "Can We Escape from Victory?" *The Freeman*, April 23, 1951, 465–468.

47. Forrest Davis, "Senator Taft's New Deal," *The Freeman*, December 25, 1950, 201–203.

48. William Bradford Huie, "Who Gave Russia the A-Bomb?" *American Mercury*, April 1951, 413–421.

49. Freda Kirchwey, "Threat out of China," *The Nation*, November 11, 1950, 423–425.

50. Andrew Roth, "Asia's New Power," *The Nation*, December 2, 1950, 504–506.

51. Freda Kirchwey, "Attlee vs. Truman," *The Nation*, December 9, 1950, 519–520. Kirchwey is here referring to MacArthur's assurances to President Truman at Wake Island in October 1950 that the Chinese would not intervene and, if they did, would suffer one of the greatest slaughters in military history.

52. "Are We at War?" *The New Leader*, November 13, 1950, 30–31.

53. "The 'New War,'" *New Leader*, December 4, 1950.

54. "Are We at War?" *The New Leader*, November 13, 1950, 30–31.

55. William E. Bohn, "The Communist Enemy Within," *The New Leader*, December 11, 1950, 5.

56. "The World Situation," *New Leader*, December 11, 1950, 30–31.

57. Forrest Davis, "Senator Taft's New Deal," *The Freeman*, December 25, 1950, 201–203. The debate over Owen Lattimore and the "agrarian reformer" thesis will be explored in detail in chapter 4.

58. "The Shape of Things," *The Nation*, January 6, 1951, 1–4.

59. In 1949, after being defeated by Mao's communist forces on the Chinese mainland

and the subsequent creation of the People's Republic of China, Chiang Kai-shek and the American-backed Kuomintang fled to the island of Formosa, where they enjoyed a) de facto control of that island despite international agreement that Formosa was part of China and b) continued control of the Chinese seat at the UN, including a permanent seat on the Security Council. Transfer of the Chinese seat at the UN to the PRC ultimately did not take place until 1971.

60. Freda Kirchwey, "Threat out of China," *The Nation*, November 11, 1950, 423–425.

61. Julio Alvarez del Vayo, "Marking Time," *The Nation*, November 25, 1950, 474.

62. Julio Alvarez del Vayo, "Mao's Counter-Proposal," *The Nation*, January 27, 1951, 73–75. Prior to moving in 1951 to its current location in Manhattan, the UN's original meeting place was at Lake Success on Long Island.

63. Julio Alvarez del Vayo, "Atomic Diplomacy," *The Nation*, December 9, 1950, 522–523.

64. Julio Alvarez del Vayo, "The UN's Grim Choice," *The Nation*, January 13, 1951, 26–28.

65. "Not by Arms Alone," *The Nation*, December 23, 1950, 667–668.

66. "The Shape of Things," *The Nation*, February 17, 1951, 145–147.

67. Freda Kirchwey, "After the UN Vote," *The Nation*, February 10, 1951, 120–121.

68. "Peace Without Appeasement," *New Republic*, December 18, 1950, 5–8.

69. "Can We Save World Peace?" *New Republic*, January 1, 1951, 5–6.

70. "Can Collective Security Work?" *New Republic*, February 5, 1951, 5–6.

71. William Henry Chamberlin, "The Blackmailer Always Returns," *New Leader*, January 1, 1951: 20.

72. William Henry Chamberlin, "Korea Must Set the Pattern," *New Leader*, October 30, 1950, 19.

73. William Henry Chamberlin, "Fuzzy Thinking in Smithfield," *New Leader*, March 12, 1951, 19.

74. William Henry Chamberlin, "Korea Must Set the Pattern," *New Leader*, October 30, 1950, 19.

75. William Henry Chamberlin, "Of Nuts and Nut-crackers," *New Leader*, February 5, 1951, 19.

76. "The Marshall Appointment," *The Freeman*, October 2, 1950, 6.

77. "Keeping Out of Bogs," *The Freeman*, December 25, 1950, 197.

78. George Langdon, "Truman Has Manila in a Frenzy," *The Freeman*, December 11, 1950, 181–182.

79. Edward Hunter, "The Suicide of Recognizing Red China," *The American Mercury*, May 1952, 44–54.

CHAPTER 3. GREAT DEBATES

1. "Blueprint for Appeasement," *The Freeman*, October 16, 1950, 39–40.

2. Rodney Gilbert, "Plan for Counter-Action," *The Freeman*, November 13, 1950, 107–109.

3. The "China Lobby" was a coalition of businessmen, publishers, and politicians who tried to pressure the US government not to recognize communist China and instead to support more fully Chiang Kai-shek and the Kuomintang. The China Lobby blamed a conspiracy of communist sympathizers within the State Department for the "loss of China" in 1949. Notable politicians supported by the China Lobby include Republican senators Joseph McCarthy and William F. Knowland. The John Birch Society is a right-wing group founded in 1958, best known for its paranoid anticommunism and conspiratorial thinking.

4. Alfred Kohlberg, "Can Chiang Trust America?" *The Freeman*, November 27, 1950, 145.

5. "The Fortnight," *The Freeman*, December 25, 1950, 196–196.

6. Malcolm Wheeler-Nicholson, "Strategy for America," *The Freeman*, February 12, 1951, 297–300.

7. "The Element of Surprise," *The Freeman*, February 26, 1951, 325–326.

8. "Keeping Out of Bogs," *The Freeman*, December 25, 1950, 197.

9. "Keeping Out of Bogs," *The Freeman*, December 25, 1950, 197.

10. I have focused on this particular editorial, as it was the clearest articulation of *The Freeman*'s preferred China policy. See also "The Fortnight," *The Freeman*, December 11, 1950, 163–165; "For a New Foreign Policy," *The Freeman*, January 8, 1951, 229–230; and "Stalin Interviews Stalin," *The Freeman*, March 12, 1951, 360.

11. Willard Shelton, "The President's Policy," *The Nation*, September 9, 1950, 221–222.

12. Julio Alvarez del Vayo, "How Europe Looks at Asia," *The Nation*, March 3, 1951, 198–199. See also "Mao at Lake Success," *The Nation*, December 2, 1950, 501–502.

13. Howard K. Smith, "Europe Says No," *The Nation*, December 9, 1950, 521–522.

14. Freda Kirchwey, "Apprehensive Allies," *The Nation*, January 27, 1951, 72–73.

15. "Washington Wire," *New Republic*, December 11, 1950, 3–4.

16. "The Decision in Korea," *New Republic*, January 22, 1951, 5–6.

17. Victor Purcell, "The U.S. Blocks Peace," *The New Republic*, February 5, 1951, 14–16.

18. "One Way Out," *Commonweal*, January 26, 1951, 388–389. See also "Sanctions," *Commonweal*, February 2, 1951, 411–412.

19. "Diplomacy," *The New Leader*, November 20, 1950, 30.

20. William Henry Chamberlin, "China Can Be Checkmated," *New Leader*, December 4, 1950, 19.

21. Chamberlin, "Crisis Strategy for the West," *New Leader*, January 15, 1951, 18.

22. Jonathan Stout, "Our Allies Inside China," *The New Leader*, December 18, 1950, 5.

23. Christopher Emmet, "Strategy for the Future," *The New Leader*, December 18, 1950, 9–10.

24. William Caldwell, "Our Second Front in China," *The New Leader*, January 22, 1951, 2–4.

25. In fairness to the Europeans, they were debating French prime minister René Pleven's 1950 proposal to create a European Defense Community during this time. A treaty to create the EDC was signed in 1952, but the plan fell apart after it failed a ratification vote in the French Parliament in 1954.

26. "Hoover's Folly," *The Nation*, December 30, 1950, 688–689.
27. "Hoover's Folly," 688–689.
28. "To a Brave New Year," *The Nation*, January 6, 1951, 1.
29. "Can We Save World Peace," *The New Republic*, January 1, 1951, 5–6.
30. "Washington Wire," *New Republic*, January 8, 1951, 3–4.
31. Harold Ickes, "Every Man a President," *New Republic*, January 8, 1951, 17–18.
32. I do not include *Commonweal* in this analysis since its editors' criticism of Hoover was rather brief, but that magazine nonetheless agreed with their liberal counterparts on this issue.
33. "The New Isolationism," *The New Leader*, January 1, 1951, 30–31.
34. August Heckscher, "Republicans Should Reject Hooverism," *The New Leader*, January 8, 1951, 2–4.
35. "The Fortnight," *The Freeman*, October 30, 1950, 67–69.
36. "For a New Foreign Policy," *The Freeman*, January 8, 1951, 229–230.
37. "The Element of Surprise," *The Freeman*, February 26, 1951, 325–326.
38. "For a New Foreign Policy," *The Freeman*, January 8, 1951, 229–230.
39. "The Fortnight," *The Freeman*, April 23, 1951, 451–452.
40. "How Brains Can Win in Europe," *American Mercury*, February 1951, 166–167.
41. "State of the Union: The Issues in 1951: I. Strength in Unity," *New Republic*, January 15, 1951, 10–11.
42. "Korea: Trial and Achievement," *New Republic*, June 25, 1951, 9–10.
43. "Our Isolationists," *Commonweal*, January 5, 1951, 315–316.
44. William Henry Chamberlin, "We Must Learn from Korea," *The New Leader*, September 30, 1950, 19.
45. William Henry Chamberlin, "1941–1951: Parallels and Differences," *The New Leader*, March 19, 1951, 21. See also Chamberlin, "The Great Debate on Foreign Policy," *The New Leader*, January 29, 1951, 21.
46. "The Fortnight," *The Freeman*, March 10, 1952, 355–356.
47. "Leading Whom Whither?" *The Freeman*, March 10, 1952, 357–359.
48. Lawrence R. Brown, "Eisenhower vs. Taft: The Vital Issue," *The Freeman*, March 24, 1952, 393–396.
49. Alexander P. de Seversky, "How to Answer Neutralism," *The Freeman*, October 6, 1952, 17–19.
50. Patrick McMahon, "Dangers, Dilemmas, and Dulles," *The American Mercury*, March–April 1953, 86–96.

CHAPTER 4. THE MACARTHUR CONTROVERSY

1. This, at least, is according to Truman's own writings, which indicate that the paramount issue was MacArthur's insubordination. For the Joint Chiefs, however, the issue was more military than political. The JCS worried that MacArthur's moves risked a wider war on the Asian mainland not only with China but potentially with Soviet

divisions in Manchuria as well. See Harry S. Truman, *Memoirs of Harry S. Truman: Years of Trial and Hope, 1946–1952* (New York: Doubleday, 1956) and William Stueck, *The Korean War: An International History* (Princeton, NJ: Princeton University Press, 1995).

2. "Drifting toward War with China," *New Republic*, August 21, 1950, 5–6.
3. "MacArthur Tries to Make Policy," *New Republic*, September 4, 1950, 7.
4. "Truman or MacArthur: The Choice in Asia," *New Republic*, September 11, 1950, 5–6.
5. "Truman Meets MacArthur," *New Republic*, October 23, 1950, 5.
6. "Truman or MacArthur: The Choice in Asia," *New Republic*, September 11, 1950, 5–6.
7. Harold L. Ickes, "Harry S. Truman is President," *New Republic*, September 11, 1950, 17.
8. Harold L. Ickes, "MacArthur Talks Too Much," *New Republic*, December 11, 1950, 18.
9. "The Shape of Things," *The Nation*, September 2, 1950, 197–198.
10. Willard Shelton, "The President's Policy," *The Nation*, September 9, 1950, 221–222.
11. "The Shape of Things," *The Nation*, December 2, 1950, 497–499.
12. "Neither MacArthur nor Truman," *New Leader*, April 16, 1951, 30–31.
13. "Formosa," *Commonweal*, September 8, 1950, 523–524.
14. "The Fortnight," *The Freeman*, October 30, 1950, 67–69.
15. "Another MacArthur Canard," *The Freeman*, November 27, 1950, 136.
16. "The Fortnight," *The Freeman*, April 23, 1951, 451–452.
17. "MacArthur's War Party," *New Republic*, April 23, 1951, 5–6.
18. "Truman or MacArthur: The Choice in Asia," *New Republic*, September 11, 1950, 5–6.
19. Harold L. Ickes, "MacArthur Talks Too Much," *New Republic*, December 11, 1950, 18.
20. Harold L. Ickes, "Nathan Hale and MacArthur," *New Republic*, May 7, 1951, 15.
21. Willard Shelton, "Notes from Capitol Hill," *The Nation*, August 19, 1950, 162.
22. "The General Sows Confusion," *The Nation*, April 28, 1951, 388–389.
23. "Futile and Foolish," *Commonweal*, April 6, 1951, 637.
24. "The Fortnight," *The Freeman*, December 11, 1950, 163–165.
25. "Americans are Expendable," *The Freeman*, April 23, 1951, 453.
26. "Neither MacArthur nor Truman," *New Leader*, April 16, 1951, 30–31.
27. See pages 69–71.
28. "Neither MacArthur nor Truman," *New Leader*, April 16, 1951, 30–31.
29. "For a New Far Eastern Policy," *New Leader*, April 23, 1951: 2–3, 30.
30. "The Shape of Things," *The Nation*, March 31, 1951, 289–291.
31. "New Phase in Korea," *New Republic*, April 9, 1951, 6.
32. "MacArthur's Offer," *New Leader*, April 2, 1951, 30.
33. William Henry Chamberlin, "A Sensible Peace Plan," *New Leader*, April 2, 1951, 21.
34. "The Fortnight," *The Freeman*, April 9, 1951, 419–420.
35. "The Fortnight," *The Freeman*, April 23, 1951, 451–452.
36. "Americans are Expendable," *The Freeman*, April 23, 1951, 453.
37. Alice Widener, "The Korean Failure," *American Mercury*, May 1952, 12–24.
38. Harold L. Ickes, "MacArthur Talks Too Much," *New Republic*, December 11, 1950, 18.

39. Harold L. Ickes, "MacArthur Home for Christmas," *New Republic*, December 25, 1950, 17.

40. "Washington Wire" and "Korea and World Politics," *New Republic*, April 16, 1951, 3–6.

41. "The Shape of Things, "*The Nation*, April 14, 1951, 337–338.

42. "MacArthur's War Party," *New Republic*, April 23, 1951, 5–6.

43. Harold L. Ickes, "Truman Has the Last Word," *New Republic*, April 23, 1951, 17.

44. Harold L. Ickes, "A Befuddled People," *New Republic*, June 25, 1951, 25.

45. Freda Kirchwey, "Next Moves," *The Nation*, April 21, 1951, 360–361.

46. Howard K. Smith, "Thou Art Soldier Only," *The Nation*, April 21, 1951, 363–364.

47. Willard Shelton, "Inevitable Showdown," *The Nation*, April 21, 1951, 362–363.

48. Alexander Werth, "Judgment Reserved," *The Nation*, April 21, 1951, 364–365.

49. Julio Alvarez del Vayo, "Relief, Hope, and Shame," *The Nation*, April 21, 1951, 365–366.

50. "In the Public Interest," *Commonweal*, April 20, 1951, 27–28.

51. "No End in Sight?" *Commonweal*, April 27, 1951, 51–53.

52. "For a New Far Eastern Policy," *New Leader*, April 23, 1951, 2–3, 30.

53. "MacArthur's Offer," *New Leader*, April 2, 1951, 30.

54. William Henry Chamberlin, "Now It's Up to Truman," *New Leader*, April 23, 1951, 9.

55. David J. Dallin, "Europe and MacArthur," *New Leader*, April 30, 1951, 15.

56. See page 89.

57. "The Fortnight," *The Freeman*, April 23, 1951, 451–452.

58. "The Risk of No-Policy in Asia," *The Freeman*, May 7, 1951, 485–486.

59. "The Shape of Things," *The Nation*, May 5, 1951, 405–408.

60. "Washington Wire," *New Republic*, April 23, 1951, 3–4.

61. "Washington Wire," *New Republic*, April 30, 1951, 3–4.

62. "Washington Wire," *New Republic*, August 6, 1951, 3–4.

63. "Peace Without Appeasement," *The Nation*, December 18, 1950, 5–8.

64. "Resolution and Restraint," *Commonweal*, January 11, 1952, 319.

65. "Now is the Time . . ." *New Leader*, April 30, 1951, 30.

66. "The Fortnight," *The Freeman*, December 29, 1952, 221–222. Here, "McLiberal" is a conservative attempt to throw liberals' preoccupation with all things "McCarthy" back in their faces.

67. "War to the Death," *New Republic*, May 14, 1951, 5; and "Washington Wire," *New Republic*, May 14, 1951, 3–4.

68. "Washington Wire," *New Republic*, May 21, 1951, 3–4.

69. "Washington Wire," *New Republic*, May 28, 1951, 3–4.

70. "Washington Wire," *New Republic*, June 4, 1951, 3–4.

71. Willard Shelton, "Confusion on the Potomac," *The Nation*, May 26, 1951, 486–487.

72. Shelton, "McCarthy-MacArthur Axis," *The Nation*, June 23, 1951, 581–582.

73. "The Shape of Things," *The Nation*, June 16, 1951, 549–552.

74. "The Fortnight," *The Freeman*, May 21, 1951, 515–516.

75. "The Fortnight," *The Freeman*, June 4, 1951, 547–548.

76. Edna Lonigan, "Letter from Washington," *The Freeman*, July 2, 1951, 624–625.

77. "Washington Wire," *New Republic*, June 18, 1951, 3–4.

78. "Texas Unconquered," *New Republic*, June 25, 1951, 7.

79. John McCully, "Not so Deep in the Heart in Texas," *The Nation*, June 30, 1951, 605–606.

80. "After the Storm," *Commonweal*, July 13, 1951, 325.

81. "They'd Rather Be Right," *Commonweal*, June 27, 1952, 286.

82. Francis Downing, "After the Tumult and the Shouting," *Commonweal*, August 1, 1952: 403–404.

83. Frazier Hunt, "MacArthur's Tragic Vindication," *The Freeman*, July 14, 1952, 687–690.

84. Frazier Hunt, "MacArthur's Tragic Vindication," *The Freeman*, July 14, 1952, 687–690.

CHAPTER 5. DUELING DOMESTIC BOGEYMEN

1. A related issue that one might expect to have been debated extensively is the economic and military mobilization that accompanied the Korean War and, indeed, became one of the conflict's greatest lasting legacies. Perhaps surprisingly, the idea that America might be slouching toward a "garrison state" was discussed relatively rarely in these journals. To the extent that the issue of mobilization was explicitly debated, it was largely subsumed into the larger debates about socialism, which are examined in the second half of this chapter. For an in-depth analysis of the domestic impact of the Truman administration's Cold War mobilization, see Michael Hogan, *A Cross of Iron: Harry S. Truman and the Origins of the National Security State, 1945–1954* (Cambridge, UK: Cambridge University Press, 2000).

2. "Gamble in Korea," *The Nation*, July 8, 1950, 23–25.

3. "To a Brave New Year," *The Nation*, January 6, 1951, 1.

4. "The Shape of Things," *The Nation*, February 17, 1951, 145–147.

5. Willard Shelton, "McCarthy-MacArthur Axis," *The Nation*, June 23, 1951, 581–582.

6. "The Present Danger," *The Nation*, June 6, 1953, 467–469.

7. Michael Straight, "The Mood of America," *New Republic*, June 26, 1950, 10–12.

8. "Washington Wire," *New Republic*, November 20, 1950, 3–4. The 1950 midterms saw Republicans gain seats in both houses of Congress, narrowing the Democratic majority in each.

9. "McCarthy on Trial," *New Republic*, October 8, 1951, 5.

10. "Enough's Enough," *Commonweal*, August 4, 1950, 406. For a more in-depth view of McCarthy's fraught relationship with his fellow American Catholics, see Donald Crosby, *God, Church, and Flag: Senator Joseph R. McCarthy and the Catholic Church, 1950–1957* (Chapel Hill: University of North Carolina Press, 1978).

11. "Outlawing the Outlaws," *Commonweal*, August 25, 1950, 475.

12. "The Anti-Anti-Communists," *Commonweal*, July 4, 1952, 307–308.

13. "Who Are the 'Subversives'?" *Commonweal*, July 18, 1952, 357.

14. "Jean Muir and 'Old Man Atom,'" *New Leader*, September 9, 1950, 30–31.

15. Most of the act's provisions were struck down by the Supreme Court in the 1960s or repealed by Congress in the early 1970s.

16. "The McCarran Curtain," *New Leader*, October 21, 1950, 30–31.

17. William Henry Chamberlin, "Making Envoys of Ill Will," *New Leader*, November 13, 1950, 20. See also David J. Dallin, "The McCarran Pro-Communist Law," *New Leader*, January 22, 1951, 9.

18. "The Refugee Muddle," *New Leader*, January 22, 1951, 30–31.

19. Norbert Muhlen, "The Phantom of McCarthyism," *New Leader*, May 21, 1951, 16–18. For a rebuttal that reveals some of the disagreement among liberals on this issue, see Granville Hicks, "Is McCarthyism a Phantom?" *New Leader*, June 4, 1951, 7.

20. William Henry Chamberlin, "'Little, Red' Is Little Read," *New Leader*, September 24, 1951, 15.

21. "Dear Editor: Charges 'New Leader' takes 'Anti-anti-Communist' Line," *New Leader*, January 21, 1952, 27–28.

22. Diana Trilling, "Mr. Russell, Communism and Civil Liberties," *New Leader*, April 28, 1952, 16–18. See also, "Is America in the Grip of Hysteria?" *New Leader*, March 3, 1952, 3–4; and William Henry Chamberlin, "Bertrand Russell and 'Hysteria,'" *New Leader*, April 7, 1952, 19.

23. Richard Rovere, "How Free is *The Nation*?" *New Leader*, July 14, 1952, 12–14. For additional criticism of *The Nation* and "anti-anti-communism," see William Henry Chamberlin, "The 'Nation's' Dud on Civil Liberties," *New Leader*, August 4, 1952, 19; "Anti-anti-Communism," *New Leader*, September 8, 1952, 31; and William Henry Chamberlin, "Two Opposites: Viereck and Werth," *New Leader*, May 4, 1953, 15.

24. "McCarthy Lays an Egg," *New Leader*, November 3, 1952, 30–31.

25. George F. Kennan, "The Triple Threat from Within," *New Leader*, June 1, 1953, 16–19. Kennan's insights on the emotional underpinnings of the McCarthyite movement here lead us to wonder whether the same critiques might also be applied with astonishing relevance to the emergence and success of Trumpism in the twenty-first century.

26. "Readers Comment Pro and Con on Kennan's Notre Dame Speech," *New Leader*, June 22, 1953, 20–21.

27. Forrest Davis, "Senator Taft's New Deal," *The Freeman*, December 25, 1950, 201–203.

28. "The Fortnight, "*The Freeman*, January 8, 1951, 227–228. Interestingly, in this same editorial, the authors first accuse Harry Truman of being a "fascist" for trying to centralize too much power in the Executive Branch, then criticize his proposal for universal health care as "socialized medicine." The president was apparently able to travel the whole length of the political spectrum within the space of a few paragraphs.

29. William F. Buckley Jr., "Senator McCarthy's Model?" *The Freeman*, May 21, 1951, 531–533. See also Buckley, "McLiberals' McCarthy," *The Freeman*, February 9, 1953, 355–356.

30. "The Times Frames a Question," *The Freeman*, June 18, 1951, 584–585. For a similar critique of the alleged progressive monopoly on faculty teaching positions, see Ludwig von Mises, "Our Leftist Economic Teaching," *The Freeman*, April 7, 1952, 425–428.

31. "The Press and Pavlov's Dogs," *The Freeman*, November 5, 1951, 72.

32. "The Fortnight," *The Freeman*, June 2, 1952, 557–558.

33. "The Fortnight," *The Freeman*, April 20, 1953, 509–510.

34. "The Fortnight," *The Freeman*, May 18, 1953, 581–582. See also "The Necessity of Red-Baiting," *The Freeman*, June 1, 1953, 619–620; and "Fifth Column Amendment," *The Freeman*, June 29, 1953, 694–695.

35. Eugene Lyons, "Is Freedom of Expression Really Threatened?" *American Mercury*, January 1953, 22–33.

36. "The Faith of The Freeman," *The Freeman*, October 2, 1950, 5–6. See also, "The Function of *The Freeman*," *The Freeman*, December 31, 1951, 197–198; and "The Faith of *The Freeman*," *The Freeman*, February 23, 1953, 369–370.

37. "The Fortnight," *The Freeman*, October 30, 1950, 67–69.

38. The most prominent target was Truman's proposal for a universal health-care system, often derided by conservatives as "socialized medicine."

39. "The Fortnight," *The Freeman*, November 13, 1950, 99–101.

40. William Faulkner, "The Duty to Be Free," *The Freeman*, January 26, 1953, 304–306.

41. George S. Schuyler, "The Pro-Slavery Propagandists," *The Freeman*, December 11, 1950, 176–177.

42. *The Freeman*, January 22, 1951, back cover. By the magazine's one-year anniversary, the editors were boasting that their circulation had reached 15,000. See "The Fortnight," *The Freeman*, October 22, 1951, 35–36.

43. Garet Garrett, "Decline of the American Republic," *The Freeman*, February 25, 1952, 331–333.

44. Neil Carothers, "Socialism is Here," *The Freeman*, May 21, 1951, 528–529.

45. John L. Beckley, "Profits vs. Socialism," *The Freeman*, September 24, 1951, 818–821. For similar arguments, see Towner Phelan, "The Weapon of Taxation," *The Freeman*, December 17, 1951, 175–178; James Monroe Madison (William Bradford Huie), "For a Second Whisky Rebellion," *American Mercury*, February 1952, 124–128; and William F. Buckley Jr., "The Rich and the Poor," *American Mercury*, July 1952, 121–127.

46. Towner Phelan, "Controls Won't Stop Inflation," *The Freeman*, November 19, 1951, 18–111. Price controls were in effect from Truman's executive action in 1951 until Eisenhower's reversal in early 1953.

47. While Mises was clearly no fan of the welfare state, his critique as expressed in *The Freeman* fell short of Hazlitt's stark characterization of his work, viz., that the welfare state would necessarily lead to totalitarianism. See Ludwig von Mises, "Agony of the Welfare State," *The Freeman*, May 4, 1953, 555–557.

48. Henry Hazlitt, "Welfare to Socialism to Communism," *The Freeman*, December 3, 1951, 133–134. For similar arguments, see Bruce Winton Knight, "Freedom Is Indivisible," *The Freeman*, January 14, 1952, 242–244; George Winder, "After Capitalism, What?" *The Freeman*, March 10, 1952, 371–373; S. Harcourt-Rivington, "Community in Bonds," *The Freeman*, May 5, 1952, 501–502.

49. "Escape from Maturity," *American Mercury*, April 1951, 393–397.

50. "Draughts of Old Bourbon," *American Mercury*, May 1951, 638–640. The references to Aneurin Bevan and London were no doubt motivated by Huie's disapproval of the former's role in creating Britain's fledgling National Health Service.

51. Felix Wittmer, "Collectivism at Yale," *The Freeman*, October 22, 1951, 58–60. *The American Mercury*, where Buckley worked on staff, featured full-page ads for the book in the November and December 1951 issues.

52. "The Fortnight," *The Freeman*, November 17, 1952, 115–116. Papers related to the Circuit Riders are currently housed at the University of Oregon.

53. Edward A. Keller, "Socialism vs. Christianity," *The Freeman*, December 1, 1952, 164–165.

54. Jack Schwartzman, "Natural Law and the Campus," *The Freeman*, December 3, 1951, 149–152.

55. Towner Phelan, "The Secret Strength of Communism," *The Freeman*, March 24, 1952, 402–404.

56. "The Wall Street Journal Fesses Up," *New Leader*, December 10, 1951, 31. The AMA was the most prominent group to lobby against Harry Truman's push for universal health care in the United States, while John T. Flynn wrote *The Road Ahead* in 1949, a warning of creeping socialism in America.

57. William Henry Chamberlin, "Socialism, Communism Are not Identical," *New Leader*, January 14, 1952, 19.

58. Attlee was British prime minister from 1945 to 1951, overseeing the creation of the modern British welfare state, including the National Health Service.

59. Max Eastman, "Can Freedom Survive under a Planned Economy?" *New Leader*, May 19, 1952, 16–19.

60. Arthur M. Schlesinger Jr., "The Vital Center: Against Communism and Reaction," *New Leader*, June 9, 1952, 16–18.

61. "Two Readers Side with Eastman in Dispute with Schlesinger," *New Leader*, June 23, 1952, 27.

62. Abba P. Lerner, "Capitalism, Socialism, and Freedom: A Reply to Max Eastman," *New Leader*, June 30, 1952, 8–11.

63. Mark Starr, "Planning with Freedom: A Reply to Max Eastman," *New Leader*, July 14, 1952, 9–10.

64. See Daniel Bell, "In Defense of Fabianism: Notes on The Freeman and Max Eastman," *New Leader*, August 11, 1952, 12–14; and Carl Landauer, "Does Planning Mean Despotism?" *New Leader*, September 22, 1952, 20–21.

65. "Friendship for the Russians," *Commonweal*, April 6, 1951, 635–636.

66. "Creeping Socialism," *Commonweal*, July 18, 1952, 355–356.

67. Notable here is Buckley's stated distaste for civil rights legislation, which would figure much more prominently in his writings in the 1960s.

68. William F. Buckley Jr., "The Party and the Deep Blue Sea," *Commonweal*, January 25, 1952, 391–393.

69. Leo R. Ward, "Buckley's Attack on Yale," *Commonweal*, February 15, 1952, 473–474.
70. "Yale vs. Harvard," *Commonweal*, June 27, 1952, 285.

CHAPTER 6. NEGOTIATIONS

1. As China was the senior partner to the North Koreans, both in military power and diplomatic influence, communist negotiators were far more concerned with the status of Chinese than North Korean prisoners. Complicating this issue, however, was the fact that many of the captured Chinese fighters had been Nationalists impressed into communist forces after the Chinese civil war ended in 1949. While these prisoners desperately wished to obtain residency in Taiwan, the Chinese Communist Party was equally desperate to avoid strengthening their Nationalist enemy, not to mention the loss of face that would come with such an arrangement. While the process of screening prisoners was incomplete, was inconsistent, and occasionally led to violence, the numbers nonetheless threatened a major propaganda defeat for the Chinese, even as American officials did their best to maximize the number of voluntary repatriates in the hopes of finalizing a negotiated settlement. See Stueck, *The Korean War: An International History* for a more in-depth discussion of these complexities.
2. See "The Chances for Peace in Korea," *New Republic*, October 22, 1951, 5; and "Washington Wire," October 29, 1951, 3–4.
3. "The Shape of Things," *The Nation*, August 4, 1951, 81–82; "The Shape of Things," *The Nation*, August 11, 1951, 102–103.
4. "The Shape of Things," *The Nation*, November 3, 1951, 365–367.
5. "Truce," *Commonweal*, December 28, 1951, 294.
6. "Korea," *Commonweal*, July 4, 1953, 385.
7. "Peace in Korea," *Commonweal*, August 7, 1953, 432–433.
8. "The Fortnight," *The Freeman*, July 16, 1951, 643–644.
9. "The Fortnight," *The Freeman*, November 19, 1951, 99–100.
10. "Peace Without Victory?" *The Freeman*, May 18, 1953, 583–584.
11. "No More UN Wars," *The Freeman*, June 29, 1953, 693–694.
12. "Dream vs. Nightmare," *The Freeman*, July 30, 1951, 678.
13. "The Fortnight," *The Freeman*, December 1, 1951, 131–132.
14. "A Test of Our Honor," *The Freeman*, June 1, 1953, 620–621.
15. David J. Dallin, "A Mistaken 'Peace Offensive,'" *New Leader*, June 18, 1951, 9.
16. David J. Dallin, "No Cease-Fire at the 38th!" *New Leader*, June 25, 1951, 11.
17. "Should We Accept Malik's Proposal?" *New Leader*, July 2, 1951, 30–31.
18. "Disengagement," *New Leader*, March 9, 1953, 30–31.
19. "Challenge and Response," *New Leader*, March 23, 1953, 30.
20. "The New Mess in Washington," *New Leader*, April 20, 1953, 30–31.
21. William Henry Chamberlin, "Half a Loaf in Korea," *New Leader*, July 23, 1951, 15.
22. "Kaesong," *New Leader*, August 27, 1951, 30–31.

23. "Again Talk?" *New Leader*, October 1, 1951, 22.

24. "The Panmunjom Trap," *New Leader*, January 28, 1952, 30.

25. "How to Make a Truce," *New Leader*, May 12, 1952, 30.

26. David J. Dallin, "The Farce of Soviet 'Neutrality,'" *New Leader*, March 24, 1952, 12.

27. Bruno Shaw, "Truce Talks Were Doomed from the Start," *New Leader*, July 7, 1952, 5–6.

28. Edward Hunter, "How We're Losing the All-Asia War," *New Leader*, August 11, 1952, 2–5.

29. "The Fortnight," *The Freeman*, September 10, 1951, 771–773.

30. "The Fortnight," *The Freeman*, December 3, 1951, 131–132.

31. "Peace in Korea?" *New Republic*, July 2, 1951, 5.

32. "Washington Wire," *New Republic*, November 19, 1951, 3–4.

33. "Washington Wire," *New Republic*, April 20, 1953, 3–4.

34. "After the Truce—The Terms for Peace," *New Republic*, June 15, 1953, 5–6.

35. "Hard Bargain," *Commonweal*, July 27, 1951, 372.

36. "Exchange of Notes," *Commonweal*, September 7, 1951, 515–516.

37. "The 'New Era,'" *Commonweal*, October 19, 1951, 28–29; "Korean Truce Parlays," *Commonweal*, November 16, 1951, 131.

38. Freda Kirchwey, "Malik's Move," *The Nation*, June 30, 1951, 599–600.

39. "The Shape of Things," *The Nation*, August 4, 1951, 81–82.

40. "The Shape of Things," *The Nation*, August 11, 1951, 102–103.

41. Freda Kirchwey, "Proof of the Pudding," *The Nation*, August 18, 1951, 122–123.

42. "The Shape of Things," *The Nation*, November 3, 1951, 365–366.

43. "The Brightening Eastern Sky," *The Nation*, April 4, 1953, 277.

44. "Hunting Booby Traps," *The Nation*, April 11, 1953, 299–300.

45. See also Freda Kirchwey, "Breaking the Circle," November 24, 1951, 435–436; and Julio Alvarez del Vayo, "Diplomacy's Hour," April 11, 1953, 301.

46. "End of the Beginning," *The Nation*, June 13, 1953, 493.

47. "Embarrassment of Deeds," *The Nation*, June 20, 1953, 513.

48. "The Panmunjom Trap," *New Leader*, January 28, 1952, 30.

49. "How to Make a Truce," *New Leader*, May 12, 1952, 30.

50. "What Now in Korea?" *New Leader*, June 2, 1952, 30–31.

51. In this demand they were joined by the editorial staff at the conservative *Freeman*; see "UN War, U.S. Fight," *The Freeman*, March 23, 1953, 441–442.

52. "The Coming Bermuda Parley," *New Leader*, June 1, 1953, 2–3.

53. "Why Not Break Off at Panmunjom?" *American Mercury*, July 1952, 8–9.

54. Styles Bridges, "Korea: A Positive Proposal," *American Mercury*, November 1952, 11–19.

55. "The 'New Era,'" *Commonweal*, October 19, 1951, 28–29.

56. "Eisenhower's Hard Choice in Korea," *New Republic*, December 1, 1952, 5.

57. "Korean Truce Mirage," *Commonweal*, February 1, 1952, 413.

58. "The War in Korea," *Commonweal*, May 9, 1952, 107–108.

59. "The Prospect in Korea," *Commonweal*, July 4, 1952, 30–310.

60. "Korea in the UN," *The Nation*, October 4, 1952, 289–290.

CHAPTER 7. THE ARMISTICE

1. David J. Dallin, "An Indictment Written in Blood," *New Leader*, February 4, 1952, 15.

2. See Dallin, "We Must Bar POW Surrender," *New Leader*, June 16, 1952, 11; and "Signs of Weakness on Truce Talks," *New Leader*, June 23, 1952, 13.

3. "Don't Betray the Korea POWs!" *New Leader*, April 21, 1952, 2, 30.

4. The implicit argument here was that Soviet prisoners who had either fought with the Germans after being captured or who otherwise did not wish to return to the Soviet Union after World War II were nonetheless repatriated, as per the Yalta agreement, and were tortured or executed by Stalin as a warning to other would-be traitors and "enemies of the people."

5. "A Test of Our Honor," *The Freeman*, June 1, 1953, 620–621.

6. Alice Widener, "The Korean Failure," *American Mercury*, May 1952, 12–24.

7. "Prisoners of War," *Commonweal*, March 21, 1952, 580–581.

8. "The Prisoners in Korea," *Commonweal*, May 23, 1952, 165–166.

9. "An Inescapable Responsibility," *Commonweal*, November 14, 1952, 133–134.

10. "Hope, Disappointment and Peace," *New Republic*, December 31, 1951, 5; "Washington Wire," *New Republic*, February 4, 1952, 3–4.

11. The communists held approximately 7,000 American POWs. The United States, by contrast, held approximately 100,000 North Korean and Chinese prisoners who did not wish to be repatriated to their communist homelands.

12. "Why Are We Fighting in Korea?" *New Republic*, August 11, 1952, 10–11.

13. "The Seoul Plan," *New Leader*, December 8, 1952, 30–31.

14. "Challenge and Response," *New Leader*, March 23, 1953, 30.

15. "Soldiers of China," *New Leader*, July 27, 1953, 30.

16. "Peace Without Victory?" *The Freeman*, May 18, 1953, 583–584.

17. See "The POWs Speak," *New Leader*, May 5, 1952, 30.

18. "The Fortnight," *The Freeman*, June 30, 1952, 637–639.

19. Edward Hunter, "Defeat by Default," *American Mercury*, September 1952, 40–51.

20. "Korean Kaleidoscope," *The Nation*, June 21, 1952, 595–596.

21. "Korean Kaleidoscope," *The Nation*, June 21, 1952, 595–596.

22. Freda Kirchwey, "The War Against the UN," *The Nation*, November 22, 1952, 457–459.

23. "Pongam: Stupidity Plus Brutality," *The Nation*, December 27, 1952, 592.

24. "The Shape of Things," *The Nation*, January 19, 1952, 49–51.

25. "Washington Wire," *New Republic*, January 14, 1952, 3–4.

26. "Peace in Korea," *Commonweal*, August 7, 1953, 432–433.

27. "The Asia Conference," *Commonweal*, August 14, 1953, 457–458.

28. "Peace in Korea?" *New Leader*, December 3, 1951, 30.

29. William Henry Chamberlin, "Why Is Red China Untouchable?" *New Leader*, March 24, 1952, 19.

30. "Dream vs. Nightmare," *The Freeman*, July 30, 1951, 678.

31. "Peace in Korea?" *New Republic*, July 2, 1951, 5.

32. "Washington Wire," *New Republic*, January 14, 1952, 3–4.

33. "Washington Wire," *New Republic*, February 25, 1952, 3–4.

34. "The War in Korea," *Commonweal*, May 9, 1952, 107–108.

35. "Balancing the Books," *Commonweal*, June 26, 1953, 287–288.

36. David J. Dallin, "Moscow's Strategic Retreat," *New Leader*, May 4, 1953, 5–6.

37. "The Communists Accept," *New Republic*, July 9, 1951, 6.

38. "Washington Wire," *New Republic*, April 20, 1953, 3–4. See also, "Washington Wire," August 3, 1953, 3.

39. "The Talk of Peace," *Commonweal*, April 18, 1952, 33. See also, "Balancing the Books," June 26, 1953, 287–288.

40. "Peace in Korea?" *New Leader*, December 3, 1951, 30.

41. "Peace in Korea?" *New Republic*, July 2, 1951, 5; "Washington Wire," *New Republic*, November 12, 1951, 3–4.

42. "Hope, Disappointment and Peace," *New Republic*, December 31, 1951, 5.

43. "After the Truce—The Terms for Peace," *New Republic*, June 15, 1953, 5–6.

44. "The UN Looks beyond Korea," *The Nation*, July 14, 1951, 25–26. See also, "End of the Beginning," July 13, 1953, 493.

45. "Peace in Korea?" *New Leader*, December 3, 1951, 30.

46. "A Beginning," *Commonweal*, July 13, 1951, 323–324.

47. "International Heroes," *Commonweal*, December 21, 1951, 269–270.

48. "Prisoners," *Commonweal*, January 4, 1952, 315.

49. "Peace in Korea," *Commonweal*, August 7, 1953, 432–433.

50. "UN War, U.S. Fight," *The Freeman*, March 23, 1953, 441–442.

51. "No More UN Wars," *The Freeman*, June 29, 1953, 693–694.

52. "The Fortnight," *The Freeman*, August 10, 1953, 797–798; "But Aggression Continues," *The Freeman*, August 10, 1953, 800–801.

53. This was a reference to Edward Gibbon, the eighteenth-century English historian who authored *The History of the Decline and Fall of the Roman Empire*.

54. "Our Korean Defeat Will Be Historic," *American Mercury*, September 1951, 16–17.

CONCLUSION

1. Michael Straight, "A Fictive Report," *New Republic*, June 2, 1952, 21–22.

2. William Appleman Williams, "Moscow Peace Drive: Victory for Containment?" *The Nation*, July 11, 1953, 28–30.

3. For more on the relationship among Stone, Williams, and the New Left, see John Ehrman, *The Rise of Neoconservatism: Intellectuals and Foreign Affairs, 1945–1994* (New

Haven, CT: Yale University Press, 1995); and Richard Pells, *The Liberal Mind in a Conservative Age: American Intellectuals in the 1940s and 1950s* (New York: Harper & Row, 1985).

4. Richard Pells, *The Liberal Mind in a Conservative Age*, ix.

Bibliography

JOURNALS/SOURCE MATERIAL

American Mercury. Accessed via microfilm, Mugar Library, Boston University.

Commonweal. Accessed via microfilm, Mugar Library, Boston University.

The Freeman. Bound by volume, Boston Public Library, Copley Square.

The Nation. Accessed via microfilm, Mugar Library, Boston University.

New Leader. Bound by volume, Boston Public Library, Copley Square.

New Republic. Accessed via microfilm, Mugar Library, Boston University.

BOOKS

Blair, Clay. *The Forgotten War: America in Korea, 1950–1953*. New York: Times Books, 1987.

Bodenheimer, Thomas, and Robert Gould. *Rollback!: Right-wing Power in U.S. Foreign Policy*. Boston: South End Press, 1989.

Bowen, Michael. *The Roots of Modern Conservatism: Dewey, Taft, and the Battle for the Soul of the Republican Party*. Chapel Hill: University of North Carolina Press, 2011.

Boyer, Paul. *By the Bomb's Early Light: American Thought and Culture at the Dawn of the Atomic Age*. New York: Pantheon, 1985.

Buckley, William, Jr. *God and Man at Yale: The Superstitions of Academic Freedom*. Chicago: Regnery, 1951.

Burnham, James. *The Coming Defeat of Communism*. New York: John Day, 1950.

Burnham, James. *Containment or Liberation? An Inquiry into the Aims of United States Foreign Policy*. New York: John Day, 1950.

Burnham, James. *The Struggle for the World*. New York: John Day, 1947.

Carter, Paul. *Another Part of the Fifties*. New York: Columbia University Press, 1983.

Casey, Steven. *Selling the Korean War: Propaganda, Politics, and Public Opinion, 1950–1953*. New York: Oxford University Press, 2008.

Chen, Jian. *China's Road to the Korean War: The Making of the Sino-American Confrontation*. New York: Columbia University Press, 1996.

Cumings, Bruce. *The Korean War: A History*. New York: Modern Library, 2010.

Cumings, Bruce. *The Origins of the Korean War*. Princeton: Princeton University Press, 1981.

Dam, Hari. *The Intellectual Odyssey of Walter Lippmann: A Study of His Protean Thought, 1910–1960*. New York: Gordon Press, 1973.

Depoe, Stephen. *Arthur M. Schlesinger, Jr., and the Ideological History of American Liberalism*. Tuscaloosa: University of Alabama Press, 1994.

Diamond, Sara. *Roads to Dominion: Right-wing Movements and Political Power in the United States.* New York: Guilford Press, 1995.

Diggins, John. *Up From Communism: Conservative Odysseys in American Intellectual Development.* New York: Columbia University Press, 1994.

Diggins, John, ed. *The Liberal Persuasion: Arthur Schlesinger, Jr., and the Challenge of the American Past.* Princeton, NJ: Princeton University Press, 1997.

Edwards, Lee. *The Conservative Revolution: The Movement that Remade America.* New York: Free Press, 1999.

Ehrman, John. *The Rise of Neoconservatism: Intellectuals and Foreign Affairs, 1945–1994.* New Haven, CT: Yale University Press, 1995.

Foot, Rosemary. *The Wrong War: American Policy and the Dimensions of the Korea Conflict, 1950–1953.* Ithaca, NY: Cornell University Press, 1985.

Fowler, Robert Booth. *Believing Skeptics: American Political Intellectuals, 1945–1964.* Westport, CT: Greenwood Press, 1978.

Francis, Samuel. *Power and History: The Political Thought of James Burnham.* Lanham, MD: University Press of America, 1984.

Goncharov, Sergei. *Uncertain Partners: Stalin, Mao, and the Korean War.* Redwood City, CA: Stanford University Press, 1993.

Gottfried, Paul. *Conservatism in America: Making Sense of the American Right.* New York: Palgrave, 2007.

Halberstam, David. *The Coldest Winter: America and the Korean War.* New York: Hyperion, 2007.

Hastings, Max. *The Korean War.* New York: Simon and Schuster, 1987.

Himmelstein, Jerome L. *To the Right: The Transformation of American Conservatism.* Berkeley: University of California Press, 1990.

Hodgson, Godfrey. *America in Our Time: From World War II to Nixon—What Happened and Why.* Princeton, NJ: Princeton University Press, 1976.

Hogan, Michael. *A Cross of Iron: Harry S. Truman and the Origins of the National Security State, 1945–1954.* Cambridge, UK: Cambridge University Press, 2000.

Holsti, Ole. *Public Opinion and American Foreign Policy.* Ann Arbor: University of Michigan Press, 2004.

Hoyt, Edwin. *The Bloody Road to Panmunjom.* New York: Stein and Day, 1985.

Hudson, Miles. *War and the Media: A Random Searchlight.* New York: New York University Press, 1998.

Hurtgen, James R. *The Divided Mind of American Liberalism.* Lanham, MD: Lexington Books, 2002.

Judis, John. *William F. Buckley, Jr.: Patron Saint of the Conservatives.* New York: Simon and Schuster, 1988.

Kadushin, Charles. *The American Intellectual Elite.* Boston: Little, Brown, 1974.

Keylor, William R. *The Twentieth Century World and Beyond: An International History since 1900.* New York: Oxford University Press, 2006.

Kirk, Russell. *The Conservative Mind: From Burke to Santayana.* Chicago: H. Regnery, 1953.

Knightly, Phillip. *The First Casualty: The War Correspondent as Hero and Myth-Maker from the Crimea to Iraq*. Baltimore: Johns Hopkins University Press, 2004.

Kuklick, Bruce. *Blind Oracles: Intellectuals and War from Kennan to Kissinger*. Princeton, NJ: Princeton University Press, 2006.

LaFeber, Walter. *America, Russia, and the Cold War, 1945–2000*. Boston: McGraw-Hill, 2002.

Lasch, Christopher. *The New Radicalism in America, 1889–1963: The Intellectual as a Social Type*. New York: Knopf, 1965.

Leffler, Melvyn. *A Preponderance of Power: National Security, the Truman Administration, and the Cold War*. Stanford: Stanford University Press, 1992.

Mao, Joyce. *Asia First: China and the Making of Modern American Conservatism*. Chicago: University of Chicago Press, 2015.

Mason, Robert, and Iwan Morgan, eds. *The Liberal Consensus Reconsidered: American Politics and Society in the Postwar Era*. Gainesville: University Press of Florida, 2017.

Mattson, Kevin. *Rebels All!: A Short History of the Conservative Mind in Postwar America*. New Brunswick, NJ: Rutgers University Press, 2008.

Mayers, David. *Cracking the Monolith: U.S. Policy against the Sino-Soviet Alliance, 1949–1955*. Baton Rouge: Louisiana State University Press, 1986.

Mayers, David. *Wars and Peace: The Future Americans Envisioned, 1861–1991*. New York: St. Martin's, 1998.

McCullough, David. *Truman*. New York: Simon and Schuster, 1992.

Moser, John. *Right Turn: John T. Flynn and the Transformation of American Liberalism*. New York: New York University Press, 2005.

Mueller, John. *War, Presidents, and Public Opinion*. Lanham, MD: University Press of America, 1985.

Nash, George. *The Conservative Intellectual Movement in America Since 1945*. New York: Basic Books, 1975.

Niebuhr, Reinhold. *The Irony of American History*. New York: Scribner, 1952.

Oberdorfer, Don. *The Two Koreas: A Contemporary History*. Reading, MA: Addison-Wesley, 1997.

Offner, Arnold. *Another Such Victory: President Truman and the Cold War, 1945–1953*. Stanford: Stanford University Press, 2002.

O'Neill, William. *A Better World: The Great Schism: Stalinism and the American Intellectuals*. New York: Simon and Schuster, 1982.

Pells, Richard. *The Liberal Mind in a Conservative Age: American Intellectuals in the 1940s and 1950s*. New York: Harper & Row, 1985.

Peterson, Merrill D. *Coming of Age with The New Republic, 1938–1950*. Columbia: University of Missouri Press, 1999.

Peterson, Theodore B. *Magazines in the Twentieth Century*. Urbana: University of Illinois Press, 1964.

Phillips-Fein, Kim. *Invisible Hands: The Making of the Conservative Movement from the New Deal to Reagan*. New York: W. W. Norton & Company, 2009.

Regnery, Alfred. *Upstream: The Ascendance of American Conservatism*. New York: Threshold Editions, 2008.

Ribuffo, Leo P. *The Old Christian Right: The Protestant Far Right from the Great Depression to the Cold War.* Philadelphia: Temple University Press, 1983.

Robin, Ron. *The Making of the Cold War Enemy: Culture and Politics in the Military-Industrial Complex.* Princeton, NJ: Princeton University Press, 2001.

Rusher, William A. *The Rise of the Right.* New York: W. Morrow, 1984.

Schlesinger, Arthur, Jr. *The Vital Center: The Politics of Freedom.* Boston: Houghton Mifflin, 1949.

Schoenwald, Jonathan M. *A Time for Choosing: The Rise of Modern American Conservatism.* New York: Oxford University Press, 2001.

Seideman, David. *The New Republic: A Voice of Modern Liberalism.* New York: Praeger, 1986.

Simmons, Robert R. *The Strained Alliance: Peking, Pyongyang, Moscow and the Politics of the Korean Civil War.* New York: Free Press, 1975.

Spalding, Elizabeth Edwards. *The First Cold Warrior: Harry Truman, Containment, and the Remaking of Liberal Internationalism.* Lexington: University Press of Kentucky, 2006.

Steel, Ronald. *Walter Lippmann and the American Century.* Boston: Little, Brown, 1980.

Straight, Michael. *After Long Silence.* New York: Norton, 1983.

Stone, I. F. *The Hidden History of the Korean War.* New York: Monthly Review Press, 1952.

Stueck, William. *The Korean War: An International History.* Princeton, NJ: Princeton University Press, 1995.

Stueck, William. *The Korean War in World History.* Lexington: University Press of Kentucky, 2004.

Stueck, William. *Rethinking the Korean War: A New Diplomatic and Strategic History.* Princeton, NJ: Princeton University Press, 2002.

Thorne, Melvin J. *American Conservative Thought since World War II: The Core Ideas.* New York: Greenwood Press, 1990.

Tomes, Robert. *Apocalypse Then: American Intellectuals and the Vietnam War, 1954–1975.* New York: New York University Press, 1998.

Truman, Harry S. *Memoirs of Harry S. Truman: Years of Trial and Hope, 1946–1952.* New York: Doubleday, 1956.

Van Allen, Rodger. *The Commonweal and American Catholicism: The Magazine, the Movement, the Meaning.* Philadelphia: Fortune Press, 1974.

Wainstock, Dennis. *Truman, MacArthur, and the Korean War.* Westport, CT: Greenwood Press, 1999.

Whelan, Richard. *Drawing the Line: The Korean War, 1950–1953.* Boston: Little, Brown, 1990.

Williams, William Appleman. *The Tragedy of American Diplomacy.* New York: Dell, 1962.

Wittkopf, Eugene. *Faces of Internationalism: Public Opinion and American Foreign Policy.* Durham, NC: Duke University Press, 1990.

Zelizer, Julian. *Arsenal of Democracy: The Politics of National Security—From World War II to the War on Terrorism.* New York: Basic Books, 2010.

Index

www.ingramcontent.com/pod-product-compliance
Lightning Source LLC
Chambersburg PA
CBHW020113281125
35938CB00063B/160/J

* 9 7 8 0 7 0 0 6 4 0 1 2 6 *